Literary Theory and the Claims of History

SATYA P. MOHANTY

Literary Theory and the Claims of History

Postmodernism,
Objectivity,
Multicultural Politics

Cornell University Press   Ithaca and London

THIS BOOK HAS BEEN PUBLISHED WITH THE AID OF A GRANT FROM
THE HULL MEMORIAL PUBLICATION FUND OF CORNELL UNIVERSITY.

Portions of this book are drawn from the following articles and are used
here, in revised form, by permission of the original publishers: "Colonial
Legacies, Multicultural Futures: Relativism, Objectivity, and the Challenge
of Otherness," *PMLA* 110 (January 1995), 108–18; "Us and Them: On the
Philosophical Bases of Political Criticism," *Yale Journal of Criticism* 2
(Spring 1989), 1–31; "History at the Edge of Discourse," *Diacritics* 12 (Fall
1982), 33–46; "Radical Teaching, Radical Theory," in *Theory in the
Classroom*, ed. C. Nelson (Urbana: University of Illinois Press, 1986), pp.
149–76; "The Epistemic Status of Cultural Identity," *Cultural Critique* 24
(Spring 1993), 41–80, by permission of Oxford University Press. Passages
from Toni Morrison's *Beloved* (Knopf, 1987) are used by permission of Toni
Morrison and International Creative Management, Inc.; copyright © 1987
by Toni Morrison.

First published 1997 by Cornell University Press.
First printing, Cornell Paperbacks, 1997.

Library of Congress Cataloging-in-Publication Data

Mohanty, Satya P.
    Literary theory and the claims of history : postmodernism,
objectivity, multicultural politics / Satya P. Mohanty.
        p.   cm.
    Includes index.
    ISBN 0-8014-2902-1 (cloth : alk. paper).—ISBN 0-8014-8135-X
(pbk. : alk. paper)
        1. Criticism—History—20th century. 2. Literature, Modern—20th
century—History and criticism. 3. Postmodernism (Literature)
4. Multiculturalism. I. Title.
PN94.M65 1997
801'.95'09045—dc21   97-3820

Printed in the United States of America.

Cloth printing   10 9 8 7 6 5 4 3 2 1
Paperback printing   10 9 8 7 6 5 4 3 2 1

dedicated

to the memory of my father

Hemanta Kumar Mohanty

1916–1996

and

to my students

Surely, I said, knowledge is the food of the soul; and we must take care, my friend, that the Sophist does not deceive us when he praises what he sells, like the dealers, wholesale or retail, who sell the food of the body, for they praise indiscriminately all their goods without knowing what is really beneficial or hurtful for the body. . . . If you know which of his wares are good and which are evil, you may safely buy knowledge of Protagoras or of anyone; but if not, then, my friend, watch out, don't take risks, don't gamble, with the most precious thing you have. For there is far greater risk in buying knowledge than in buying food and drink. The one you purchase of the wholesale or retail dealer, and carry them away in other vessels, and before you receive them into the body as food or drink, you may deposit them at home and call in an expert to give you advice—who knows what is good to be eaten and drunk, and what not, and how much, and when; and then the risk of purchasing them is not so great. But you cannot buy knowledge and carry it away in another vessel; when you have paid for it you must receive it into the soul and go on your way, either greatly harmed or greatly benefited. These things let us investigate with our elders, for we are still young—too young to determine such a matter. And now let us go, as we were intending, and hear Protagoras.

SOCRATES IN PLATO'S *Protagoras*

CONTENTS

CONTENTS

ACKNOWLEDGMENTS

This book is very different from the one I set out to write several years ago. It is still an exploration and analysis of postmodernism, but now it also provides a detailed sketch of a theoretical alternative to it. At critical moments, Margaret Ferguson and Shekhar Pradhan helped me see what was implicit in what I was saying. My thanks to them for their attentive and thoughtful readings. The central ideas were worked out in my undergraduate and graduate seminars at Cornell, and I owe my students more than I can convey here. My thanks also to Dick Boyd, whose commitment to cross-disciplinary dialogue about cultural and political issues has been inspiring. I first presented the arguments of the final chapter in the form of lectures for our jointly taught course "The Politics of Knowledge and Interpretation"; the second half of that chapter is an attempt to convince Dick on a point where we disagreed (and now perhaps don't).

I want to thank Jonathan Arac, Donald Marshall, and John McGowan for their comments on earlier versions of the book. Biodun Jeyifo, Dominick LaCapra, Kenneth McClane, and Paul St. Pierre served as sounding boards for many of the arguments as they evolved; I thank them for their responses, and for their friendship over these years. Members of the Moral Theory Group at Cornell helped make many of my ideas concrete: I thank Carol Acree-Cavalier, David Alvarez, Amy Carroll, Caroline Hau, Mario Hernandez, Juan Mah y Busch, Sarah McGrath, Minh Nguyen, and Furaha Norton for their probing questions. My thanks also to Dionne Espinoza, Philip Lewis, David Lloyd, Lisa Lowe, Kavita Panjabi, Reeve Parker, Shalini Puri, Domna Stanton, Ed White, Allen Wood, and Alok Yadav for helpful advice or feedback. Members of the English Department staff—Vicky Brevetti, Robin Doxtater, Darlene Flint, Hope Mandeville, Marianne Marsh, Lisa Melton, and Suzanne Sager—helped in more ways than they might realize.

Bernhard Kendler of Cornell University Press has been an insightful and patient editor; Carol Betsch and Judith Bailey have been superb copyeditors. Paula Moya read the last chapter with exemplary care and rigor, and the final version is stronger because of her comments. Minh Nguyen was a sensitive, intelligent, and sympathetic reader; she also helped in the preparation of the index. Charlene Gima, Juan Mah y Busch, and Minh Nguyen were excellent research assistants who provided not only assistance and helpful criticism but much needed good cheer as well.

Finally—Chandra Talpade Mohanty, with whom I have discussed virtually every idea in this book, and who has always provided unstinting help, advice, and support: I thank her for her intellectual integrity and generosity and, above all, for the yogic attitude of *shraddhā* she brings to everything she does.

S. P. M.

PREFACE

For many writers and scholars, the current prominence of literary theory is evidenced in the "postmodernist" consensus that seems to exist among progressive thinkers, activists, and cultural workers. Those on the Left who defend theory often point to the need for a thoroughgoing critique of some of the traditionally enshrined ideals of the dominant culture: truth, rationality, the objectivity of knowledge and values. What is specifically postmodernist, however, is not the critique of tradition itself—for such a critique was central to the Enlightenment project of modernity as well—but rather the more far-reaching claim that truth and rationality are always socially and discursively constructed and their validity and applicability are necessarily limited to their particular contexts or situations. They have, it is claimed in principle, no general or universal import.

One of my intentions in this book is to examine this postmodernist claim by breaking it down into some of its constituent assertions and presuppositions. Since I believe postmodernism is a popular intellectual position on the Left, I look at it critically and politically to decipher both the reasons for its attractiveness and the theoretical conclusions it implies or entails. My critique attempts to cut a bit deeper than standard arguments for or against postmodernism (or, in literary-critical circles, specific versions of poststructuralism) have allowed us to do. Thus I recast the issues by focusing most centrally on the various postmodernist arguments against objectivity, examining the move from local discussions about textual meaning or the complexity of cultural interpretation to the larger claims about the status of knowledge.

My other aim in this book is to explore and develop a theoretical alternative to the notion of objectivity which is assailed by postmodernists, an alternative position that can be characterized in philosophical terms as "realist." Since I believe that a strong and defensible notion of objectivity best serves our progressive cultural and political projects, my critique of postmodernism's epistemological claims and my elaboration of a realist alternative should be seen as a left critique of what is now the dominant current within the Left. They also constitute an invitation to readers to reexamine some of the key arguments and positions in contemporary cultural theory and politics. That is why I have organized the book as a more or less continuously developed argument, with the first part (Chapters 1–4) examining familiar positions and debates in literary theory and the second part (Chapters 5–7) urging the need for a reformulation of the epistemological issues underlying our cultural debates.

For polemical purposes, my central theses can be summarized and situated in the following way: The key postmodernist claims I identify derive from well-motivated political desires and agendas but are seriously underdemonstrated. Underlying these claims is a cluster of arguments about the untenability of objective knowledge, but these arguments cannot be adequately examined without a consideration of strong theoretical alternatives such as those realism provides. Seen in this comparative light, postmodernism does not appear very attractive as a philosophical position or as a political perspective. I maintain that a postpositivist realism (of the kind developed in the 1970s and the 1980s) would be attentive to the postmodernist's cautions about the social and historical entanglements of knowledge and would enable us to explain the distortions of ideology and political power. At the same time, however, it can provide us with a sophisticated and usable notion of objectivity as an ideal of inquiry, as a reasonable social hope rather than the dream of transcendence.

It is on the basis of such a notion of objectivity that I sketch (in Chapter 7) the outlines of a cultural politics that can combine a radical universalist moral vision with a genuine multiculturalism. I thus implicitly reformulate the terms of a very old debate over the Enlightenment's claims to a progressive epistemology and politics. Since Johann Georg Hamann and Johann Gottfried Herder mounted their powerful attacks on the Enlightenment's universalist conceptions of reason, morality, and history, arguing instead for the irreducibility of cultural particularity and diversity, many writers and scholars have tended to see universalism and particularism as inevitably opposed ideals. European romanticism defined and deepened this tendency, seeing its project as a defense of culture against reason, of diversity of values against monism and uniformity. My realist accounts of cultural identity, reason, and value are meant to take us beyond this opposition by showing how moral universalism and multiculturalism are compatible and indeed complementary ideals. I outline a vision of cultural diversity based on the claim that "cultures" are fields of moral inquiry, with room for objective knowledge as well as for error or mystification. Multiculturalism, I argue, should be defined as a form of epistemic cooperation across cultures.

A serious critical debate between postmodernism and the realist position thus requires clarity about the underlying theoretical issues and questions. While these theoretical issues surface in current debates in literary and cultural criticism, they in fact also reflect the urgencies of our progressive social and political movements, the deepest challenges posed by contemporary history. My understanding of the issues and questions I write about here is shaped by my personal engagement with these problems and these ideals. The decolonization of the third world and our postcolonial dreams of *both* internationalist solidarity and cultural pluralism; the ongoing struggles against racism, sexism, and social inequalities of all kinds; the democratic and anti-imperialist movements of our own day as well as the ethical imperative to reexamine and transform our personal and social identities—these are some of the contexts that have defined for me the tasks and goals of theory, including literary theory. This book is an attempt at a certain kind of clarification. It is also a call to reformulate and extend the terms of our theoretical debates.

SATYA P. MOHANTY

Ithaca, New York

**Literary Theory
and the
Claims of History**

INTRODUCTION: CRITICISM AS POLITICS

When Theodor Adorno and Max Horkheimer declared in a 1947 essay that the Enlightenment was "totalitarian," they revealed the deep anxiety many intellectuals in our times have felt about the founding age of modern criticism.[1] That this anxiety has crystalized as a political concern in contemporary critical debates is an irony in need of some explanation. For the Enlightenment, declaring itself the "age of criticism" and of faith in reason to battle human superstition and servitude, saw *itself* as inherently radical and subversive. So while Voltaire based his critique of the Roman Catholic church on pleas for religious toleration, for instance, he mounted a powerful attack on clericalism in all its forms. And the publication of Diderot's *Encyclopedia* was suppressed, at least for a while, for the "irreparable damage" it was supposed to do to "morality and religion." Even Kant, after the publication of *Religion within the Limits of Reason Alone*, was forbidden by royal decree from writing anything further on the subject. There is thus an irony in the desire of any "critical" discourse to define itself in political opposition to the principles of the Enlightenment, but the fact is that Adorno and Horkheimer were not alone. Indeed, their wariness about the Enlightenment's faith in reason is shared by most contemporary theorists influenced by postmodernism. If faith in the power of reason to liberate us is an essential characteristic of (Enlightenment) critical modernity, the

1. Max Horkheimer and Theodor Adorno, *The Dialectic of Enlightenment*, trans. John Cumming (New York: Continuum, 1993), p. 6, and see p. 24.

limits of this faith—and of this reason—seem to constitute recent criticism's deepest concern.

But if we are to discuss the claims of criticism as a political practice, we need to begin by acknowledging that it was the singular achievement of the Enlightenment thinkers to have granted to "criticism" (*Kritik*) a status and a function that were essentially tied to a vision of the social. When Kant declared in the first *Critique* that his age was, "in every sense of the word, the age of criticism," he wanted to assert simultaneously that every social discourse or institution "must submit" to the "reason" that criticism serves. "Religion, on the strength of its sanctity, and law, on the strength of its majesty, try to withdraw themselves from it," Kant warned, "but by so doing they arouse just suspicions, and cannot claim that sincere respect which reason pays to those only who have been able to stand its free and open examination."[2] Reason's task, as Kant says elsewhere, is to make possible *"man's emergence from his self-incurred immaturity."*[3] Reason can achieve this goal by being *self*-critical in a principled way: the "critique of pure reason" is really the "tribunal for all disputes of reason. . . . [It] is intended to fix and to determine the rights of reason in general."[4] It is the dual task of criticism to submit everything to reason and to "determine" reason's "rights." Without such a powerful and ever vigilant "tribunal," reason would revert to a "state of nature." Invoking the Hobbesian distinction between the state of nature, which is the "state of injustice and violence," and that "constraint of law" which would ensure "the freedom of others and . . . the common good," Kant points directly, in substance as well as through metaphor, to the political vision underlying his notion of criticism:

> It is part of . . . freedom that we should be allowed openly to state our thoughts and our doubts which we cannot solve ourselves, without running the risk of being decried on that account as turbulent and

2. This quotation is from the famous preface to the first edition. See *Critique of Pure Reason*, trans. F. Max Muller (Garden City, N.Y.: Doubleday Anchor, 1966), p. xxiv, note.

3. Kant, "An Answer to the Question: 'What is Enlightenment?' " in *Kant: Political Writings*, ed. Hans Reiss, trans. H. B. Nisbet, 2d enlarged ed. (Cambridge: Cambridge University Press, 1991), p. 54. For good introductory accounts of the Enlightenment which emphasize the Kantian theme of rational self-determination, see Onora O'Neill, "Enlightenment as Autonomy: Kant's Vindication of Reason," in *The Enlightenment and Its Shadows*, ed. Peter Hulme and Ludmilla Jordanova (New York: Routledge, 1990), pp. 184–99, and Allen Wood, "The Enlightenment," *The Encyclopedia of Religion*, vol. 5 (New York: Macmillan, 1987), pp. 109–13. I am indebted to both these essays.

4. Kant, *Critique of Pure Reason*, p. 486.

dangerous citizens. This follows from the inherent rights of reason, which recognises no other judge but universal human reason itself. Here everybody has a vote; and, as all improvements of which our state is capable must spring from thence, such rights are sacred and must never be diminished.[5]

Kant's conception of criticism is based on his view of reason as a practical capacity. Shorn of its speculative theoretical excesses, reason serves the cause of a just polity in which "everybody [would have] a vote." In Kant's view criticism is rational and reflexive, and a form of practical intervention in our conventional understanding of society—its values, ideas, and institutions. Critical activity is necessarily part of Kant's vision of freedom and justice, and the basis on which reason can claim "inherent rights" is presumably that it is "universal *human* reason" and thus points to a moral potential latent in all humans.

This powerful and grand Kantian conception of criticism is tied historically to the growth of what Jürgen Habermas calls the classical "public sphere," and thus its claims to a rationality can be historically and politically specified in some ways. The transition from the critical discourses of the seventeenth century to the epistemic and political values of the Enlightenment is marked mainly by a new function: the valuing of rationality over authority. The imperative of Enlightenment rationalism is to create a new reason based on the new image of the polis (compare Kant's concern with the "freedom of others" and "the common good") through the forms of open debate, controversy, and discussion which the bourgeois public sphere makes possible in a limited but important way. The public sphere, particularly in Habermas's formulation, "mediates between society and state" and appears in its specifically modern form as the rising bourgeois class consolidates its political power:

> Though mere opinions (cultural assumptions, normative attitudes, collective prejudices and values) seem to persist unchanged in their natural form as a kind of sediment of history, public opinion can by definition only come into existence when a reasoning public is presupposed. Public discussions about the exercise of political power which are both critical in intent and institutionally guaranteed have not always existed—they grew out of a specific phase of bourgeois society and could enter into the order of the bourgeois constitutional state only as a result of a particular constellation of interests. . . .

5. Ibid., pp. 486–87.

Society, now a private realm occupying a position in opposition to the state, stood on the one hand as if in clear contrast to the state. On the other hand, that society had become a concern of public interest to the degree that the reproduction of life in the wake of the developing market economy had grown beyond the bounds of private domestic authority. The bourgeois public sphere could be understood as the sphere of private individuals assembled into a public body, which almost immediately laid claim to the officially regulated "intellectual newspapers" for use against the public authority itself. In those newspapers, and in moralistic and critical journals, they debated that public authority on the general rules of social intercourse.[6]

In its ideal intentions, Habermas goes on to say, the public sphere of the liberal bourgeoisie sought to transform absolutist political authority into rational authority. The "general interest" was the underlying criterion by which such a "rationality" was judged, "according to the presuppositions of a society of free commodity exchange, when the activities of private individuals in the marketplace were freed from social compulsion and from political pressure" (p. 53). Even within the limited ideological context (of "free commodity exchange") the conception of criticism that emerges is both social and revolutionary. Criticism questions authority in a principled way, with the "general interest" in view, and thus the principle and the underlying political conception of criticism are relevant beyond their immediate contexts.

Given this vision of critical activity as a radical and demanding social praxis, a specifically cultural criticism, whether textual interpretation or theoretical analysis, can often play a valuable utopian role in society. Many modern conceptions of cultural and aesthetic criticism have implicitly relied on political ideals embodied in individuals and their moral and imaginative growth. Whether in the garb of a Schillerian aesthetic education, which posits the freedom of "play" as its telos, or in the "best spiritual work" Matthew Arnold ascribes to criticism—that it will prevent a "self-satisfaction which is retarding and vulgarising" and lead humans "towards perfection"[7]—the most influential visions of the critical task have always asserted that cultural-critical activity has a useful social and pedagogical function. Closer to us in time and place, T. S. Eliot, even as he enhanced our appreciation of the value of the

6. Jürgen Habermas, "The Public Sphere: An Encyclopedia Article," *New German Critique* 1 (Fall 1974), 50, 52.

7. Matthew Arnold, "The Function of Criticism at the Present Time," in *"Culture and Anarchy" and Other Writings*, ed. Stefan Collini (Cambridge: Cambridge University Press, 1993), p. 38.

practical criticism of literature and prepared the ground for the advent of New Criticism, nevertheless never forgot to emphasize the vision of an alternative community that criticism (and literary culture in general) was supposed to create. And Leavisite criticism, despite its nostalgia for lost agrarian communal forms and values, was at least concerned to fight its battles not in the name of "mere 'literary' values"—as Terry Eagleton reminds us—but with the insistence that "how one evaluated literary works was deeply bound up with deeper judgements about the nature of history and society as a whole."[8]

The more recent rise of a purely technical understanding of criticism naturally involves a change in its intellectual and political conception as well. At least in the Anglophone world, the success of New Criticism in supplanting the philological schools in the forties and the fifties was tied to the relative efficiency of New Critical methods of close reading in the college classroom. The cogency of textual criticism as a pedagogical model may have led to a lack of commitment to the self-critical or the inherently metacritical imperatives of all critical activity. The emphasis in New Critical discourses and practices was not purely on the text as artifact; the analyses always led to—or were founded on—visions of order or anarchy, community or alienation. But these were isolatable thematic elements, divorced from any necessary connection with the theory of reading or interpretation. Criticism became technical not because it lost the nerve to talk about society but primarily because it took its nature and its role in society for granted. It took as unproblematical its status as knowledge (about literature and culture, of course, but about the social and the political as well). Criticism as interpretation was relegated to the task of distinguishing between a valid reading and those that seemed inadequately justified by the text. There is a curious prehermeneutical reification of the text in the New Critical approach, evident, for instance, in the following passage from an essay by Cleanth Brooks called "What Does Poetry Communicate?":

> Our examination has carried us further and further into the poem itself in a process of exploration. As we have made this exploration, it has become more and more clear that the poem is not only the linguistic vehicle which conveys the thing communicated most "poetically," but that it is also the sole linguistic vehicle which conveys the things communicated accurately. In fact, if we are to speak exactly,

8. Terry Eagleton, *Literary Theory* (Minneapolis: University of Minnesota Press, 1983), p. 33.

the poem itself is the *only* medium that communicates the particular "what" that is communicated.[9]

Brooks is arguing against the notion of a poem as a mere vehicle for some transcendental or more fundamental meaning—hence his insistence on the poem as the "only medium" or the "sole linguistic vehicle." But the process of interpretation is not considered hermeneutical here; the right reading confines itself to the text, which is seen as the sole repository of meaning. The reader, situated in a certain time and place, imbued with a subjectivity that is socially shaped even as it reads the poem, is not really encountered in this theoretical paradigm.

What is equally significant is that such a reification of the text sees itself as coexisting, quite unselfconsciously, with a simultaneous insistence on the moral tasks of critical activity. In another essay in *The Well-Wrought Urn*, Brooks argues against a critical relativism, calling for a more engaged understanding of criticism's function: "The Humanities are in their present plight largely because their teachers have more and more ceased to raise normative questions, have refrained from evaluation. In their anxiety to avoid meaningless 'emoting,' in their desire to be objective and 'scientific,' the proponents of the Humanities have tended to give up any claim to making a peculiar and special contribution. . . . If the Humanities are to endure, they must be themselves—and that means, among other things, frankly accepting the burden of making normative judgments" (p. 235). Brooks makes his point even more specific: the humanities must not "comply with the spirit of the age," but "resist it" (p. 235). But this desire to "resist" is an individualist and narrowly circumscribed ethical gesture, for there is no theoretical support for it. There is no continuity between the ethical demand and an understanding that the interpretive context is itself value-laden (and even political). From the laboratorylike situation of the study we emerge into the open arena of the classroom, and it is only here that (public and moral) values become relevant for Brooks. The New Critic's ethics are supplementary to the reading of texts—which are conceived as autonomous linguistic objects. In this theoretical perspective, the critic's social values play no necessary interpretive role, positive or negative. They have no epistemic import.

The New Critical project succeeds to the extent that it takes its own discursive and contextual situation less than seriously. It ignores com-

9. Cleanth Brooks, *The Well-Wrought Urn* (New York: Harcourt Brace & World, 1947), p. 74.

plex questions about what we might call, drawing on modern herme-neutical theory, the historical "horizon" of interpretation and understanding.[10] Here is I. A. Richards, for instance, on the relation be-tween evaluation and interpretation:

> That the one and only goal of all critical endeavours, of all interpreta-tion, appreciation, exhortation, praise or abuse, is improvement in communication may seem an exaggeration. But in practice it is so. The whole apparatus of critical rules and principles is a means to the attainment of finer, more precise, more discriminating communica-tion. There is, it is true, a valuation side to criticism. When we have solved, completely, the communication problem, when we have got, perfectly, the experience, the mental condition relevant to the poem, we have still to judge it, still to decide upon its worth. But the latter question nearly always settles itself; or rather, our own inmost nature and the nature of the world in which we live decide it for us. Our prime endeavour must be to get the relevant mental condition and then see what happens.[11]

This passage from *Practical Criticism*, arguably one of the most influ-ential texts in the New Critical corpus, may seem a little quaint now with its interest in "mental conditions," but it also suggests the way crucial metacritical questions are avoided in the course of a rather cir-cumscribed discussion of the "valuation" involved in criticism. Aes-thetic evaluation is shaped by "our own inmost nature and the nature of the world in which we live," but the nature of that influence or its implications for literary interpretation are not issues worth pondering. All the talk about text and value serves merely to direct attention away

10. In defining the concept of "horizon," Hans-Georg Gadamer explains why an analy-sis of the situatedness of interpretation is essential: "We should learn to understand our-selves better and recognize that in all understanding, whether we are expressly aware of it or not, the efficacy of history is at work. . . . Consciousness of being affected by history . . . is primarily consciousness of the hermeneutical situation. . . . Every finite present has its limitations. We define the concept of 'situation' by saying that it represents a standpoint that limits the possibility of vision. Hence essential to the concept of situation is the con-cept of 'horizon.' The horizon is the range of vision that includes everything that can be seen from a particular vantage point. Applying this to the thinking mind, we speak of narrowness of horizon, of the possible expansion of horizon, of the opening up of new horizons, and so forth. . . . [W]orking out the hermeneutical situation means acquiring the right horizon of inquiry for the questions evoked by the encounter with tradition." *Truth and Method*, 2d revised ed., trans. Joel Weinsheimer and Donald Marshall (New York: Crossroad, 1989), pp. 301–2; for the relevant general discussion, see pp. 265–379.

11. I. A. Richards, *Practical Criticism: A Study of Literary Judgment* (New York: Har-court Brace Jovanovich, n.d.), p. 10.

from the hermeneutical and social dimension of the critical enterprise, since it defines critical reading as an essentially private activity. What is barely acknowledged is the alternative theoretical possibility that our aesthetic valuations are always linked to deeper and often implicit social and historical values. It would follow from this alternative view that good readings of texts would need to deal reflexively with such values and their social contexts, in particular with how they together influence our critical responses.

In the United States, where New Criticism maintained hegemony for several decades, there were some significant challenges to its technical-textual orientation. If the New Critics themselves saw their work as implicitly opposed to the kind of philological research residual in the reigning "historical" criticism, which sought to explicate texts in terms of historical data about sources, social contexts, and a general understanding of biographical facts, some major alternatives were available in both critical writing and pedagogical models. Such critics as Lionel Trilling, F. O. Matthiessen, and Edmund Wilson exhibited a strong moral dissatisfaction with the New Critical devaluation of historical context and sought to reassert the social dimensions of literary criticism while respecting the formal and linguistic complexity of the literary text. Trilling, for instance, read Freud and Nietzsche quite avidly and knew Marx with enough sympathy to describe his sense of history as an essential "sixth sense."[12] Trilling's concern in *The Liberal Imagination* was to develop a less turgid sense of "reality in America" than was prevalent in his time, but "reality" was for him a process of active and acute engagement with history and the "operating forces" of the culture, which were never available without reference to "gross institutional facts" (p. 197). Trilling considered Nietzsche exemplary for his attempt to achieve a critical and active fusion of the "historical sense" and the "sense of art" (p. 197). He saw criticism as providing a valuable corrective to the dominant culture of his society: it can bring, he argued, a "lively sense of contingency and possibility, and of those exceptions to the rule which may be the beginning of the end of the rule" (p. xv). Trilling's own achievement—as well as that of the major critics of this varied group—was to have claimed for critical discourse a complex and nuanced public function. His conception of criticism is reminiscent in its own way of the Enlightenment's emphasis on, say, "taste" as involving a cognitive and social dimension.[13]

12. Lionel Trilling, *The Liberal Imagination* (New York: Viking, 1950), p. 195.
13. See Ernst Cassirer, *The Philosophy of the Enlightenment*, trans. Fritz C. A. Koelln and James P. Pettegrove (Princeton: Princeton University Press, 1951), pp. 297–312; and

So there has always been a version of criticism in the recent past that has seen criticism's very nature as unavoidably social and historical. "History" becomes a political slogan for literary critics only when the technical and formalist conception of critical activity has repressed criticism's essential hermeneutical nature, its emphasis on the social situatedness of textual interpretation. The social vocation of criticism is reasserted in different ways in the works of Trilling and Wilson (or F. R. Leavis, in his own way, in Britain), and there is at least one kind of continuity between their understanding of the critical enterprise and that expressed in an influential book by a critic of a later generation: "The works of culture come to us as signs in an all-but-forgotten code, as symptoms of diseases no longer even recognized as such, as fragments of a totality we have long since lost the organs to see. . . . Now . . . the literary fact, like the other objects that make up our social reality, cries out for commentary, for interpretation, for decipherment, for diagnosis. . . . It . . . [is] literary criticism [that must] continue to compare the inside and the outside, existence and history, . . . continue to pass judgment on the abstract quality of life in the present, and to keep alive the idea of a concrete future."[14] Criticism must interpret, in the strongest sense of the word, if it is to compare and connect "existence and history," and that act of interpretation is simultaneously an evaluation of social life. Implicit in this passage is a deeper claim that "decipherment" and "judgment" are interdependent, especially since the impoverished abstraction of modern life produces a distorted understanding of literary texts. This view of the nature and goals of criticism is distinctly post–New Critical; it points to a richer and more complex conception of the critical enterprise because it refuses to sunder fact from value, or reading from history.

Such an antipositivist conception sometimes becomes evident in contemporary theory's critique of the Enlightenment. Adorno and Horkheimer's attack on the Enlightenment, for instance, is more than a mere gesture of defiance, for it is also a call for a more reflexive conception of critical discourse. Their primary charge is that Enlightenment principles have "extinguished any trace of [their] own self-consciousness," and hence the Enlightenment is "as totalitarian as any system. Its untruth consist[s] . . . in the fact that for [it] the process is

Gadamer's discussion of the social and cognitive basis of the concepts of taste, "common sense," and judgment in *Truth and Method*, esp. pp. 19–42.

14. Fredric Jameson, *Marxism and Form* (Princeton: Princeton University Press, 1971), p. 416.

always decided from the start."[15] They are against the dominating power of abstract systems over historical reality; "discursive logic," which posits the "universality of ideas," ignores the possibility that its own universal claim is based on "actual domination" (p. 14). The radical vision of Enlightenment critical principles may seem rather ambiguous from this perspective. If Adorno and Horkheimer are right, the antiabsolutist politics inherent in the universal claims of rationality is in fact compromised by the tendency of Enlightenment reason to ignore its own complex historical function. Reason, they argue in effect, can freeze into a false objectivity. Many literary and cultural theorists extend this claim to suggest that reason is always politically suspect, and that objectivity is neither possible nor desirable. The political critique of reason, together with its implications for the nature of genuine objectivity, are thus central questions for contemporary criticism and theory.

The Political Claims of Theory

This book begins with the thesis that the polemic and the internal differences notwithstanding, the field of discourse we identify as "literary theory" is organized around a few related assumptions about the nature of objective knowledge. It is my intention to examine some of these related assumptions and provide a critical alternative to what I see as the central thesis of contemporary theory. This thesis is evident in domains other than literary criticism, for "literary theory" does not in fact refer to a theory of literature today. Rather, it points to a larger area of theoretical investigation informed by film and media studies, anthropology, ethnic and third-world cultural studies, feminism, and various kinds of interpretive projects in the social sciences. As will be evident from the following chapters, contemporary literary theory opens out onto fundamental issues in social and political theory.

In the Preface, I identified the core thesis of postmodernist literary and cultural theory as a denial of objectivity, and suggested that this denial is based on an extreme form of (social or linguistic) constructivism. As an assumption, constructivism cuts across theoretical schools and movements. Various intellectual developments are seen as contributing to the constructivist consensus: Thomas Kuhn's account of the paradigm relativity of scientific theories; Richard Rorty's critique of epistemological foundationalism; the analyses of traditional notions of

15. Horkheimer and Adorno, *Dialectic*, pp. 4, 24.

language, signification, and human subjectivity developed by Saussurean semiotics and contemporary psychoanalysis; the deconstruction of phenomenology and idealism by various kinds of poststructuralist thought; and finally, the critique of ideology developed in contemporary marxist and feminist scholarship, based on examination of the strategic exclusions that sustain hegemonic belief systems or theories. In the light of all these developments, postmodernist constructivism may be defined most basically as the idea that all those epistemological norms which were so dear to the Enlightenment—rationality, objectivity, and truth—are no more than social conventions, historically variable and hence without claim to universality. In the particularly influential poststructuralist formulation of this thesis, all knowledge is seen as tied to the necessary miscognition of human subjects caught in a network of forces they cannot evade or comprehend. What sets knowledge into motion, what creates the "knowledge-effect," to draw on structuralist terminology, are these larger impersonal, asubjective forces and dynamics—language, the unconscious, history. Our claims of impartial knowledge are thus spurious.

In its most reasonable and interesting form, the poststructuralist critique of objective knowledge is cast as a more local debate, a critique of idealist conceptions of "absolute knowledge." Drawing on Lacanian psychoanalytic theory, with its claim that "the discovery of the unconscious . . . is that the implications of meaning infinitely exceed the signs manipulated by the individual," the literary theorist Shoshana Felman, for instance, proposes, against the Hegelian ideal of absolute knowledge, an alternative conception of the relation between human subjects and the discourses in which they formulate what they know.

> There can . . . be no such thing as absolute knowledge; absolute knowledge is knowledge that has exhausted its own articulation; but articulated knowledge is by definition what cannot exhaust its own self-knowledge. For knowledge to be spoken, linguistically articulated, it would constitutively have to be supported by the ignorance carried by language, the ignorance of the *excess of signs* that of necessity its language—its articulation—"mobilizes." Thus, human knowledge is, by definition, that which is *untotalizable*, that which rules out any possibility of totalizing what it knows or of eradicating its own ignorance.[16]

16. Shoshana Felman, "Psychoanalysis and Education: Teaching Terminable and Interminable," *Yale French Studies* no. 63 (1982), 29, and see 28–31. In Chapter 1, I briefly discuss the theoretical kernel of Felman's Lacanian thesis (i.e., the idea that "ignorance" is not the simple absence of knowledge but should rather be conceived dynamically in relation to a socially situated knowing subject).

This is a suggestive critique of idealist conceptions of the cognizing subject, but if we are to generalize beyond the local critique to a claim about the nature of knowledge as such, as Felman seems to do in this passage, we cannot get very far until we have made the meanings of "knowledge" and "articulation" much less vague than they are here. We need at the very least to indicate the different social ways in which knowledges are produced and the difference that different kinds of articulation (in "languages" organized at varying degrees of formalization, from the natural languages to the symbols of the mathematician or the computer scientist) make. We need, in other words, a more developed account of how various kinds of knowledge are produced in various social contexts before we can generalize from this interesting but limited suggestion.

But the poststructuralist claim is in fact often cast in more extreme terms. In a dialogue in which she outlines the political aims of the postmodernists, Gayatri Spivak accurately summarizes the postmodernist critique of "objectivity" as "a radical acceptance of vulnerability," what we may gloss as an acknowledgment of epistemic fallibility.[17] For Spivak the argument does not rest on a claim about the nature of a specifically linguistic articulation or the individual subject's relation to the signs she "mobilizes" in order to seek or formulate knowledge; rather, it is an argument about the relation between knowledge and narrativity in general. It is also not just that whenever we narrate (that is, explain or organize reality in some way) "something is left out" (p. 18). What makes the view poststructuralist is the contention that narration is by definition necessary but suspect: something in its very nature undermines knowledge. "I think if one can lump Derrida and Lyotard together in this way, I think what they are noticing is that we cannot but narrate. . . . [W]hat they're interested in is looking at the limits of narration, looking at narrativity" (p. 20).

What they consider the "limits" of narration becomes evident a little later in the same discussion. When asked why poststructuralists or postmodernists do not generally provide arguments or evidence in support of their suggestive theses, Spivak's answer reveals that much more than the status of "narration" is at stake. Notice in the following exchange how the claim about the nature of narrativity is linked up with an account of not just idealist conceptions of absolute knowledge but also of the very standards and expectations of reasonable argumentation we usually rely on:

17. Gayatri Chakravorty Spivak, *The Postcolonial Critic* (New York: Routledge, 1991), p. 18.

[Question] [The postmodernists] have to persuade us. One of the standard ways of persuading us is to use arguments. One of the standard ways of arguing is to appeal to reason, and one of the standard ways of making a rational argument is to appeal to evidence, to point to things. But it seems that at the end of the line in the arguments that they're producing, they are pointing to an absence. And therefore I'm slightly puzzled as to how one is supposed to take their argument as an argument.

[Answer] It really asks for, as it were, to use a very old term, a transformation of consciousness—a changing mind set. It's in that sense, again to use an old-fashioned word, [an] ideological project. To develop a mind set which allows one not to be nervous about *the fact that what one is saying is undermined by the way one says it, radically.* (p. 20, emphasis added)

The more far-reaching claim is expressed indirectly in this response in the italicized portion of the passage, and it is more general than the specifically antiidealist thesis Felman extracts from Lacanian theory. It is in the nature of discourse—language, narrative, and so on—to destabilize knowledge, to "undermine" any substantive thesis being asserted. In other words, what Spivak calls the "radical acceptance of vulnerability" is based on the deeper belief that nothing is ever epistemically reliable. The corollary suggestion in this passage about the necessity of changing one's "mind set" in response to requests for cogent arguments or evidence may strike some readers as bizarre, but fortunately it does not have to be seen as entailed by the poststructuralist critique of objectivity.[18] This critique, as may be evident in the two instances I have

18. This argument, that in critically evaluating poststructuralism we need to make a leap of faith rather than look for arguments or evidence, is clearly an uncomfortable corner into which the movement's defenders sometimes find themselves backing. Even a critic such as Jonathan Culler, who generally values lucidity and careful argumentation, makes a tortuously qualified version of this kind of point in defending Paul de Man's manner of reasoning. See his *Framing the Sign* (Norman: University of Oklahoma Press, 1988), p. 134: "While [de Man's] analyses focus on the resistant or disruptive and insistently oppose modes of understanding that overcome textual difficulties so as to hear in the text what it is thought to say, the character of his own writing makes this the only way to understand or interpret him. One can only make sense of his writings if one already has a sense of what they must be saying and can bear with the slippage of concepts, the elusiveness of idiosyncratically employed philosophical and linguistic terms. One works to get over or around the puzzling valuations, the apparently incompatible claims. To learn from his writings, one must read him also in the ways he warns us against, giving in to the teleology of meaning." The problem with an injunction of this kind is that, without any further specification of where a bad argument is simply a bad argument and in which generic contexts it is to be "read" as something else, it becomes unnecessary ever to evaluate an argument.

quoted, draws on substantive claims about the nature of such things as language, narrative, discourse in general, as well as the relations between interpretation and the object or "text" interpreted. Knowledge, it is said, is always constructed in very specific ways through discourse, and in one way or another this constructedness renders knowledge unstable, less than "objective."[19]

Now, many contemporary theoretical positions share one or another version of this skepticism about objective knowledge. Rationality is equated with the philosopher's vain dream, objectivity with the self-deceiving claim of the masculinist imagination.[20] Many feminists and marxists, for instance, who reject extreme forms of epistemological nihilism since they wish to leave open the possibility of valid political belief and judgment, are often content with general skepticism toward claims about objective truth. Whether or not they accept the specifically poststructuralist thesis I have just identified, many progressive scholars adopt the postmodernist position that the search for objective knowledge is at best a form of nostalgia, at worst a desire to dominate and control. According to the social theorist Linda Nicholson, for instance, postmodernism not only reveals the oppositions of truth and falsehood, fact and superstition to be arbitrary, historically produced schemes for organizing what we study, it also claims that we do not need a theory of knowledge at all.[21] This position is based on an epistemological relativism, the claim that *in principle* human thought cannot

19. "The defining feature of post-structuralism is the breakdown of the distinction between language and metalanguage—a theory of narrative is itself a narrative, a theory of writing is itself writing, a discourse on metaphor does not escape metaphor, a theory of repression involves repression" (Culler, *Framing*, p. 139). This series of theoretical claims can be developed, qualified, or refuted through empirical inquiry, but the metatheoretical claim (about the status of the explanation a metalanguage provides, about the status of theory as such) can be specified only if we understand the substantive nature of "language" in such a way that it will always undermine the explanatory role a "metalanguage" usually claims to play. Rejections of "grand theory" (see p. 140) are not quite to the point here, since one does not need to be a poststructuralist to be wary of overly general theoretical explanations. See Richard Miller, *Fact and Method* (Princeton: Princeton University Press, 1987), on the modern worship of generality. The bite of the specifically poststructuralist thesis is evident more in its explicit or implicit denial that *objective* interpretations, explanations, or theories are possible to come by. Much depends, then, on how we define objectivity in the context of human inquiry and, in particular, on whether we conflate objectivity with certainty.

20. For a useful account of the "maleness" of traditional Western conceptions of reason, which acknowledges, however, that rationality can be a valuable epistemic ideal, see Genevieve Lloyd, *The Man of Reason* (Minneapolis: University of Minnesota Press, 1989).

21. Linda Nicholson, Introduction to *Feminism/Postmodernism*, ed. Nicholson (New York: Routledge, 1990), pp. 1–16.

transcend its social moorings, that it can make no claims that are supposed to have transcultural or transhistorical validity.

> Postmodernists have gone beyond earlier historicist claims about the inevitable "situatednesss" of human thought within culture to focus on the very criteria by which claims to knowledge are legitimized. The . . . radical move in the postmodern turn was to claim that the very criteria demarcating the true and the false, as well as such related distinctions as science and myth or fact and superstition, were internal to the traditions of modernity and could not be legitimized outside of those traditions. . . . Therefore the postmodern critique has come to focus on philosophy and the very idea of a possible theory of knowledge, justice, or beauty. The claim is that the pursuit itself of such theories rests upon the modernist conception of a transcendent reason, a reason able to separate itself from the body and from historical time and place. (pp. 3–4)

The suspicion of "philosophy and the very idea of a possible theory of knowledge" is of course very general, and in order to examine the postmodernist case we need to make the claim much more precise. For one thing, it needs to be made clear whether the critique involves simply the rejection of epistemological foundationalism, the idea that once we have found an ideal ahistorical method or theory of knowledge it will ground our various sciences and permanently guide our different practices of inquiry. Understood as an antifoundationalist sentiment, postmodernism's suspicion of a "possible theory of knowledge" can have much theoretical support, drawing on the work of Richard Rorty, among others. But antifoundationalism does not entail a relativistic rejection of "the very criteria demarcating the true and the false," nor does it render irrelevant and unnecessary the search for a nonfoundationalist theory of knowledge, an empirically grounded philosophical account of the varieties of socially based truth and error, of the standards and criteria by which we justify knowledge claims or consider them erroneous.

That such a "philosophical account" would have political ramifications becomes clear when we realize that the postmodernist denial of the possibility of such an account is itself also a claim about the spurious "political baggage" that often comes with searches for such accounts. This baggage is seen as tied to the interests of the hegemonic Euro-American culture and society that "produced" this ideal of reason and science. "Postmodernists," says Nicholson, "describe modern ideals of science, justice, and art *as* merely modern ideals carrying with them specific political agendas and ultimately unable to legitimize themselves as universals. Thus, postmodernists urge us to recognize the highest ideals of modernity in the West as immanent to a specific historical time and geographical region and also associated with certain political baggage. Such baggage includes notions of the supremacy of the West, of the legitimacy of science to tell us how to use and view our bodies, and of the distinction between art and mass culture."[22] One of the theoretical questions I raise in this book concerns the ability of postmodernists to examine this political baggage adequately without a context-sensitive and yet generalizable understanding of objectivity as an ideal of human inquiry. But what Nicholson suggests here and what Felman and Spivak have pointed to in their own ways is that for most of us today progressive politics—feminist, antiracist, anticolonialist, and so forth—has increasingly become identified with a critical and de-mystificatory project that not only interrogates the smugness of tradi-tional claims to truth but is also skeptical of any attempt to seek objectivity.

One of my central theses, developed cumulatively in the following chapters, is that this skeptical stance and the constructivist theoretical view that underlies or accompanies it are no longer adequate for pro-gressive politics and they lead to serious confusion in cultural—and par-ticularly cross-cultural—studies. I would like to situate my argument in an immediate political context. Contemporary political culture renders contructivist denials of "objective knowledge," even when they are couched in demands for plural explanations, social diversity, and cul-

22. Ibid., p. 4. For a similar formulation of the political implications of the postmodern-ist critique, see the introduction to another widely cited volume of left writings on post-modernism, Andrew Ross, ed. *Universal Abandon? The Politics of Postmodernism* (Minneapolis: University of Minnesota Press, 1988), pp. xii–xviii. Ross: "The political and philosophical traditions that underlie or 'ground' Western liberal capitalism and its various socialist alternatives . . . [are] rooted in the Enlightenment project of social, cultural, and political rationality, [and] they are also tied to propositions about the universality of that project—as a social logic through which the world ought to transform itself in the image of Western men" (p. xii). Ross maintains (as do many of the authors in the volume) that the critique of claims to universality is the hallmark of postmodernist thought. I suggest in this book that the discussion of postmodernism is best conducted not by an examination of claims to universalism, which always need to be further specified in the discursive con-texts in which the claims are advanced, but rather in terms of the underlying epistemologi-cal issues concerning objectivity. Our views about objectivity both explain and justify particular universalist claims.

tural tolerance, socially conservative instead of radical. Whereas in the late sixties when arguments for the recognition of social diversity and difference had a political edge in Western Europe and the United States, now diversity and "multiculturalism" are just as often used as slogans by the corporate establishment. In fact, to take contemporary race politics in Britain as an example, both Labour and Tory governments have used arguments for cultural diversity based on a notion of cultural particularism to divide and depoliticize the "black" Left. The singular achievement of the antiracist Left in Britain is that, over the course of the sixties and seventies, it created a viable unity of people of Asian and Afro-Caribbean descent under the political term "black." "Race" was a political category in this context because it emphasized the class solidarity of Asian and Afro-Caribbean workers and identified their common interests against the discriminatory practices of the state. In the midseventies, however, the British government adopted a policy of "liberal multiculturalism" that in effect promoted separatism in the name of cultural diversity. Funds were poured into local black organizations to encourage exploration of cultural differences and backgrounds; a public discourse that recognized diversity and emphasized cultural pluralism in fact ended up depoliticizing race and substituting (a narrowly defined) "culture" for antiracist consciousness. One of Britain's foremost black activists diagnosed this situation in a pioneering critique of the ambiguities of contemporary liberalism:

The combined strategy of promoting individual cultures, funding self-help groups and setting down antidiscriminatory and equal opportunity guidelines . . . began finally to break down the earlier cohesion of culture, community and class. Multiculturalism deflected the political concerns of the black community into the cultural concerns of different communities, the struggle against racism to the struggle for culture. Government funding of self-help groups undermined the self-reliance, the self-created social and economic base, of these groups: they were no longer responsive to or responsible for the people they served—and service itself became a profitable concern.[23]

23. A. Sivanandan, "RAT and the Degradation of Black Struggle," *Race and Class* 26 (Spring 1985), 6. Sivanandan provides an excellent bibliography in his notes; the reader may also wish to consult Paul Gilroy, *There Ain't No Black in the Union Jack* (London: Hutchinson, 1987), and Peter Fryer, *Staying Power: The History of Black People in Britain* (London: Pluto Press, 1984). Back issues of *Race and Class* are an invaluable resource. See also Sivanandan's collection of essays *A Different Hunger* (London: Pluto Press, 1982).

Such examples offer us an important lesson: the political value of slogans about difference and pluralism is not self-evident. In particular, the ambiguous politics of hegemony in contemporary societies, the processes through which cultural ideas are reshaped and consent manufactured, teaches us why the antiobjectivist pluralist stance of "theory" needs to be historically specified and evaluated. Is, for instance, the black British activists' emphasis on the *reality* of "race" as a *fact* of both social domination and oppositional identity merely an "objectivist" delusion or an essentialist nostalgia, to be theoretically liberated by the (state-sponsored) idea of multiculturalism? In the United States, Michael Omi and Howard Winant have shown how an objective analysis of racist domination was obscured by an intellectual agenda that emphasized the cultural multiplicity of "ethnic" identities, but the ideology of ethnicity did not emerge out of a neoconservative conspiracy; it was a vision (much like British multiculturalism) of liberal intellectuals.[24] In this context, our political questioning of objectivity and reason, with the attendant suspicion of the universalizing tendency in modern thought, needs to be situated in history. Certain kinds of pluralism and relativism have been, at best, ambiguous allies of the Left.

Outlining an Alternative Theory and Politics

My position in this book originates in the belief that the constructivism that informs so much of postmodernist literary theory is *intellectually* inadequate or outdated. The arguments against objectivity and rationality are largely intended to displace notions of reason, explanation, and science that we have inherited from positivism. Some of the defining features of positivism are: (a) a hard and rigid distinction between science and non-science; (b) a similar demarcation of the world of "facts" from the world of "values"; and (c) a conception of objective knowledge as a goal that is reached by eliminating all subjective bias, all social or political interest. Postmodernism's denial of objectivity is a critique of this particular conception of objectivity and the related notions of science, fact, and value. But the postmodernist critique of knowledge is limited because it does not consider reasonable alternatives to the positivist view. At least since the 1970s, a nonconstructivist alternative to positivism has been emerging. This postpositivist tradi-

24. See Michael Omi and Howard Winant, *Racial Formation in the United States* (London: Routledge & Kegan Paul, 1986), esp. chap. 1.

tion, which is a version of philosophical realism, offers sophisticated accounts of objectivity and reason, basing itself on a reexamination of the actual nature of the "hard" sciences as complexly coordinated social practices. Postpositivist realists claim, for instance, that the "hard" sciences are not as hard as the positivists thought they were, for scientists typically rely on more than direct observation in the testing of theories. Not unlike their colleagues in the human sciences, they also rely on a whole host of background assumptions and theories, and on untested and nonexperimental "lore." Scientific knowledge, then, is holistic and relational in some of the ways the various hermeneutical traditions suggest knowledge in the human sciences is. If our traditional understanding of scientific norms and criteria is not accurate, how must we reorient our political critiques of them?

This is the question that frames my book. I begin with two chapters that deal directly with language and meaning, of central concern in contemporary literary-critical thought. I argue against a popular poststructuralist view of language and explore alternatives to it. Finding the view of linguistic reference held by Paul de Man inadequate in crucial respects, I propose that a cogent theory of language needs to explain both how language is capable of autonomous productivity and how it is socially determined. The de Manian position is representative because it elevated to the status of doctrine some of the unease poststructuralist theories about language have always expressed about reference, in particular about the extent to which it "fixes" meaning. More than Jacques Derrida's, Paul de Man's writings reveal a desire to go beyond any kind of determinacy (and hence objectivity of interpretation) that linguistic reference might require. De Man's theologization of language as endlessly disruptive of secure interpretation is predicated in part on a dubious reading of Charles Sanders Peirce's notion of the interpretant, which de Man sees as a refutation of the idea that the way words refer to the world might limit the range of interpretations we consider legitimate. The key de Manian claim is that the semiotic productivity of language can be adequately understood only when we have rid ourselves of our beliefs in "extralinguistic" (referential) determination of meaning. I think this key claim is false, and I explain in Chapters 1 and 2 how the much-misunderstood Peirce in fact showed that we can account for the productivity of language (its unceasing "semiosis") only when we have understood how reference is culturally and historically determined. Drawing on Mikhail Bakhtin, Hilary Putnam, and Saul Kripke, I also explain how the social moorings of language might be understood as essential to it. That is, if we are going to explain how language works, we cannot relegate the social processes of reference to the realm of the "extralinguistic" as de Man and every other formalist wish to do. My discussion attempts to show that reference is best conceived as an epistemological notion involving a variety of practices and traditions of social inquiry and that an adequate theory of language (and, by implication, of linguistic texts) needs to address both epistemic and social-theoretical questions.

In Chapters 3 and 4 I discuss how Louis Althusser and Fredric Jameson, both marxists working in very close contact with poststructuralism, particularly its worries about reference, usefully translate the more extreme and abstract claims about indeterminacy of meaning (and objective interpretation) into a more productive concern with how historical interpretation is inevitably textual and dialogic, and why historical knowledge cannot be conceived in positivist terms. Hence these theorists make an advance over the formalist position(s) against which I argue in the first two chapters.

But both Althusser and Jameson, especially in some of their key theoretical formulations, show an inadequate understanding of the social bases of knowledge, importing wholesale the reigning poststructuralist ideas about epistemology and the subject. Thus Althusser's theory of ideology, while elucidating the complexly material ways in which human creatures become social subjects by incorporating beliefs and values of the dominant order, remains within a curiously formalist notion of the human subject, which is philosophically impoverished since it sees individuals as mere products of the dominant ideology. What his theory cannot explain are agency, reason, and creativity; like all (post)-structuralists, Althusser (in the essay on Lacan) hints at but does not elaborate a philosophical anthropology, an account of human needs and capacities which might explain why humans are not only the subjects of ideology but also agents of their own freedom, of rational struggle and creative social change. The problem (as will be evident in retrospect from the vantage point of Chapters 5, 6, and 7) is that Althusser's theory of ideology lacks an understanding of the dialectical relation between error and truth, between socially produced mystification and socially produced objective knowledge. It lacks such an understanding in part because Althusser has no conception of how our deepest evaluative terms—freedom or rational agency, for instance—might be epistemically justified.

The problem, similar to the one I point out in the case of Jameson (see the last section of Chapter 4), is that poststructuralist marxists are often weakest in their theory of knowledge, since they assume in advance that poststructuralist theories of language, signification, and subjectivity provide us with all the epistemology we need. Jameson, who synthesizes the Hegelian marxist tradition and the Althusserian one, providing in the process a useful and complex theory of textual interpretation, nevertheless leaves unaddressed more basic questions about historical-materialist epistemology and metaphysics. He takes over a weak view of subjectivity and knowledge from structuralism and poststructuralism, never questioning their unyielding skepticism about metaphysical questions. The result is the curious paradox that the marxist Jameson often relies on an individualist and asocial epistemology.

At best, this situation leads to a kind of vagueness, in the case of Jameson and others like him; at worst, the underexamined problems of reference and knowledge lead to relativism of one variety or another. Cultural relativism, for instance, is sanctioned by some vague notion that if textual meanings are in principle indeterminate and (in some formulations, because) objective interpretations are always unstable, then it must be impossible for us to understand other cultures. Their commitment to historical materialism fortunately prevents both Althusser and Jameson from espousing any kind of extreme cultural or historical relativism, but it is evidence of their status as transitional figures (in terms of intellectual history, in the encounter with poststructuralism, as well as for the purposes of my exposition) that they remain so unconcerned about the need to develop an adequate materialist epistemology, one that will help link science with politics, reason with value. It is the goal of the second part of this book to tackle more directly a few of the key issues that such an epistemology would face, building on the discussion of the social and epistemic nature of linguistic reference in Chapter 2.

Chapter 5 interrogates the pervasive rhetoric of otherness in contemporary theory and criticism, raising doubts about the value of the various kinds of relativism implied by the postmodernist slogans of fragmentation and discontinuity. Focusing on cultural and historical relativism in particular, especially in debates within anthropology and cultural studies, I examine the claim that relativism leads to greater tolerance of the unfamiliar or the new. In my view, relativism of any kind is inadequate for cross-cultural understanding, and unless we find terms with which we can begin to understand others, and in particular our real differences—and similarities—with them, we cannot conceive what genuine tolerance might mean and what a genuinely multiculturalist society would look like.

The key antipositivist insight of contemporary culture consists in the recognition of epistemological holism, whether of the Heideggerian or Gadamerian "hermeneutical" variety or the kind evident in, say, W. V. O. Quine's or Thomas Kuhn's demonstration that even seemingly innocent scientific "observations" are in crucial respects theory dependent. I implicitly draw on the first variety in Chapter 5 and directly discuss the second in Chapter 6, and in each case my goal is to show that holism does not necessary lead to relativism. The recognition that it is impossible to evaluate statements and texts from other cultures in isolation—by excluding, for instance, an examination of the prejudices and presuppositions we bring with us from our culture—should not lead us to conclude that we cannot ever objectively interpret or evaluate such statements and texts. In Chapter 5, among other things, I maintain against postmodernists that we have much in common across cultures (human agency, for one thing), so that cultural relativism should be seen as intellectually underjustified as well as politically misguided.

The final two chapters turn to the task of outlining a realist conception of knowledge and politics. The first part of Chapter 6 examines the pragmatist argument for postmodernism, especially through a consideration of Richard Rorty's powerful critique of epistemological foundationalism. I show how the critique is valuable, as well as how it accounts for the social bases of knowledge production, but I argue that it does not necessarily lead to postmodernist conclusions. By pointing out the central issues involved in the critique of foundationalism and positivist methodology, I show that a thoroughgoing antifoundationalism is equally compatible with a realist view of scientific inquiry as a social practice and the naturalistic conception of knowledge that goes with it. The discussion focuses on the central concepts that underlie the claims of postmodernism (of both the poststructuralist and the pragmatist varieties), whether or not they are explicitly discussed in contemporary debates in literary and cultural theory. I both identify these concepts and explain what is at stake in the different ways of defining them, especially when we consider the postpositivist realist alternative. I thus specify the implications of epistemological holism, outline alternative definitions of explanation and causation, and discuss the relations among the different domains of human inquiry. I explain exactly how the lessons of holism can be incorporated into a postpositivist realist view of human inquiry, a view that is nonrelativist and yet (thus?) open to epistemic fallibility. It is on a hermeneutical basis, I contend, that we need to understand the idea of objective knowledge or objective social interests not only in the natural sciences but in social and moral inquiry as well. The last two chapters find that a naturalist conception of human inquiry would be central to this postpositivist understanding of objectivity as socially conditioned and produced (and hence radically revisable and antifoundationalist). In this conception, what we know about successful or unsuccessful explanations, for instance, or about the phenomenon of causation, is limited to the empirical and theoretical knowledge we glean from our various domains of inquiry. And these domains of inquiry, whether in the natural or the human sciences, are open to revision, even radical and wholesale self-correction, not only because of their methodological "reflexivity" but also because they draw and build on empirical knowledge about the world, which is always subject to change. This naturalist conception of epistemology à la Quine thus ensures that realism will remain fallibilistic (Peirce's term), open to revision and correction.

At the same time, however, this nonfoundationalist naturalist approach would not be skeptical of all universal claims a priori, the way postmodernism is. Chapter 7 demonstrates how we might elaborate an objective theoretical account of cultural identity by examining the epistemic status of personal experience and cultural identity. I outline a realist account of experience and identity and indicate, through a detailed interpretation of Toni Morrison's important novel *Beloved*, how powerful contemporary notions of cultural politics—feminist, anticolonial, socialist—might be built out of a refigured image of objectivity. I also suggest how we might see writers such as Morrison as engaged in a project that is simultaneously historical and theoretical, a project that is in some ways continuous with the political concerns of postmodernist theorists. If my general account of the relation between experience and identity is convincing, it might suggest how we can avoid some blind alleys that postmodernist theory has created for us. If my interpretation of *Beloved* encourages readers to take Morrison's underlying vision of history, cultural memory, and community seriously as social and moral philosophy, it might also suggest to these readers how many of our contemporary political writers are engaged in a theoretical project that can take us beyond the debilitating skepticism of postmodernist thought. Toni Morrison and other writers are engaged in a realist project with a deep belief in the possibility of objective knowledge. In the context of their work we can see clearly why the positivist demarcation of a world of hard facts from a world of soft values leads to an impossibly constricted view of what responsible and reliable human inquiry is, and we can also see how we need to reconceptualize objectivity.

In particular, the concluding section of the book draws together and reemphasizes the various theoretical and political themes of the previous chapters by focusing on the epistemic status of "values." I also extend the realist theory of identity to a full-blown account of multiculturalism as a form of epistemic cooperation, based on a cognitivist view of culture as a field of moral inquiry, involving practice, experimentation, and rational conjecture. I show why a strong defense of multiculturalism ought to be based not on relativism but on a sound form of moral universalism and how such a radical universalism is compatible with the ideals of a healthy cultural—and indeed even moral—pluralism.

As I said earlier, this book grows out of the belief that for immediate historical reasons as well as more general intellectual ones, the extreme constructivism of many postmodernists is not satisfactory today. It will be evident in the following chapters why I do not think that an emphasis on the constructed, conventional nature of social meanings and institutions is incompatible with a postpositivist realist view of knowledge and the world. My presentation of the realist alternative is, however, necessarily sketchy, outlining a few core proposals rather than providing anything like a comprehensive defense of them. My primary goal in this book is to indicate how the central theses of postmodernism might be fruitfully identified as epistemological claims, where and why these claims are untenable, and what sort of alternative to them we can conceive. It is from a realist perspective, I suggest, that we can best understand the social distortions of knowledge and justify the social and political goals for which we struggle.

Part One

1

PAUL DE MAN, LANGUAGE,
AND THE POLITICS OF MEANING

If, as Richard Rorty suggests, American literary criticism since World War II has increasingly compensated for the "professionalization" of philosophy and its withdrawal into purely technical and academic concerns, then contemporary "criticism" is not merely a professional discipline but a larger social phenomenon, supplanting history, philosophy, or religion as the site of cultural and moral pedagogy par excellence.[1] The renaissance of "theory" in the American literary academy since the early seventies may, however, suggest a significantly different cultural prospect. The development of highly specialized languages of critical practice, assumptions about the inherent superiority of theory over immediate questions of textual interpretation, the particular combination of the prophetic tone with the desire for scientific rigor—all these point to a substantial change in the cultural role and function of contemporary literary criticism. Less a culturally effective discourse than a specialized set of language games, contemporary criticism may indeed resemble academic philosophy in its most technical modes, appealing to a trained coterie.

1. See Richard Rorty, "Professionalized Philosophy and Transcendentalist Culture," in *Consequences of Pragmatism* (Minneapolis: University of Minnesota Press, 1982), pp. 60–71. Harold Bloom stresses the responsibility the teacher of literature now has for a general moral pedagogy: "The teacher of literature now in America, far more than the teacher of history or philosophy or religion, is condemned to teach the presentness of the past, because history, philosophy and religion have withdrawn as agents from the Scene of Instruction" (cited in Rorty, p. 68). We may or may not respond to the plaintive tone of Bloom's

From the outside, it is possible to lament this truncation of the public functions of criticism. Edward Said, whose career straddles both high theory and the popular cultural critical modes, has attacked much of contemporary theory on the grounds of its political ineffectuality. By implicit contrast to the very critics Rorty would identify as the previous generation's culture heroes (including Lionel Trilling and Edmund Wilson), Said chides even marxist critics for their apparent contentment with the discursive contexts of academic institutions.[2] For anyone concerned with the politics of culture, this is certainly a significant charge and needs to be thought through. There are institutional pressures toward insularity and irrelevance. It is safer and more comfortable for an American cultural critic to write about theories of ideology than to analyze the hidden racist agenda of the state and its implications for immediate educational and cultural issues. But Said may be too hasty in assuming that critics such as Paul de Man and Harold Bloom are ineffectual angels, for the college literature classroom is often the register of fundamentally new aesthetic-cultural ideologies. The death of the author; the valorization of *jouissance*, not pleasure, the text, not the work; the play of mobile signifiers, not the search for determinable meaning—the slogans point to a basic systemic change that touches our discourses of society as well as of art. Such a phenomenon, then, requires at least an intrinsic theoretical critique, rather than a purely sociological diagnosis.

Theory and Pedagogy

The 1982 issue of *Yale French Studies* titled "The Pedagogical Imperative: Teaching as a Literary Genre"[3] may be in this instance an ideally representative text. Its emphasis on teaching—the theater, the politics, the discourses—grounds its theoretical discussion in a context with which all of us are familiar. Some of the essays are in the form of manifestos (Paul de Man's, for instance, or the editor's preface) and are thus easier to analyze. Others provide detailed textual analyses that enable

---

assertion, particularly in this passage, but it identifies a phenomenon both Rorty and Bloom describe in the same general terms.

2. See Edward W. Said, "Reflections on American 'Left' Criticism," in *The World, the Text, and the Critic* (Cambridge: Harvard University Press, 1983), pp. 158–79; and Said, "Opponents, Audiences, Constituencies, and Community," *Critical Inquiry* 9 (September 1982), 1-26, special issue "The Politics of Interpretation."

3. *Yale French Studies*, no. 63 (1982), hereafter abbreviated *TPI* and cited parenthetically in the text.

the authors to generalize about text, genre, social context, and their ideological interpenetrations (see, for example, Richard Terdiman's "Structures of Initiation: On Semiotic Education and Its Contradictions in Balzac"). Several of the other essays are models of witty, *nouvelle vague* criticism of individual texts with a desire to recapture itinerant meanings and impulses, the play of power or desire (Jane Gallop and Neil Hertz are the best examples here). In addition, there are short extracts from Derrida and Lyotard and essays by Barbara Johnson, Andrew McKenna, Michael Ryan, and others. At the heart of the volume, however, is Shoshana Felman's provocative essay "Psychoanalysis and Education: Teaching Terminable and Interminable," which formulates and clarifies the central implication of the title of the collection. Given the obviously rich diversity of the volume and the significance of its subject, it may be useful for any critical or ideological analysis to begin here. In these meditations on teaching the larger politics of contemporary theorizing about literature becomes evident, and it is possible to analyze both the politics and the theory in detail. My main emphasis in this chapter is on the work of Paul de Man, which has had a major influence in contemporary theory.

Let me begin by quoting from two of the essays in the first section of the volume:

> Whenever [the] autonomous potential of language can be revealed by analysis, we are dealing with literariness. (Paul de Man, "The Resistance to Theory," p. 10)

> One cannot determine the function of language and literature . . . without taking into account the political and economic functions and uses of language. (Michael Ryan, "Deconstruction and Radical Teaching," p. 55)

On one obvious level, these two quotations from the same volume might indicate a basic schism in methodology or approach. On the one hand, de Man, Barbara Johnson, Joan de Jean, and others appear to advocate something like an *intrinsic* approach in literary matters which would respect the internal dynamism of texts, of language and literature. On the other hand, marxists such as Ryan and Terdiman, it would seem at first glance, stress the *extrinsic*, the sociological dimension, opposing "history" to "language," and insisting that language and literature are defined in their "political and economic functions and uses." This division between the extrinsic and the intrinsic is, however, fundamentally misleading, particularly in a collection of essays such as this.

Much of the radical basis of contemporary theory—psychoanalytic, marxist, or what is called poststructuralist[4]—suggests that there is a fundamental commonality between the two approaches. Any understanding of American literary criticism today needs to start from an acknowledgment of this shared basis, this common ground so unlike the theoretical foundations of, say, New Criticism. This common idea is evident in claims about the text (and textuality), about language, about literature and literariness, about notions of context and history—in short in every major idea or term that is being debated in literary-critical journals. For convenience, let me call this a debate about textual "meaning." What guided much of the older debate about meaning was a concern for validity and correctness: Is this what this passage from *Finnegans Wake* or *The Faerie Queene* means? Under what conditions, with what guarantee, will we know what the limits of its meaning are? History, in these views, is either the (inert) context that must be recovered to clarify and instruct us in our search or (as with the New Critics) a covertly installed myth of literary and cultural history which sanctions "purely immanent" textual analysis and evaluation.[5] In the older context, then, we needed to be clear about what was being represented and about the form of the representation, but the new theoretical view renders many of these questions obsolete. Now the discussion is not about the *what* of meaning but about the *how*. A text is considered to be less a discrete and bounded object to be analyzed, with strata or levels to be unearthed, than a dynamic intertextual process, and the death of meaning is proclaimed because it is not the stable instances

4. For a critique of at least the terms "poststructuralism" and "deconstruction" as they are used in the United States, see Philip Lewis, "The Post-structuralist Condition," *Diacritics* 12 (Spring 1982), 2-24. I use "poststructuralist" to refer to the dominant strand of postmodernist theory, whose focus is on language and signifying systems but whose claims are basically epistemological.

5. Cf. Fredric Jameson's comment on New Criticism made in the context of his general discussion of "theories of history": "The New Critics—long thought by themselves as well as by others to be resolutely ahistorical—in reality devoted significant energies to the construction of historical paradigms: the dissociation of sensibility from Donne to Shelley, the reconquest of style and image from Swinburne to Yeats; such characteristic frameworks for analysis amount to Hegelian models of literary change. . . . Indeed . . . the individual analysis inevitably projects its own diachronic framework, it could not have been otherwise. Only this model now tries to pass itself off as a theory of history in its own right, and at once the characteristic marks of pseudohistory reappear: the obsession with historical rise and decline, the never-ending search for the date of the fall and the name of the serpent. . . . Such false problems . . . are in turn pressed into ideological service, in which an eschatological framework helps conservative politics masquerade as ethics in an ostensibly aesthetic enterprise." *Marxism and Form* (Princeton: Princeton University Press, 1971), pp. 323–24.

of meaning that critics wish to analyze now but rather its discursive mobility.

The political basis of this new emphasis can be appreciated only when we acknowledge the underlying claim that particular meanings are conventional or social, and hence "ideological" in their apparent naturalness. To attempt to deny meaning in theory, then, is to attempt to suspend the transmission of culturally dominant ideas in the natural course of things. Teaching our English 101 students to value "order," for instance, is not an innocent teaching of *Troilus and Cressida*; it is a specific form of acculturation. To oppose order to chaos, form (and culture) to nature, method to madness, is to be complicitous with the transmission of political *doxa*, to aid in the reproduction of the dominant ethical binarisms or ideologically coded hierarchies. Against this background, the new theory's para-doxical teaching is that meanings do not exist as such but are produced; what we thought we knew was an illusion of meaning, an effect of our subjective desires or our (political) positionings.

At their best, many of the essays in this issue (no matter what their methodology or ideological tag) implicitly display this concern. Paul de Man, for instance, rejects traditional aesthetic categories on the ground that they conjure up in one form or another a prediscursive connectedness of word and thing, valuing an ideal notion of experience and meaning over the instability of linguistic processes. For de Man, this instability is indeed "literariness," revealed in the "figurality" of language. Barbara Johnson, in much the same spirit, would see the "pedagogical moment" as best represented by a "blank" space, for it inherently seeks to transmit and codify that which cannot be known. In her essay on Molière's *Ecole des Femmes*, she substantiates this idea along much the same lines as I have just done:

> The question of education, in both Molière and Plato, is the question not of how to transmit but of how to *suspend* knowledge. . . . In a negative sense, not knowing results from repression, whether conscious or unconscious. Such negative ignorance may be the necessary by-product—or even the precondition—of any education whatsoever. But positive ignorance, the pursuit of what is forever in the act of escaping, the inhabiting of that space where knowledge becomes the obstacle to knowing—*that* is the pedagogical imperative we can nei-

jyther fulfill nor disobey. ("Teaching Ignorance: *L'Ecole des Femmes*,"
p. 182)

The ideal, then, is to "suspend knowledge," not to "transmit" it, to
foster a "positive ignorance" of that which is culturally coded and determined. As in the case of de Man, Johnson sees the role of literature as
constitutive in this process: literariness is the self-deconstructing play
of language over and within the discourses of the conventional and the
ideological. Jane Gallop reads Sade's *Philosophy in the Bedroom* as a
celebration of an "irrational bodily materiality" that subverts "rational
order," the guarantor of cultural meaning. Michael Ryan, enlarging the
analysis to what we more familiarly call "institutions" (such as the university), considers the institutional codedness of knowledges and values. The assumption of objectivity in teaching, Ryan says, operates on
the basis of an exclusion of what cannot be thought within the institutional power hierarchies; the norms of "propriety" and "integrity" can
be deconstructed to show how they guarantee the persistence of existing power relations. It follows from all these accounts, then, that meanings are highly charged *values*, not innocent counters of literary-critical
discourse. The repudiation of objective meaning is based on the recognition of its implication in politics; to suspend it is to enable us to progress from coded knowledges to positive and liberating "ignorance." The
critical emphasis on the social constructedness of meanings thus reflects an interest in a wide range of cultural and political issues that
may well be central to contemporary intellectual culture.[6]

The general critique of objective meaning can be understood on another theoretical level. This is a specifically poststructuralist point,
often made by Althusserian marxism, psychoanalysis (especially after
Lacan), and post-Saussurean philosophies of language. The common and
far-reaching assertion is that "meaning" must be attacked in its superficial homogeneity, its ideality, because it always implies the corresponding categories of consciousness and self-present experience. The
speciousness of such categories is shown in the context of the Coperni-

6. The current influence of literary theory on other fields—social and political theory,
anthropology, history—is largely due to the popular acceptance of the constructivist thesis.
See, e.g., *Social Postmodernism: Beyond Identity Politics*, ed. Linda Nicholson and Steven
Seidman (Cambridge: Cambridge University Press, 1995); Joan Wallach Scott, *Gender and
the Politics of History* (New York: Columbia University Press, 1988), esp. chap. 2; Judith
Butler and Joan W. Scott, Introduction to *Feminists Theorize the Political*, ed. Butler and
Scott (London: Routledge, 1992), pp. xiii–xvii; James Clifford, *The Predicament of Culture*
(Cambridge: Harvard University Press, 1988), esp. pp. 21–54.

can discoveries that are said to inform literary theory: the radical alterity of the unconscious in Lacanian psychoanalytic theory, not the unplumbed depths of consciousness but its unrepresentable blank edge; the Althusserian thesis, in marxism, that history is not inert context or linear narrative but a text that can be grasped only in the symptomatic gaps within our discourses; and finally the postmodernist claim that language is not so much a human instrument as the very index of our finitude, speaking its own alien history through us. The central lesson is that the mastery of the human subject over its meanings and its consciousness is uncertain and spurious.[7]

In these accounts true knowledge is less a substance to be learned or transmitted than what Shoshana Felman (in her essay in *TPI*) calls a veritable "structure of address," an acknowledgment of the complex transsubjective play of our positionings within desire and ideology, ignorance and insight. Pedagogy, particularly in the realm of culture, needs, then, to face the fundamental challenge to escape both the transmission of coded knowledge and the coded transmission of knowledge. It must suspend this continuity, question the self-evidence of meanings by invoking the radical, but determining, alterities that disrupt our flawless discourses of knowledge. In a valuable discussion of psychoanalysis as a pedagogic process, Felman concludes that pedagogy is itself akin to psychoanalysis:

> Teaching, like analysis, has to deal not so much with *lack* of knowledge as with *resistances* to knowledge. Ignorance, suggests Lacan, is a "passion." . . . Ignorance, in other words[,] is nothing other than a *desire to ignore*: its nature is less cognitive than performative; . . . it is not a simple lack of information but the incapacity—or the refusal—to acknowledge *one's own implication* in the information. (p. 30)

Learning is dialogic, but not in the traditional Socratic sense. For it involves a necessary implication not only in the desire not to know, but also in the radical alterity of the unconscious. Teaching is a fundamentally ideological act to the extent that it ignores the political ruses of

7. The general inspiration for this last idea is Nietzsche, especially his "naturalist" critique of rationalism. See, e.g., *The Will to Power*, trans. Walter Kaufmann and R. J. Hollingdale, ed. Kaufmann (New York: Vintage, 1968), pp. 263–67, secs. 477–80. But Nietzsche's hopeful views about the possibility of objective knowledge (e.g., *On the Genealogy of Morals*, in *Basic Writings of Nietzsche*, trans. and ed. Walter Kaufmann [New York: Modern Library, 1968], p. 555, Third Essay, sec. 12) should also be kept in mind, especially since these are generally ignored by literary theorists (see below, pp. 40–42).

desire and ignorance and focuses on self-evident or even "objective" knowledge.

It is in this general intellectual context, then, that we need to understand the polemics about language or textuality. When the deconstructionist wants to put the text *en abîme*, to show how the "tropics" of discourse unravel the sutured text and reveal an imbricated intertextuality, we need at least to appreciate the political implications of the constructivist thesis. Meanings, structures, totalities are revealed in their pure conventionality—declared to be provisional and produced. The inner harmony of textual meaning is disrupted by the alien music that refuses to respect the convenient dichotomies of inner and outer, text and context. It is in this sense that the politics of Paul de Man's influential position is best appreciated. The appeal of de Man's work derives not so much from its analytical rigor as from what one critic identifies as the "rhetoric of authority."[8] The political claims of his theory, however, depend on his constructivist critique of some of the central categories of criticism and philosophy.

De Man's contribution to "The Pedagogical Imperative," "The Resistance to Theory," is almost a manifesto, and may thus be an opportune place to begin an analysis. The essay was originally commissioned by the Committee on the Research Activities of the Modern Language Association of America for a volume titled *Introduction to Scholarship in*

---

8. Frank Lentricchia, *After the New Criticism* (Chicago: University of Chicago Press, 1980), pp. 282–317. This may also be the place to indicate the main reason I find Lentricchia's critique of de Man not entirely convincing. It is not because Lentricchia reads de Man (as Jonathan Culler puts it—see *On Deconstruction* [Ithaca: Cornell University Press, 1982], p. 229) "as an existentialist," but because I find that after accepting that it is "necessary to agree" with de Man's theoretical arguments, Lentricchia falls back on the familiar (and weak) "But what about politics?" kind of criticism. Lentricchia's critique—we accept the necessity of the aporetic within an insular "wall-to-wall discourse," but "we must resist" it—is inadequate: "Where has de Man left things? Even should we agree that in the world of wall-to-wall discourse the *aporia* is inevitable—and I believe it is necessary to agree to this and to the poststructuralist problematic upon which the idea rests—we must resist being pushed there, unless we wish to find ourselves with de Man and other avant-garde critics into the realm of the thoroughly predictable linguistic transcendental, where all literature speaks synchronically and endlessly the same tale. . . . In this realm the discourse of literature would suppress the powerfully situating and coercive discourses of politics, economics, and other languages of social manipulation" (Lentricchia, p. 317). One of my implicit claims is that to want to "resist" the cogency of "wall-to-wall discourse" is to have misconceived the issues from the start; any insular perspective cannot be significantly analyzed by merely stressing that the world "outside" exists and that it would be healthy to acknowledge it. Rather, an adequate critique must expose the complicity of the insular "inside" with its domesticated notion of the "outside."

Modern Languages and Literatures, but the editors, as de Man tells us himself, subsequently rejected it. The reason may not be too difficult to assess. De Man, who was supposed to write on the state of the art of research in literary theory, chose to emphasize the general de Manian thesis that the "main theoretical interest of literary theory consists in the impossibility of its definition" and to support this claim by stressing the unstable basis of any scholarly field that has as its focus language or literature. This approach may seem reasonable, especially considering the peculiar resistance of literature to reductive exegesis and commentary. As we go on, however, problems begin to arise. What purported to be a survey of the field turns out to be a peculiarly de Manian version of things: "The resistance to theory is a resistance to the rhetorical or tropological dimension of language, a dimension which is perhaps more explicitly in the foreground in literature (broadly conceived) than in other verbal manifestations" (p. 17). Elsewhere in the essay we have been told that "literariness" is revealed when we are dealing with the "autonomous potential" of language, when we move beyond naive representational conceptions of language that posit a natural and primordial link between sign and referent, the name and the thing named. The critique of reductionist views of language forms the basis of de Man's thought; much of his work is intended to challenge our notions of reference or expression and their role in linguistic and literary processes. Hence de Man's insistent emphasis on the tropological dimension, on language as unstable and (more important) self-deconstructing play. Powerful and strategic as this view may be in contemporary literary-theoretical debates, this is only one view, and an E. D. Hirsch or an Edward Said may have considerable difficulty accepting it as the constitutive claim of contemporary theory. It is easier now to understand the hesitation of the editors who rejected the essay; but its open biases may make the piece all that much more valuable for my discussion.

De Man's theory is formulated through a rejection of all those theories of language which would deny what he considers its autonomously productive nature. Whether it be the legacy of phenomenology or hermeneutics, on the one hand, or the residual phenomenalism of some versions of semiotics, on the other, de Man's critique seeks to displace and problematize the source and locus of secure interpretations. Therefore, his main targets of attack are those theories that short-circuit the aleatory dynamics of language by a hasty assimilation of these processes into uncritical notions of the phenomenal world as the source and guarantor of the meanings of linguistic texts. The problem with de Man's view of language, however, is that it proceeds a little too hastily from a rejection of crude notions of reference as a guarantee of meaning to an implausible theory of language (and literature) as essentially figural, defined by the indeterminable rhetorical play that subverts the security of any meaning. As a negative gesture, rhetoric is a useful deconstructive tool, and literariness a valuable political slogan. When rhetoric itself is hypostatized, however, a new essentialism emerges. Meanings are no longer insistently derived from the "world," but they are denied with a similar insistence, invoking an unchanging machinery of tropical self-dissolution.

The first major issue that is obscured by de Man's extreme and unqualified opposition between referential meaning and rhetorical play is what both semiotics and contemporary analytic philosophy identify as a genuine philosophical issue—the complexly mediated relations between "words" and "the world," the causal interactions between language and the contexts in which it is produced or interpreted. If we refuse to consider the referent as a real object that guarantees the artificial circumscription of every semiotic operation and provides a theological security to interpretation, then, such theorists of the sign as Peirce and Hilary Putnam would say, *reference* points to a larger question, which deals with the *social determination* of signifying practices, linguistic or otherwise. This question opens out onto the entire problematic that preoccupied such founders of our intellectual modernity as Marx and Freud (note, for instance, the transposed history of the concept of "overdetermination" borrowed from *The Interpretation of Dreams* by the marxist philosopher Althusser),[9] as well as such radical thinkers as Derrida, whose "grammatological" project would pose, in (re)considering the "problems of critical reading, . . . the question of the text, its historical status, its proper time and space."[10] But de Man, with

9. See particularly "Contradiction and Overdetermination," in Louis Althusser, *For Marx*, trans. Ben Brewster (London: New Left Books, 1977), pp. 87–128. Althusser's essay on Lacan may also be of interest in this context. See "Freud and Lacan," in *Lenin and Philosophy and Other Essays*, trans. Ben Brewster (New York: Monthly Review Press, 1971), pp. 189–219.

10. Jacques Derrida, *Of Grammatology*, trans. Gayatri Chakravorty Spivak (Baltimore: Johns Hopkins University Press, 1976), p. lxxxix. But although Derrida asserts that "the science of writing—*grammatology*—shows signs of liberation all over the world," he must be cautious, for to think *history* (or the "text's historical status") is a far from simple problem, and needs, first of all, to be *posed*. The question can be posed only if it recognizes its dependence on a complex network of determinations: "The idea of science and the idea of writing—therefore also of the science of writing—is meaningful for us only in terms of an origin and within a world to which a certain concept of the sign . . . and a certain concept of the relationships between speech and writing, have *already* been assigned. A most determined relationship, in spite of its privilege, its necessity" (p. 4).

his emphasis on the "autonomy" of language, is unable to see the relation between such autonomy and (social) determination as anything but purely oppositional. The reason is that de Man understands such determination only in the most simplistic way, as a monocausal relation between "signs" and "things" which is essentially self-evident without the mediation of theories, cultures, or paradigms. The conception of reference which underlies de Man's theory of the productivity of language is narrowly empiricist. In this chapter and the next, I would like to substantiate my claim about de Man and show what a more adequate theory of reference would need to explain. I argue implicitly that we can begin to understand the productivity of language and signification only when we have a better account of reference which explains the complex *variety* of (causal) relations between language and the world and, in particular, between signs and their social contexts.

"Language" as a Model for Critical Reading

De Man's criticism is most powerful when we treat its hypotheses about language and literature as purely heuristic, as methodological fictions. But de Man's claims about literariness, reference, and the nature of language are not isolated theses that arise only in the context of his textual readings; they are themselves supported by an identifiable epistemological position, which I would like to elucidate and then critique.

De Man's view of language points to a substantial metaphysical thesis, one that underwrites a distinct epistemological position. In *Blindness and Insight*, de Man declares his intention to examine the constitutive problem of all criticism as the "necessary immanence of the [critical] reading in relation to the [literary] text."[11] His interest is thus in the (unstable) "cognitive status" of "the language of criticism in general" (p. 119). In examining the works of such critics as Georg Lukács, Georges Poulet, and even Derrida, de Man means to delineate the gap between their "method" and their "insight" (p. 106). The uneasy encounter between critics and the (literary) texts they write about is symptomatic of a more general epistemological uncertainty; the unease, de Man claims, is unavoidable. In *Allegories of Reading*, de Man deconstructs the totalizations of meaning which inhere in critical

11. Paul de Man, *Blindness and Insight*, 2d ed., rev. (Minneapolis: University of Minnesota Press, 1983), p. 110, hereafter *BI*.

methods (for example, semiology) and in philosophical and aesthetic concepts (for instance, the classical notion of trope or the coherence of logic). The implication of such readings for literary criticism becomes even clearer in de Man's later collection *The Rhetoric of Romanticism*, where the period concept of "romanticism" is shown, through readings of Wordsworth, Shelley, Hölderlin, and Kleist, to have no more than a fictional coherence, to be unable to sustain a plausible literary history. Criticism, de Man implies, can do no more than project coherent fictions of history and knowledge; its necessary dependence on the literariness of the literary text severely qualifies its cognitive claims.

De Man's readings are critiques of critique; but as meta- or paracriticism such readings are effective only to the extent that they take the literary text (that is, that in relation to which the original critic's language has an "immanent" existence) as a contingent unknown, as the model of the unformulatable Other unwittingly manifested in the critic's discourse. The positive status of the literary, then, needs to be an open and variable question, to be "read" contextually rather than determined in advance. It ought to be approached asymptotically in the interplay of blindness and insight in specific critical texts, in critical readings themselves considered as ideologies of reading, of the text, indeed of the literary itself. The uncompromisingly critical nature of de Man's project depends, then, on its radicalization of *reading*: insofar as it is irreducibly intertextual or interstitial, its deconstructive movement keeps speculative and essentialist metaphysical assertions at bay.

But underlying de Man's criticism is a theory of language (and a related notion of literariness) which renders such radical reading impossible. For in all his works, there has always been the assertion that it is a certain essential property of language which performs the deconstruction of critical and interpretive discourses. In the opening essay of *Allegories of Reading* "rhetoric" or the "figural potentiality of language" is equated with "literature itself."[12] Hence, "poetic writing is the most advanced and refined mode of deconstruction; it may differ from critical or discursive writing in the economy of its articulation, but not in kind" (p. 17). "Literariness" performs the most rigorous criticism, and in his own critical work, de Man claims, he is only "trying to come closer to being as rigorous a reader as the author had to be in order to write the [text] in the first place" (p. 17). No simple intentional fallacy is involved here, however. In "The Rhetoric of Blindness" de Man had disclaimed

12. Paul de Man, *Allegories of Reading* (New Haven: Yale University Press, 1979), p. 10, hereafter *AR*.

any such notion, pointing rather to the "knowledge that [Rousseau's] language, as language, conveys about itself, thereby asserting the priority of the category of language over that of presence" (*BI*, p. 119). This characteristic of Rousseau's language, that is, its knowledge of itself, is what distinguishes it as literary. More fundamentally, this definition of the literary is predicated on a prior understanding of all language as primarily figural. For like music, language is a "diachronic system of relationships" but essentially, again by analogy, "a mere structure because it is hollow at the core" (p. 128). (This is the insight of Rousseau's which de Man chastises Derrida for being blind to.) The metaphoricity that exists as the "origin" of all languages has no "literal referent. Its only referent is 'le néant des choses humaines' " (p. 135). This thesis about language is never seriously examined in de Man's work. Indeed, many of the details of his critical project depend on such a view of language and the related thesis about literature as that language which "implicitly or explicitly signifies its own rhetorical mode" (*BI*, p. 136).

In *Allegories of Reading* the chapter titled "Metaphor," which also deals with Rousseau, makes the metaphysical and epistemological underpinnings of this view of language quite explicit. The human condition is such that there is a "discrepancy between the outer and the inner properties of entities" (p. 150), and we need to accept this "condition of permanent suspense between a literal world in which appearance and nature coincide and a figural world in which this correspondence is no longer *a priori* posited" (p. 151). The "literal world," one may infer, is the world in which "reference" guarantees objective meaning, where meanings are self-evidently there ("appearance and nature coincide") since words simply mirror the external world with no need for mediating concepts or theories. Such an image of direct and absolute "correspondence" amounts to more than a view of language; it is also a foundationalist theory of knowledge, and foundationalism is what de Man wishes to avoid. What he opposes to such a foundationalist theory is an alternative account of the relation between language and knowledge. Language, he says, is inherently reflexive—"language is about language" (p. 153)—and this reflexivity secures for it a kind of epistemic privilege over all forms of human thought. Thus, for instance, "the self-reflective moment of the *cogito* . . . is not an original event but itself an allegorical (or metaphorical) version of an intralinguistic structure, with all the negative epistemological consequences this entails" (p. 153 n. 28). The epistemological consequences are negative because language denies not only that there is an a priori correspondence between words and the world which can secure the objectivity of human knowledge but also that objective knowledge as such is ever possible: "*All* language is . . . a conceptual, figural, metaphorical metalanguage. As such, it partakes of the blindness of metaphor when metaphor literalizes its referential indetermination into a specific unit of meaning" (pp. 152–53, emphasis added).

How do we explain this unique reflexivity that makes language an exemplary model for all human inquiry? We don't. It is quite simply the essential nature of language, for at its heart is a "conceptualization" that "consists first of all of a wild, spontaneous metaphor which is, to some degree, aberrant" (*AR*, p. 153). But it is "not intentional, because it does not involve the interests of the subject in any way" (p. 154): the aberration "results exclusively from a formal, rhetorical potential of the language" (p. 154). This thesis about the "wild" and "spontaneous" origin of language explains de Man's epistemological view. It is this thesis that subtends (and accounts for) the *necessary* "blindness" of the critical texts de Man reads: in one way or another, these works misread—in a manner they cannot avoid, for it is constitutive of their implication in the "literary" text—the more "enlightened" texts de Man would call "literary." The "light" that is the property of literary texts blinds rather than reveals, because of its abyssal vision of the "nothingness" (*le néant*) we glimpsed earlier. Aberration is constitutive of metaphoricity, and so, it must be stressed here, are its wildness and its "spontaneous" springing forth. In de Man's theory, we can read no further.[13] The negative epistemological thesis is supported by a deep and unwavering metaphysical conviction about the nature of language and the human condition, and this conviction is not open to examination. That explains why every critical reading can, a priori, be translated as an attempt at mastery, and deconstructed by language.[14]

13. Rousseau, for de Man, is a "non-blinded author" whose "first readers" are always "blinded": "These blinded first readers . . . then need, in turn, a critical reader who reverses the tradition [of their misreadings] and momentarily takes us closer to the original insight. The existence of a particularly rich aberrant tradition in the case of the writers who can legitimately be called the most enlightened, is therefore no accident, but a constitutive part of all literature" (*BI*, p. 141).

14. It should be clear that I am suggesting that there is a fundamental continuity between de Man's early work (*BI* in particular) and the later essays collected in *AR*. This is an issue that has been the subject of the most fruitful debate surrounding de Man's work; the two best essays I have read on de Man are sharply opposed. See Rodolphe Gasché, " 'Setzung' and 'Übersetzung': Notes on Paul de Man," *Diacritics* 11 (Winter 1981), 36–57, and Suzanne Gearhart, "Philosophy *before* Literature: Deconstruction, Historicity, and the Work of Paul de Man," *Diacritics* 13 (Winter 1983), 63–81. On the whole, my position here is closer to Gearhart's.

I think it would be useful to understand exactly how de Man's views evolved, but the

So this view of language is based on more than a simple description of how literary texts work, for what we have here is not an independent account of language or literature so much as a more fundamental theory of *knowledge*, presented in the form of propositions about literature, rhetoric, or tropes. In "Rhetoric of Tropes (Nietzsche)" (*AR*, pp. 103–18) this underlying theory becomes explicit; de Man endorses an argument he ascribes to Nietzsche: "Philosophy [that is, epistemology] turns out to be an endless reflection on its own destruction at the hands of literature [that is, the kind of language that is most aware of its rhetorical nature]" (p.115) because "all rhetorical structures . . . are based on substitutive reversals [of such epistemological terms and values as "truth" and "error"], and it seems unlikely that one more such reversal over and above the ones that have already taken place would suffice to restore things to their proper order. One more 'turn' or trope added to a series of earlier reversals will not stop the turn towards error" (p. 113). There is thus no distinction to be made between *grades* of truth or error, for once we have given up our "naïve belief in the proper meaning of . . . metaphor" (p. 111)—which is like our naive belief in the referential meaning of words—we come to acknowledge "the necessary subversion of truth by rhetoric as the distinctive feature of all language" (p. 110). This subverted "truth" is not the property of a particular theory that is deficient in some respect but rather the very idea of a truth that can in principle *be distinguished from* error.

It might be instructive to reexamine the passage from Nietzsche de

---

critical assessment of a substantive account of language and knowledge is unavoidable. Many progressive writers have tended to focus exclusively on faithful exegesis of de Man's views or on showing how they can be either politically useful or dangerous. The faithful exegeses amount to a serious underreading, I think, and it is premature to debate the "political" uses. Before we can discuss whether de Man's ideas are politically progressive, we must analyze them as ideas, as evaluatable claims. For a useful but analytically limited account of the evolution of de Man's views, see Lindsay Waters, "Introduction: Paul de Man, Life and Works," in de Man, *Critical Writings, 1953–1978*, ed. Waters (Minneapolis: University of Minnesota Press, 1989), pp. ix–lxxiv; the brief discussion of Walter Benjamin's influence is relevant background for the development of de Man's epistemological views. For a good example of a progressive critic's defense of de Man as politically useful, as providing a view of language which can be used for the purposes of ideology critique, see Michael Sprinker, *Imaginary Relations* (London: Verso, 1987), pp. 237–66. Sprinker does not evaluate de Man's claims but interprets them by showing how they are compatible with (or analogous to) the Althusserian claim that "*ideology is eternal*, exactly like the unconscious" (quoted on p. 264). My own position in this book is that such claims, and the epistemological theories that underlie them, need to be examined carefully to see whether they are sound.

Man is explicating: "What therefore is truth? A mobile army of metaphors, metonymies, anthropomorphisms: in short a sum of human relations which became poetically and rhetorically intensified, metamorphosed, adorned, and after long usage seem to a nation fixed, canonic, and binding; truths are illusions of which one has forgotten that they *are* illusions; worn-out metaphors which have become powerless to affect the senses; coins with their images effaced and now no longer of account as coins but merely as metal."[15] Nietzsche is pointing out that what we consider truth is often an "illusion" because we have forgotten ("after long usage") that such illusions used to have a particular social function in the past—they corresponded to certain needs, and thus reflected "a sum of human relations." Now that we have forgotten the original pragmatic value of social truths we consider them "fixed, canonic, and binding." Moreover, we do so not as individuals but as "a nation" or a community of individuals. Truths are now mere dogmatic beliefs because we have forgotten their original social function, their therapeutic role, as it were. Myths that are harmless during times of economic crisis or privation (national character, self-sufficiency) can later turn into dangerous ideologies (jingoism or racist xenophobia). Nietzsche wishes to point out that truths are after all human constructions, that they serve certain needs and, in fact, reflect certain values. He is thus offering a critique of the notion of truth as static and incorrigible, the truth of the idealist or the positivist. The passage de Man cites expresses the Nietzschean view that we cannot conceive of a purely rational subject of knowledge, devoid of presupposition or bias. His perspectivism urges us to recognize that we cannot conceive of an "objective knowledge" that is free of interest and based on pure asubjective contemplation.

It is difficult to argue, however, that Nietzsche has no commitment to retaining the distinction between truth and error, for he wants to explain the precise differences that different kinds of error make. Error, bias, and interest need to be specified and understood if we want to gain objectivity and knowledge. Consider, for instance, this passage from *On the Genealogy of Morals*:

> But precisely because we seek knowledge, let us not be ungrateful to
> such resolute reversals of accustomed perspectives and valuations

15. Friedrich Nietzsche, "On Truth and Falsity in Their Extramoral Sense," trans. Maximilian A. Mügge, in *Philosophical Writings*, ed. Reinhold Grimm and Caroline Molina y Vedia (New York: Continuum, 1995), p. 92.

with which the spirit has, with apparent mischievousness and futility, raged against itself for so long: to see differently in this way for once, to *want* to see differently, is no small discipline and preparation of the intellect for its future "objectivity"—the latter understood not as "contemplation without interest" (which is a nonsensical absurdity), but as the ability *to control* one's Pro and Con and to dispose of them, so that one knows how to employ a *variety* of perspectives and affective interpretations in the service of knowledge.[16]

Nietzsche is advocating an antipositivist and naturalistic conception of epistemic activity. We seek knowledge in much the same way we do other things; imperfect epistemic agents that we are, we invest what we seek to know with our biases and prejudices, with our half-formed "theories." But doing so shows us the way to greater objectivity, how to "control [our] Pro and Con" and "how to employ a *variety* of perspectives in the service of knowledge." The unavoidability of "perspectives" means that we err when we seek to know from a presupposition-free god's-eye view. But that positivist image of objectivity is not the only one we have; Nietzsche thinks objective knowledge is gained precisely through our various perspectives, through our critical uses of them, the way we "control" and "employ" them. The passage I have just quoted goes on to warn against conceptions of "pure reason" and "knowledge in itself," for "there is *only* a perspective seeing, *only* a perspective 'knowing'; and the *more* affects we allow to speak about one thing, the *more* eyes, different eyes, we can use to observe one thing, the more complete will our 'concept' of this thing, our 'objectivity,' be."

When we return to de Man's brief but forcefully stated interpretation of the Nietzschean passage about truth as a moving "army of metaphors," we are struck by the way notions of truth and error have been flattened, admitting no variety or degree. "What is being forgotten," writes de Man of the transition from "sum of human relations" to "fixed, canonic, and binding," is "precisely the rhetorical, symbolic quality of all language. The degradation of metaphor into literal meaning is not condemned [by Nietzsche] because it is the forgetting of a truth but much rather because it forgets the un-truth, the lie that the metaphor was in the first place" (*AR*, p. 111). But what exactly does it mean, in the context of what Nietzsche says, to say that the metaphor was a "lie" in the first place? Lie as opposed to what? If the metaphor was once "a sum of human relations," we have seen why it needs to be

16. Nietzsche, *On the Genealogy of Morals*, in *Basic Writings*, p. 555, Third Essay, sec. 12.

understood in its practical role, serving to fulfill needs or desires that are never purely epistemic. What sense would it make then to call the metaphor a "lie . . . in the first place"? De Man seems to conceive truth (the opposite of lie) in the very way Nietzsche cautions against, as something to which we might have access bereft of all our perspectives (our needs, prejudices, theories). Since such a truth is not possible to achieve, de Man concludes that all else is error, a lie.[17] The fiction of a truth arrived at through "contemplation without interest" (Nietzsche's phrase) is presupposed so as to engender the category of necessary and unavoidable error. But in that case both the truth and the error are reductive fictions, hypostatized extremes that lock us into a chimerical battle between literature and philosophy. All epistemic distinctions are erased in this absolute opposition that is presupposed rather than theorized, asserted but not justified through argument or demonstration.

Reference and the "Autonomy" of Language

It should be clear by now how reference and truth play parallel roles in de Man's theory. Both are defined reductively in ways that are fundamentally positivist, since neither allows for the productive mediation of bias, perspective, or "theory." Given this narrow and artificial circumscription of these concepts, the opposed concepts of "figurality" and "error" are so idealized that they explain very little. Error, as we have seen, is inflated to an unavoidable condition, and the variety of kinds (or degrees) of error remains unanalyzable. Similarly, and ironically, the very phenomenon de Man wishes to explain through his discussion of figurality—the productivity of language—is explained inadequately. It is asserted, but it cannot be accounted for. I would like to suggest that in order to explain the productivity of language, how meanings and interpretations change in part because of a property of language, we need a more complex understanding of reference than the one de Man has. Interestingly, it is Peirce, whose work de Man and other poststructuralists often cite with admiration, who provides us

17. The move from the rejection of an empiricist or positivist (or even idealist) model of objective knowledge to the opposite extreme, the adoption of a full-blown skepticism about knowledge, is fairly typical. Postmodernist skeptics implicitly assume that the only kind of objective knowledge that can be conceived at all is positivist (or idealist). When they find this conception (the aperspectival knower or the subject of Hegelian absolute knowledge) defective for one reason or another, they assume that a thoroughgoing skepticism is warranted.

with such an understanding. As is true in the case of Nietzsche's episte-mological views, Peirce's theory of reference (in particular his notion of the interpretant) does not support a postmodernist or poststructuralist position in any clear-cut way. Indeed, Peirce's theory explains the pro-ductivity of language because it emphasizes how "reference" has sig-nificant epistemic content.

Peirce insisted on the constitutive function of the interpretant in all signification: "A sign stands *for* something *to* the idea which it pro-duces, or modifies. . . . That for which it stands is called its *object*; that which it conveys, its *meaning*; and the idea to which it gives rise, its *interpretant*."[18] The interpretant is not another interpreter but itself a sign, dependent on the cultural space in which signification occurs. As Umberto Eco points out in a study informed by and building on Peirce's work, in the context of any signification we need to consider the dy-namic nature of reference, not the referent as a mere object or thing:

> Let us try to understand the nature of the object that corresponds to an expression. Take the term /dog/. The referent will certainly not be the dog *x* standing by me while I am pronouncing the word. For any-one who holds to the doctrine of the referent, the referent, in such a case, will be all existing dogs (and also all past and future dogs). But "all existing dogs" is not an object which can be perceived with the senses. It is a set, a class. . . . *Every attempt to establish what the referent of a sign is forces us to define the referent in terms of an abstract entity which moreover is only a cultural convention. . . .* What, then, is the meaning of a term? From a semiotic point of view it can only be a *cultural unit. . . .*
> . . . [S]ignification (as well as communication), by means of contin-ual shiftings which refer a sign back to another sign or string of signs, circumscribes cultural units in an asymptotic fashion, without ever allowing one to touch them directly. . . . *Semiosis explains itself by itself*; this continual circularity is the normal condition of significa-tion.[19]

For Eco, "dog" is what philosophers call a "social kind," since its mean-ing and reference are defined through social convention. The Peircean notion of the interpretant thus links reference to the wider textual field of human signification. Thus, linguistic production cannot be consid-

18. Charles Sanders Peirce, *Collected Papers* (Cambridge: Harvard University Press, 1960), p. 171, sec. 1:339.

19. Umberto Eco, *A Theory of Semiotics* (Bloomington: Indiana University Press, 1976), pp. 66–67, 71.

ered outside the network that constitutes the social text. De Man refers to Peirce in his discussion of rhetoricity in *Allegories of Reading*, but the passage is a curious one, revealing no real contact with the theoretical implications of the notion of "unlimited semiosis," which should be so significant to de Man's own project:

> Charles Sanders Peirce, who, with Nietzsche and Saussure, laid the philosophical foundation for modern semiology, stressed the distinction between grammar and rhetoric in his celebrated and so suggestively unfathomable definition of the sign. He insists, as is well known, on the necessary presence of a third element, called the interpretant, within any relationship that the sign entertains with its object. . . . The interpretation of the sign is not, for Peirce, a meaning but another sign; it is a reading, not a decodage, and this reading has, in its turn, to be interpreted into another sign, and so on *ad infinitum*. Peirce calls this process by means of which "one sign gives birth to another" pure rhetoric, as distinguished from pure grammar, which postulates the possibility of unproblematic, dyadic meaning, and pure logic, which postulates the possibility of the universal truth of meanings. Only if the sign engendered meaning in the same way that the object endenders the sign, that is, by representation, would there be no need to distinguish between grammar and rhetoric. (*AR*, pp. 8–9)

The reference to Peirce may do, at a very simple level, what de Man wants it to do: that is, it may help him reestablish the distinction between semiology (in the model of a grammar) and rhetoric. But it brings with it more problems than it is worth, for there is a significant and necessary misreading of Peirce here.[20] How, for instance, does the *object*

20. Here is the passage from Peirce de Man probably has in mind: "In consequence of every representamen being thus connected with three things, the ground, the object, and the interpretant, the science of semiotic has three branches. The first is called by Duns Scotus *grammatica speculativa*. We may term it *pure grammar*. It has for its task to ascertain what must be true of the representamen used by every scientific intelligence in order that they may embody any *meaning*. The second is logic proper. It is the science of what is quasi-necessarily true of the representamina of any scientific intelligence in order that they may hold good of any *object*, that is, may be true. Or say, logic proper is the formal science of the conditions of the truth of representations. The third, in imitation of Kant's fashion of preserving old associations of words in finding nomenclature for new conceptions, I call *pure rhetoric*. Its task is to ascertain the laws by which in every scientific intelligence one sign gives birth to another." Charles Sanders Peirce, "Logic as Semiotic: The Theory of Signs," in *Philosophical Writings of Peirce*, ed. Justus Buchler (New York: Dover, 1955), p. 99. (Derrida quotes a portion of this passage in *Of Grammatology*.) For an interpretation of Peirce's complex and difficult theory of the interpretant, especially with the intent of explaining how it can account for the semiotic productivity of language, see Chapter 2.

"engender the sign"? What exactly does the answer de Man takes for granted ("by representation") mean in a Peircean context?

Peirce's claim about the relation among sign, object, and interpretant is that it is *irreducibly triadic*. So Peirce asserts immediately after the passage de Man is most probably alluding to: "A *Sign*, or *Representamen*, is a First which stands in such a genuine triadic relation to a Second, called its *Object*, as to be capable of determining a Third, called its *Interpretant*, to assume the same triadic relation to its Object in which it stands itself to the same Object. The triadic relation is *genuine*, that is its three members are bound together by it in a way that does not consist in any complexus of dyadic relations."[21] De Man, by contrast, privileges the relation between the sign and the interpretant (another sign) over what he considers to be the unproblematical relation between the object and the sign. He can do so only because he sees the Peircean "object" as merely the "given," the thing in the world, of no great significance in the processes of sign production.

But for Peirce, "the object of representation can be nothing but a representation of which the first representation is the interpretant."[22] Thus, the relation between the sign and the interpretant can be seen only *in the context of the object they "interpret" together*. The relation of the sign or the interpretant to the "object" is not purely internal to the sign but is based, as another commentator maintains, implicitly agreeing with Eco's account, on such "collateral information" as an "insistent environment common to all three terms."[23] Such an environment cannot, by definition, be purely intrinsic to the sign; the sign has no pure interior as its defining characteristic. The obdurate facticity of the object needs to be understood in social and semiotic terms. For Peirce the facticity of the object is not a precultural (or pretheoretical and unmediated) "given." Since the object presupposes cultural information, one cannot define it by abstracting it from the social and epistemic context of this information. The refractory at the heart of semiotic processes is what we saw in Eco's definition of the referent as a "cultural convention," and it indicates that such notions of process as de Man seems to suggest (rhetoric: pure generation of signs) are fundamentally misleading. Signifying processes are defined by complex relations, since the "insistent environment" that ties together sign, object, and

21. Ibid., pp. 99–100.
22. Peirce, *Collected Papers*, p. 171, sec. 1:339.
23. David Savan, *An Introduction to C. S. Peirce's Semiotics, Part 1*, Toronto Semiotic Circle Monograph 1 (Toronto: Toronto Semiotic Circle, 1976), p. 55. I develop Savan's suggestion through an exegesis of what Peirce says in his "Logic as Semiotic." See Chapter 2.

interpretant makes it possible for them (as terms of analysis) to come into existence in the first place. The "purity" of the pure logic, grammar, and rhetoric de Man alludes to can only asphyxiate the semiosis that Peirce sees as the basis of language and signification.

To summarize, then, in de Manian theory the linguistic is too hastily opposed to the real world. A more productive approach to reference, such as we see in the works of Peirce or Eco, would suggest that linguistic play might indeed have social and cognitive content. De Manian literary theory moves too easily from rejection of an extrinsic notion of determination of meaning (as in the referential fallacy) to hypostatization of certain notions of the linguistic ("rhetoricity," "figurality") as essential and constitutive features of language and literature. Consequently, the danger is that the reading of texts can take on a mechanical form; at a certain point, "reading" congeals into "Reading," which is an unyieldingly noncognitivist enterprise: "Language" sanctions a "Reading" that is itself "forever impossible to read" (AR, p. 77). In the classroom this strategy can devolve into a predictable maneuver: text after text would be revealed in its subtextual play of emptiness, for an unceasing and unchanging allegory of textuality always "Reads" itself to reveal the hand of the new God in all its creation. "The task of literary criticism in the coming years," writes de Man in the assured tone of both prophecy and power, will be such a predictable operation. This oft-cited passage from the opening essay of *Allegories of Reading*, after a reading of a passage from Proust, concludes with a characteristic vision of the "whole of literature" being read in a similar way. There is only the *minor* qualification that "the techniques and the patterns would have to vary considerably . . . from author to author. But there is absolutely no reason," de Man asserts, "why analyses of the kind here suggested for Proust would not be applicable, with proper modifications of technique, to Milton or to Dante or to Hölderlin" (AR, pp. 16–17).

In sharp opposition to this view, a criticism that would deal with the specificity of the literary would need a more adequate conception of the social phenomenon we call language. To achieve such a conception, it would have to take the cognitive content of *reading* and interpretation more seriously. Building on Peirce, Saussure, and Eco's development of their ideas, such criticism would have to make contact with accounts of reference which have been developed in recent analytic philosophy. Several epistemological and social-theoretical issues need to be addressed more directly if we are to develop anything like an adequate theory of linguistic reference. The next chapter suggests why this is so.

2

REFERENCE AND THE SOCIAL
BASIS OF LANGUAGE

I began the preceding chapter by staging my discussion of various competing positions in contemporary literary theory around a notion of the "meaning" of texts. It became evident that understood in this general way, such seemingly diverse projects as marxist criticism, feminism, and deconstruction in fact have a great deal in common. They share in particular an emphasis on the conventional nature of social meanings, and thus on the ideological nature of textual interpretation itself. But in exploring Paul de Man's claim about language, I ran up against several underexamined issues having to do with the nature of "reference" and the exact nature of the "sociality" of language. These issues are important in debates over specific interpretations and, primarily, because they point to theoretical questions involved in all social and cultural explanation. Meanings may be conventional and hence ideologically decomposable, but how exactly is the meaning of a linguistic text related to the nature of language as a social phenomenon? Linguistic texts are polysemous and productive, but in what nonessentialist way can we explain this productivity? Is the ineliminable heteroglossia of language or even the self-deconstructing nature of "literary" language as de Man defines it an ontological "given," or is it to be itself interpreted and specified relationally (as the Peircean notion of the interpretant suggests)—in relation to the various contexts of linguistic use? Finally, how does language hook up with "the world," and what basic account of the referential dimensions of language must we have to understand its ongoing semiosis? It is the aim of the present chapter to begin to sketch an alternative to the view of language underlying the de Manian position, and the discussion is organized around questions about reference and the social contexts of language. I draw primarily on the work of the Bakhtin school to explain the social nature of language and then develop the discussion I began in the preceding chapter of Peirce's notion of the interpretant. Finally, drawing on the work of Hilary Putnam, I suggest how linguistic reference can be defined "causally" in relation to social practices. Together, these ideas are intended to contribute to a nonreductive social and historical account of language; they are also intended to suggest how our understanding of language, if developed through an exploration of these questions, might be more adequately responsive to general epistemological concerns (including the ones de Man addresses).

On Social Determination

To begin to talk about the social bases of language is to understand some of the ways in which the primary features of language are "determined" by its social conditions of production and consumption. But "determination" is a large and complex issue, opening out onto questions about the nature of interpretation and explanation. One may or may not agree with Borges's suggestion that human history is the history of a few metaphors, but it is difficult to deny the tension, evident in particular in the social sciences, between metaphors and historical understanding. The influence of such famous models as that of base and superstructure in marxism attest to this difficulty. First formulated by Marx in its classic form in the preface to *A Contribution to the Critique of Political Economy* (1859) and then handled in various ways by marxists and non-marxists, this figure has oscillated between the extremes of a topological image with its notions of "zones" or "levels," on the one hand, and the image of an almost undifferentiated continuum of overlapping areas of productivity, on the other.[1] The central issue in this figural drama, the notion of "determination," refers to some idea of causal pressure that one dimension of social life exerts upon another. However we formulate the problem, the model raises several meta-analytic issues that are central to theories of culture or society. For theories

---

1. Perhaps the best example of this latter kind of claim is Gilles Deleuze and Félix Guattari, *Anti-Oedipus*, trans. Robert Hurley, Mark Seem, and Helen R. Lane (New York: Viking, 1977), where a notion of universal productivity is developed far beyond the traditional marxist understanding of the term.

of "culture" or of the "aesthetic," to the extent that they propose powerful explanatory models or principles, also project images of the social space in which culture finds its definition.[2]

Thus it would be prudent to recognize that even the model of base and superstructure which is now often dismissed as simplistic and crude has a history that is not always understood clearly. Marx provides the most succinct formulation of the image in the course of what he warns us is to be regarded as only a brief summary, only the "general result," a "guiding thread" for future research as it was for his own investigations.[3] Here is the passage that can lead to problems of interpretation if we fail to heed these contextual warnings:

> In the social production of their lives, men enter into definite relations that are indispensable and independent of their will, relations of production which correspond to a definite stage of development of their material productive forces. The sum total of these relations of production constitutes the economic structure of society, the real foundation, on which rises a legal and political superstructure and to which correspond definite forms of social consciousness. The mode of production of material life conditions the social, political and intellectual life process in general. It is not the consciousness of men that determines their being, but, on the contrary, their social being that determines their consciousness. (p. 503)

It might be argued that "the real foundation" is a crude explanatory notion in this passage, since it reduces the "legal and political superstructure" to mere epiphenomena or, at best, rigidly determined elements that "rise" effortlessly upon the basis of such reality. Moreover, the term "correspond" could be read as a further corroboration of the strict determinism inherent in this model. But such an acontextual reading would be neither fair nor particularly illuminating. In fact the image is much more complex. In earlier texts Marx and Engels recognize that the relation between the two elements that constitute "the real foundation" ("material productive forces" and the "relations of production") itself results from what Engels calls "a reciprocal action."

2. For a brief but useful survey of different marxist definitions of culture and of the implications of such definitions, see the essay on culture by William Outhwaite in *A Dictionary of Marxist Thought*, ed. Tom Bottomore (Cambridge: Harvard University Press, 1983), pp. 109–12.

3. Karl Marx, Preface to *A Contribution to a Critique of Political Economy*, in Karl Marx and Frederick Engels, *Selected Works in Three Volumes* (Moscow: Progress Publishers, 1977), 1:503.

The crucial idea is that this is an action "of two *unequal* forces,"[4] pointing to the specifically historical-materialist thesis against the idealist claim that "ideas" or the "Spirit" absolutely determine the direction of world history. For Marx and Engels, "productive forces" do not refer only to technology. The German term *Produktivkräfte* was originally a reference to Adam Smith and David Ricardo's "productive powers," and thus better rendered in a way that can suggest a range of human abilities rather than merely the materials and instruments of production. Whether we translate it as "productive powers" or "productive forces," we need to keep in mind the expansive sense that Marx intends in using the term, by referring us to the forms of "determinate" human relations and faculties involved in social production and labor. Productive powers thus include forms of cooperation and social division that human societies use in production.[5] On this view, then, simple determinism is excluded in principle, for primacy is accorded to the political and economic *relations* that constitute social existence, and the instruments of production are never defined outside the context of these relations.[6] Marx understood the theoretical framework sketched here as merely a guideline for concrete empirical research that would in turn correct and develop these general theses. Speculation was never the goal of materialist inquiry.

What was an interactive model for Marx and Engels, to be used as a general thesis directing and itself corrected and modified by actual research, became a more popular notion in precisely the most simplistic forms of unilinear determinism. As Raymond Williams has suggested, the later ossification of the model derives from the crucial shift from understanding the base-superstructure metaphor as primarily *relational* to understanding it as "(a) relatively enclosed categories or (b) relatively enclosed areas of activity."[7] With such a solidification of what was once a dynamic and potentially quite supple explanatory model, the central

4. Engels, quoted in Allen Wood, *Karl Marx* (London: Routledge and Kegan Paul, 1981), p. 64.
5. For an excellent discussion of these questions, see ibid., chap. 5.
6. On the question of determination in Marx's theory of history, see the following essays in *After Marx*, ed. Terence Ball and James Farr (Cambridge: Cambridge University Press, 1984): William H. Shaw, "Marxism, Revolution, and Rationality," pp. 12–35; Jon Elster, "Historical Materialism and Economic Backwardness," pp. 36–58; Richard W. Miller, "Producing Change: Work, Technology, and Power in Marx's Theory of History," pp. 59–87; Philippe Van Parijs, "Marxism's Central Puzzle," pp. 88–104; and James Noble, "Marxian Functionalism," pp. 105–20.
7. Raymond Williams, *Marxism and Literature* (Oxford: Oxford University Press, 1977), pp. 77–78.

problem of social determination became the less illuminating process of relating two autonomous levels. Consequently, the semiosis and internal dynamism of the "base" or the "real foundation" were transformed into physical fixity; the superstructural levels were allowed to proliferate only with the intention of determining their "places" in this topological hierarchy. For any kind of cultural criticism or analysis, this kind of simplification is singularly debilitating, for such elements as language must merely be externally situated in relation to art, religion, law, the economy, and so on in what can only be a predetermined and predefined social whole. What ideological criticism might gain in certitude and clarity it loses in the suppleness of its explanatory terms.

Williams, whose main experience was with literary and cultural texts, suggests a solution to this problem which is now an accepted tenet of many versions of cultural marxism. For Williams, the way out of the dilemma between a reductive but powerful ideological account of culture, on the one hand, and a purely immanent formalism without any critical potential, on the other, is to extend the understanding of "productive forces" to superstructural phenomena such as language and literature. Thus, Williams suggests that we retain the relative autonomy of the levels but consider each a "dynamic and internally contradictory process." The enlarged notion of productive forces or powers makes it possible to do so because the idea of determination retains the hierarchy of "social being" over "consciousness," and the "modes of production of material life" still condition "the social, political and intellectual life process in general," but there is also room for a more complex notion of interaction and dependency between the various aspects of social existence.[8] Above all, the dominant mode of production may determine artistic or cultural practice, but we can better appreciate what Williams calls the "residual" and the "emergent" social formations and their multivalent ideological status. Forms of commonality and cooperation as modes of economic being both survive in and emerge from the dominant ethos, and to brush these away as ineffectual epiphenomena is to ignore the internal dynamism and contradiction that characterize the material complexity of human histories. At the core of the historical-materialist conception of social determination, however, is

8. Ibid., p. 82; see pp. 79–94. For extreme interpretations of Williams's general point, see Rosalind Coward and John Ellis, *Language and Materialism* (London: Routledge and Kegan Paul, 1977), as well as the more recent developments in "postmodern" media studies. In such interpretations, the causal—and hence explanatory—priority of economic or political practices over, say, cultural ones often disappears almost completely, and the political efficacy of cultural practices is overestimated.

the idea, no matter how qualified, that social phenomena are *causally* related to one another. One of the primary challenges for explanation is thus to go beyond the mere description of how social forms are constructed to identification of the complex hierarchy of causal forces and principles.

Bakhtin on Linguistic Production

It is against the background of such questions that Bakhtin's contributions to our understanding of language are best appreciated.[9] His sense of the historicity of languages (and in fact of all signs) lies at the basis of his conception of the internal determination of language by social existence. Unlike Saussure, who inspired the Russian formalists and was so influential at the time Bakhtin was writing, the Bakhtin school sees language more as a heterogeneous field and medium of activity than as a system. Bakhtin recognizes the necessity of the abstraction that linguistics performs in order to study what it determines as its object, but he considers language as "discourse," that is, language "in its concrete living totality," more significant.[10] First, then, we need to pay attention to the heterogeneity essential to language as a social phenomenon. According to Bakhtin, "At any given moment of its historical existence, language is heteroglot from top to bottom: it represents the co-existence of socio-ideological contradictions between the present and the past, between differing epochs of the past, between different socio-ideological groups in the present, between tendencies, schools, circles and so forth, all given a bodily form" (*DI*, p. 291). But this "co-existence of socio-ideological contradictions" is not an external and inessential fact. If it is our intention to understand language in its "concrete" and "living" human reality, Bakhtin insists that we cannot afford

9. Almost all recent textual and biographical studies of the works of the Bakhtin school (including Pavel Medvedev and V. N. Volosinov) have concluded that the major publications of the group were, in fact, substantially authored by Bakhtin. Without going into the details of this argument, I will indicate that I find the continuity of the ideas of the Bakhtin school quite remarkable, and thus I use Bakhtin's name as a convenient abbreviation for the works of the group as a whole. The two main texts on language on which I draw are M. M. Bakhtin, *The Dialogic Imagination*, trans. Caryl Emerson and Michael Holquist, ed. Holquist (Austin: University of Texas Press, 1981); and V. N. Volosinov, *Marxism and the Philosophy of Language*, trans. Ladislav Matejka and I. R. Titunik (Cambridge: Harvard University Press, 1986). These are henceforth referred to as *DI* and *MPL*. Similar ideas are explored in Bakhtin, *Speech Genres and Other Late Essays*, trans. Vern McGee (Austin: University of Texas Press, 1986), esp. pp. 60–131.

10. Mikhail Bakhtin, *Problems of Dostoevsky's Poetics*, trans. and ed. Caryl Emerson (Minneapolis: University of Minnesota Press, 1984), p. 181, henceforth cited as *PDP*.

to ignore these contradictions. In a constitutive and necessary way, language (or, for that matter, the sign) is conflictive, formed and produced in this dialogue that defines it. Sociality inheres in the sign, for Bakhtin, in the form of an "otherness" it must face up to in order to come into being as a word in the first place. For at an elementary level, signs "arise only on *interindividual territory* . . . [only on the basis] that the two individuals be organized socially, that they compose a group (a social unit)" (*MPL*, p. 12). This is a strong thesis, worth emphasizing in the context of the previous chapter. At one level, it is the commonsensical point that language is a social fact, but Bakhtin, like Peirce, is making a deeper claim that will develop into a theory of how the semiotic nature of language is essentially and constitutively social.

Given his focus on *parole* (as opposed to *langue*, which was Saussure's main concern), on the utterance rather than on the systemic aspects of language, Bakhtin is interested in the creative relation with the other which determines the word from within. The production of the individual speech act, he says, must contend with the multiplicity of particular uses of the word—the range of (socially specific) connotative energies that intersect in it. In this sense, the alien, the other, is already present in each word utterance, directing both the way in which the word conceives of its object ("the alien word is already in the object," Bakhtin points out) and the orientation of every word "toward a future answer word" (*DI*, p. 280). Thus every speech act is an implicit acknowledgment of its situatedness, its conflicted or cooperative production. Every instance of speech is always inherently reflexive, social, and "metacommunicative," and "to speak" (as Gary Saul Morson glosses Bakhtin) "is to speak about speech."[11] For Bakhtin, reflexivity is the property of all language to the extent that language is a situated act. The word (our text, that which we interpret) carries its own context within it, not as extra baggage but as the very condition of its coming into existence.

If the context inheres in the word, then, implicated in its very production and understanding, the notion of contextual determination becomes a matter quite different from our original sense of an external relation of power or pressure. "The word in language is half someone else's," says Bakhtin, emphasizing how the other, within the word, internally limits and puts pressure on what the word can be made to mean. Context exists within the word much as what Fredric Jameson

11. Gary Saul Morson, "The Heresiarch of *META*," *PTL: A Journal for Descriptive Poetics and Theory of Literature* 3 (October 1978), 413.

(borrowing an idea from Wilhelm von Humboldt and Goethe) would call its "inner form."[12] This is the real (social) content of the word (or, for Jameson, the literary work). Naturally, the determination of language by the socioeconomic is not a relationship of exteriority. Rather, for the Bakhtin school, it is imperative in understanding the utterance to lay bare the mediating instances of (historical) convention, of genre, and sedimented ideological meanings. Each utterance is like a palimpsest and has inscribed in it a multiplicity of historical meanings and forms. Thus for Bakhtinians the larger task of a theory of language is to formulate a preliminary typology of forms:

> Each period and each social group has had and has its own repertoire of speech forms for ideological communication in human behavior. Each set of cognate forms, i.e., each behavioral speech genre, has its own corresponding set of themes.
> An interlocking organic unity joins the form of communication (for example, on-the-job communication of the strictly technical kind), the form of the utterance (the concise, businesslike statement) and its theme. Therefore, *classification of the forms of utterance must rely upon classification of the forms of verbal communication.* The latter are entirely determined by production relations and the sociopolitical order. . . . Enormous significance belongs to *the hierarchical factor* in the processes of verbal interchange and . . . a powerful influence is exerted on forms of utterance by the hierarchical organization of communication. (*MPL*, pp. 20–21)

The key idea here is that "communication" is a social activity, and its forms are ultimately determined by the "sociopolitical order." These forms of communication are not like external shells, however, which we bring to bear on the appropriate kernel of meaning ("theme" in Bakhtin's terminology here); rather, the meanings constitute themselves only in this larger matrix in which they already exist, the "unity" among the theme, the form of the communication, and the form of the utterance. Anticipating the poststructuralist views discussed in Chapter 1, the Bakhtinian account of how meaning works draws attention away from the "what" of meaning to the "how." But the "how" is here defined by the hierarchical set of relations that constitute the social order, and it is to this that words and texts refer.

It would be useful to elaborate on Bakhtin's emphasis on language as

12. Fredric Jameson, *Marxism and Form* (Princeton: Princeton University Press, 1971), pp. 401–4.

parole, as the speech act, for if it is the basic communicative model that defines language (see the passage just quoted), then Bakhtin's primary emphasis is on the productive aspect of the utterance. Instead of considering linguistic behavior as a reflection of or homologous to another, more primordial level of social life, this approach to language reveals the contradictory and conflictive practice that language is in its generation and use. In its dimension as productive play language becomes a sensitive register of social life. Simultaneously the register and the response, such linguistic (and textual) process provides a supple model of contextual determination, a model suggestive of both a multiplicity of (autonomous) practices and their interdependency and mutual conditioning.

Thus even the most seemingly ordinary usages contain a deeper contextual significance. The linguistic sign, as it exists outside the dictionary or the philologist's study, is necessarily imbued with ideological choice and conflict:

> In point of fact, the linguistic form . . . exists for the speaker only in the context of specific utterances, exists, consequently, only in a specific ideological context. In actuality, we never say or hear *words*, we say and hear what is true or false, good or bad, important or unimportant, pleasant or unpleasant, and so on. *Words are always filled with content and meaning drawn from behavior or ideology*. That is the way we understand words, and we can respond only to words that engage us behaviorally or ideologically. (*MPL*, p. 70)

Signs, which must always be read and uttered evaluatively, are opposed to what Bakhtin would call signals—inert, fixed in their self-identity, meant to be recognized rather than understood. The red traffic light that impels me to stop is a signal: I recognize its import in a context that is not constitutively ideological. But when someone says, "Stop," the contextual determinants are many and necessary. From the tone of the speaker to even such matters as dress, manner, and the particular (socially constituted) communicative relationship that exists between us, I attempt to understand the word as context-specific sign. We experience this active understanding every day, taking into account the minutest details of social accentuation which shape the utterance. Even in the most conventional situations, much of our specific experience of language comes in instances of deviation from or adherence to the norm as it is defined in the ideological context, that is, at least the hierarchies inherent in the communicative situation. Even an "ordinary" utterance is often a complex unity of understanding, response, and creativity which refers outward to its multiply determined contexts.

There is a more general theoretical point involved here. The deeper Bakhtinian claim is that the truest features of language are revealed only in moments of crisis or change. Although Bakhtin does not amplify this claim in much detail, it constitutes a crucial emphasis of marxist theory and I would like to develop it systematically. A central claim of marxism is that a good explanation must be diagnostic, revealing latent forces beneath the manifest level of phenomena. This constitutes the interpretive, hermeneutic dimension of marxian thought. More specifically, however, there is the thesis that conflict and struggle are central to historical (and hence also linguistic) processes. This notion of the essentially conflictive nature of language—its concrete uses and their historical contexts—lies at the heart of Bakhtin's view of language. If forms of communication are always hierarchically organized, engaged (and defined) in relationships of power, then the history of language is the history of these conflicts, these dynamic instances of contestation and productivity. "Conventions," or the forms and genres of linguistic behavior, are thus hardly exhausted by their present usage. In fact, even the utterance remains always already implicated in this history of "traces." Janus-like, oriented both toward the past and toward the future, each utterance negotiates its own complicated presentness.

Bakhtin's notion of language as a sedimented and generative process can be understood only if we keep in mind the complementary claim that any historical process—and the history of language is one instance—must inevitably exist at different levels of explicitness and clarity. In "normal," "ordinary" times, the conflict inherent in language and history remains obscured by the smoothness of the surface. The creases of ideological conflict appear only in the "lucid" moments of radical change: the crises in the history of a language or in the sociopolitical order, the moments of "revolution." In such moments the inherent pluralities in every historical or linguistic moment surface, and the idea of peaceful coexistence explodes under the pressure of deeper tensions and struggles.[13]

13. Compare Bakhtin's view (as I am developing it) with that of the scientists Richard Levins and Richard Lewontin on the essence of the "dialectical" approach to history and nature: "Things change because of the actions of opposing forces on them, and things are the way they are because of the temporary balance of opposing forces. . . . The dialectical view insists that persistence and equilibrium are not the natural state of things but require explanation, which must be sought in the actions of opposing forces. The conditions under which the opposing forces balance and the system as a whole is in stable equilibrium are quite special. They require the simultaneous satisfaction of as many mathematical rela-

Bakhtin's emphasis on the socially determined nature of language is thus closely linked to his analysis of the semiotic nature of the word. Bakhtin stresses how the word utterance is to be interpreted as an always already semiotized entity that comes into its own in a shared and contested space. Thus any question about the productivity of language should only be raised in the context of this socially determined contestation and struggle that shape the word's internal unity or incoherence. Against the de Manian view of language, Bakhtin would maintain that to empty out the referential sedimentations in the word, its generic and conventional being, is to do violence to the semiotic core of language and thus to engage in a kind of formalistic reductionism.

The Bakhtinian account describes semiotization of meanings as a necessarily social and historical process. In the book on Dostoevsky, Bakhtin explains how we can arrive at an adequate understanding of the "idea" as a social fact. Dostoevsky is an exemplary writer for Bakhtin because his texts adequately "dialogize" the "idea," revealing how it lacks a purely internal coherence since it is constituted in a network of socially specific implications and connotations. Such "dialogization" involves an emptying out of the idea as a psychological unit:

> The idea—as it was *seen* by Dostoevsky the artist—is not a subjective individual-psychological formation with "permanent resident rights" in a person's head; no, the idea is inter-individual and inter-subjective—the realm of its existence is not individual consciousness but dialogic communion *between* consciousnesses. The idea is a *live event*, played out at the point of dialogic meeting between two or several consciousnesses. In this sense the idea is similar to the *word*, with which it is dialogically united. Like the word, the idea wants to be heard, understood, and "answered" by other voices from other positions. Like the word, the idea is by nature dialogic. (*PDP*, p. 88)

The "word" and the "idea" are then less self-evident entities than "positions" in a social semiotic that is itself composed of many such positions, real and potential, past, present, and future. The semiotization of both "word" and "idea" is possible only when we take their social existence seriously. Any adequate interpretation of linguistic or

tions as there are variables in the system, usually expressed as inequalities among the parameters of that system." Richard Levins and Richard Lewontin, *The Dialectical Biologist* (Cambridge: Harvard University Press, 1985), p. 280. Levins and Lewontin see the dialectical view as profoundly opposed to the dominant view, "Cartesian reductionism," which conceives both nature and society in "reified" or "alienated" ways. See esp. pp. 267–88.

ideological phenomena would need to pay attention to this referential network within which they exist. Dostoevsky is a unique antenna of his times because he possesses an understanding of the mediated and textual nature of social reality:

> As an artist, Dostoevsky did not create his ideas in the same way philosophers or scholars create theirs—he created images of ideas found, heard, sometimes divined by him *in reality itself*, that is, ideas already living or entering life as idea-forces. Dostoevsky possessed an extraordinary gift for hearing the dialogue of his epoch, or, more precisely, for hearing his epoch as a great dialogue, for detecting in it not only individual voices, but precisely and predominantly the *dialogic relationship* among voices, their dialogic *interaction*. He heard both the loud, recognized, reigning voices of the epoch, that is, the reigning dominant ideas (official and unofficial), as well as voices still weak, ideas not yet fully emerged, latent ideas heard as yet by no one but himself, and ideas that were just beginning to ripen, embryos of future worldviews. "Reality in its entirety," Dostoevsky himself wrote, "is not to be exhausted by what is immediately at hand, for an overwhelming part of this reality is contained in the form of a still *latent, unuttered future Word*." (*PDP*, p. 90)

Bakhtin finds Dostoevsky a valuable interpreter of the social precisely because he is able to see that the word and the idea are interactive social phenomena that are *constituted* in this interaction. The semiosis (or the textuality) of such phenomena provides us access to the social meanings they embody. Interpretation is thus dependent on such semiotization and textualization, which themselves refer to wider social processes. Bakhtin's theory of the referential contexts of linguistic signs suggests the outlines of a theory of textual and historical interpretation.

Peirce, Semiosis, and the Interpretant

Charles Sanders Peirce's theory of the interpretant, discussed in the last chapter, complements and extends the Bakhtinian account of the social basis of language. Like Bakhtin, Peirce describes the social nature of linguistic reference. Both Bakhtin and Peirce thus provide valuable correctives to the Saussurean account of language as a system, since they emphasize and explain theoretically the extent to which signification and language are historical and are shaped by changing cultural and social conventions.

We saw in the last chapter how Peirce's definition of signification involves a triadic relation among the Sign, the Object, and the Interpretant.[14] The point about this triadic relation, Peirce makes clear, is that none of the three can be seen in isolation, and it would be a mistake to see the triad as "any complexus of dyadic relations."[15] The Interpretant, not a person but an interpretive position or perspective (and therefore itself like a sign), interprets the Object just as the Sign does. But what defines the Interpretant ("the Third") as a Sign is its standing in a relation to another Sign, which is its "Third." Herein lies a basic reason why signification is part of an unending chain; and it suggests why reference and signification, again contrary to the de Manian view, are necessarily and irreducibly social. It is this crucial point that I would like to develop in this section.

Peirce's claim that the Interpretant is like a Sign presupposes that the Sign is itself not insular but dependent on external (that is, "collateral") information. Peirce recognizes that this concept is not immediately familiar to most people, but it is his definition of the Sign nonetheless. The representing activity of the Sign cannot be conceived, Peirce argues, without keeping in mind that the Sign represents within a social space, drawing on information available publicly. The Peircean Object is essential to the Peircean Sign, for it is an already interpreted entity that is reinterpreted by the Sign. The Object is not the thing-in-itself but rather a culturally and socially defined unit; the Peircean theory of signification presupposes a cultural space. Here is the relevant passage:

> The Sign can only represent the Object and tell about it. It cannot furnish acquaintance with or recognition of that Object; for that is what is meant in this volume by the Object of a Sign; namely, that with which it presupposes an acquaintance in order to convey some further information concerning it. No doubt there will be readers who will say they cannot comprehend this. They think a Sign need not relate to anything otherwise known, and can make neither head nor

14. To avoid confusion in the following account, I capitalize the Peircean terms Sign, Object, and Interpretant; uncapitalized, they bear their conventional meanings. In addition to the bibliographic references provided in Chapter 1, the reader might wish to consult David Savan's updated publication *An Introduction to C. S. Peirce's Full System of Semiotics*, Toronto Semiotic Circle Monograph Series 1 (Toronto: Toronto Semiotic Circle, 1987–88). For a brief but useful discussion of Peirce's pragmatism in the context of contemporary philosophy of science, see Ian Hacking, *Representing and Intervening* (Cambridge: Cambridge University Press, 1983), chap. 4.

15. Charles Sanders Peirce, "Logic as Semiotic: The Theory of Signs," in *Philosophical Writings of Peirce*, ed. Justus Buchler (New York: Dover, 1955), p. 100.

tail of the statement that every Sign must relate to such an Object. But if there be anything that conveys information and yet has absolutely no relation nor reference to anything with which the person to whom it conveys the information has, when he comprehends that information, the slightest acquaintance, direct or indirect—and a very strange sort of information that would be—the vehicle of that sort of information is not, in this volume, called a Sign. (p. 100)

The Sign and the Object do not encounter each other in a state of cultural or historical innocence. The Sign modifies an already existing interpretation of the Object. "Interpretation" might seem like a strong word here, but as I shall explain, it is in fact quite appropriate given the last sentence in the passage quoted.

The "information" the Sign conveys about the Object, Peirce says, must be related to (or must refer to) the information the interpreter already has (or else it would be "a very strange sort of information"). This new information the Sign conveys to the interpreter is something that makes a difference then, a difference to the interpreter *in her role as interpreter*. It is in this sense that it is nontrivial, and we are justified in calling the information the interpreter already possesses about the Object a preexisting "interpretation." It must have roughly the same degree of significance as the information the Sign provides. Thus at the core of signification is the relation of one interpretation to another, or the extension, revision, or modification of meanings by other meanings. Signification is by definition not purely "autonomous" if by that we mean that it has no reference to anything that preexists; indeed it is predicated on a prior definition of meanings as significant information, which implies in turn a shared culture, a shared social and historical space. The Sign and the Object are always already in this space.[16]

16. The account of Peirce I am developing here is indebted in a general way to Eco (see the citations in Chapter 1, and more specifically *Semiotics and the Philosophy of Language* [Bloomington: Indiana University Press, 1984], pp. 43–45), but our textual emphases and our readings differ. These differences are probably due to differences in our views about reference, specifically about the explanatory adequacy of a view of reference as ultimately conventional. Contrast, e.g., Eco's reading of Hilary Putnam on reference (*Semiotics*, pp. 73–78) with the one I develop in the next section of this chapter. The differences in detail notwithstanding, however, my account of Peirce's conception of the Interpretant can be seen as a critical elaboration and specification of what Eco suggests in passages such as these: "The criterion of interpretability allows us to start from a sign in order to cover, step by step, the entire circle of semiosis. . . . To interpret a sign means to define the portion of a continuum which serves as its vehicle in its relationship with the other portions of the continuum derived from its global segmentation by the content. It means to define a portion through the use of other portions, conveyed by other expressions" (*Semiotics*, pp. 41–42).

Peirce's general claim here is that any interpretation of a linguistic sign presupposes a wider network of background theories or assumptions. Such a conception is profoundly antiempiricist; indeed, it anticipates Heidegger's hermeneutical view, developed in the oft-cited section 32 of *Being and Time*, that every "interpretation" (*Auslegung*) presupposes a prior and more primordial "understanding."[17] For Peirce's theory of signification is clearly also holistic, and his thesis is cognitivist: the Sign's Object exists (for the person who interprets the Sign) in a context of explicit or implicit interpretations, and only in such a context can the interpreter apprehend it. The presence of existing interpretations indicates why the Peircean Object should be conceived not as any "given" isolatable entity but as (part of) a network of relationships. Often, in fact, as Peirce maintains, the Object of the Sign involves various modalities of existence: "The Objects—for a Sign may have any number of them—may each be a single known existing thing or thing believed formerly to have existed or expected to exist, or a collection of such things, or a known quality or relation or fact, which single Object may be a collection, or whole of parts, or it may have some other mode of being, such as some act permitted whose being does not prevent its negation from being equally permitted, or something of a general nature desired, required, or invariably found under certain general circumstances" (p. 101). The Object may in fact be unobservable; indeed it may be a theoretical entity impossible to account for within the empiricist's observation-based epistemology: not only chairs and pencils and human

17. See Martin Heidegger, *Being and Time*, trans. John Macquarrie and Edward Robinson (New York: Harper and Row, 1962), sec. 32, pp. 188–95. *Auslegung* is a form of "laying out" of what is implicit in the more primordial level of "understanding." "In Interpreting," Heidegger says, "we do not, so to speak, throw a 'signification' over some naked thing which is present-at-hand, we do not stick a value on it; but when something within-the-world is encountered as such, the thing in question already has an involvement which is disclosed in our understanding of the world, and this involvement is one which gets laid out by the interpretation" (pp. 190–91). The structural parallel I am suggesting between Peirce's view of signification and Heidegger's hermeneutics is most clearly evident in the antiempiricist epistemology both wish to outline.

The parallel should not be overdrawn, however. Peirce's view of the complex dimensions of reference draws him (via the notion of the Interpretant) toward a holistic account, but his central emphasis is on cognitive and epistemic aspects of signification. Heidegger's hermeneutical holism, on the other hand, includes more than conscious beliefs or theoretical propositions. Section 32 of *Being and Time* talks about various practical (i.e., pretheoretical) ways in which the fore-structure of understanding exists (see, e.g., p. 191). Heideggerian holism is also to be contrasted with the epistemological holism Quine espouses; see my discussion of Quine and the more general issues involved in Chapter 6. On the question of Heidegger's "practical holism," I am indebted to Hubert L. Dreyfus, "Holism and Hermeneutics," *Review of Metaphysics* 34 (September 1980), 3–23.

bodies, then, but also (necessarily unobservable) theories of atomic structure or planetary motion. Peirce's view of signification includes an understanding of the complex epistemic dimensions of reference, and the "facticity" of the Peircean Object is indeed deeply theory-laden.

How, Then, Do We "Fix" Meanings?

But how, within this cultural and epistemic environment that pervades the Sign-Object relation, do particular instances of signification take place? In other words, how does one "fix" meaning? And equally important, how does signification lead (paradoxically) to an endless process of semiosis, the unending play of meaning and interpretation? The key to both problems is in the concept of the Interpretant, without which, Peirce insists, his definitions of the Sign and the Object would be incomplete (the relation, we recall, is "genuinely triadic"). The oft-cited passage in which Peirce discusses his theory of the sign (based on the triadic relation among Sign, Interpretant, and Object) is quite dense. I have alluded to it already (in Chapter 1), but since it is obscure in some crucial places it might be best to quote it in its entirety before I develop my analysis of it:

> A *Sign*, or *Representamen*, is a First which stands in such a genuine triadic relation to a Second, called its *Object*, as to be capable of determining a Third, called its *Interpretant*, to assume the same triadic relation to its Object in which it stands itself to the same Object. The triadic relation is *genuine*, that is its three members are bound together by it in a way that does not consist in any complexus of dyadic relations. That is the reason the Interpretant, or Third, cannot stand in a mere dyadic relation to the Object, but must stand in such a relation to it as the Representamen itself does. Nor can the triadic relation in which the Third stands be merely similar to that in which the First stands, for this would make the relation of the Third to the First a degenerate Secondness merely. The Third must indeed stand in such a relation, and thus must be capable of determining a Third of its own; but besides that, it must have a second triadic relation in which the Representamen, or rather the relation thereof to its Object, shall be its own (the Third's) Object, and must be capable of determining a Third to this relation. All this must equally be true of the Third's Thirds and so on endlessly. (pp. 99–100)

I suggested that it is the Interpretant that helps "fix" the relationship between the Sign and the Object. How does it do this? My proposal, on the basis of what Peirce says in this passage, is that the Interpretant provides a *more specific* kind of "information" about the Object than was evident in the initial (general and abstract) relation between the Sign and the Object. For Peirce makes it clear that the Interpretant's relation to the Object is in some ways similar to that of the Sign to the Object, but that it cannot be "merely similar." And since the Sign and the Object, as I have already shown, are related to each other against a background of cultural or social information, to see how the Sign "reinterprets" the interpretation the Object brings with it, we must need the help of some more specific angle. That is what the Interpretant provides. For in any given instance of signification, when a Sign is "read" or understood, the Interpretant delimits the information that is relevant in some way to (part of) the Interpreter's context. This event should not be reduced to its conscious psychological components, for the Interpretant simply outlines that slice of contextually relevant cultural and social information which makes a specific interpretation of the Sign-Object relation possible.

In the Peircean triad, what makes a Representamen a Sign is "a mental Interpretant" (p. 100), but the Interpretant implies the perspective of interpreting persons without being limited to ideas in people's heads. It is also not necessary that the Interpretant be conceived individualistically: an Interpretant may be a collectivity of sign users. All that is required, it seems clear, is that they share a common agenda of (culturally and socially analyzable) needs, interests, and goals. Peircean semiotics presupposes a social relationship among people but does not imply that we must reduce all aspects of signification to actual psychological processes. Many kinds of social meaning exist in various degrees of anonymity. The Peircean theory of the Interpretant helps us understand how (to put it in our familiar, everyday terms) signs point "outward," how they are related not only to things or objects in the (natural and social) world but also, inevitably, to socially organized bodies of information. Together these relations define the deeply theoretical and socially mediated phenomenon called linguistic "reference."

How Do Meanings Change?

This way of defining the Interpretant helps us understand the pragmatic dimension of signification and the necessary function of the reference to social and cultural contexts, but in what way does it explain the unending semiosis for which Peircean theory is so famous? I think the answer is to be found in the successive stages by which Peirce defines the relations among Sign, Interpretant, and Object. The Third (the Interpretant) stands in a different relation to the triad from the First (the Sign): "for this would make the relation of the Third to the First a degenerate Secondness merely." Now this difference would follow if my account of the Interpretant as specifier of cultural and social information is accepted, for then the "circle" of signification is never neatly or tightly drawn, since the Third (the Interpretant) involves a contextual element that is essentially historically contingent, and not related to the Sign (the First) in a purely *logical* way. The Interpretant is defined both as a relational term and as one that is open to the empirically new. This definition is what explains Peirce's additional condition that the Third can itself be further specified, is "capable of determining a Third of its own." It is by definition not a free-floating element but one that is socially and culturally localizable and thus further contextualized. Peirce's insight consists in seeing this "fixing" of and by context to be itself a semiotic process that is in principle unending, since it involves new and revisable empirical information. Such information is both sought through and organized by (interest- and need-relative) cognitive agendas; it is available in the form of (culturally and historically specific) interpretations. It goes without saying that such agendas and interpretations can be critically evaluated, and the information they provide or draw upon is itself subject to (theoretical and empirical) interrogation.

Let me return to the passage from Peirce to round out the account I have been providing here. After stating the crucial condition that the Third must be able to determine its own Third, Peirce adds: "Besides that, it must have a second triadic relation in which the Representamen [the Sign], or rather the relation thereof to its Object, shall be its own (the Third's) Object, and must be capable of determining a Third to this relation." As we have seen, the unending semiosis is generated out of the Third's relation to its Third (and its own Object); this triadic relationship stands in a skewed relation to the original triad which ensures openness to new information. But Peirce complicates this picture further by making the additional claim that every Third is doubly related to the Sign (and the Object): the Sign of the first triad can be seen as its Third's Object in yet another complex relationship. The relation between the Sign and the Interpretant is always, in principle, contextually overdetermined.

The abstract-specific opposition I have been proposing here can itself be modified contextually. The practice of fixing relations of signification is perspectival, almost in the Nietzschean sense: the mobile army of signs and their contexts, to adapt Nietzsche's image, collectively refer to "the sum of human relations" and the processes of their metamorphosis. Human social activity is presupposed by Peirce's understanding of signification, and the history of such activity explains the semiosis (and is partly constituted by it). In the face of poststructuralist denials of the theoretical significance of linguistic reference, one obvious advantage of the Peircean account is that it demonstrates how signification can be both relatively autonomous and part of the causal structure of the social world. It is only because signs exist in a dense referential network, Peirce says, that they reproduce and move about endlessly. Central to his theory is the conception of the Sign as involved in overlapping but not entirely commensurable triadic referential relationships. The referential dimension of signs is irreducible, since cultural and social contexts can never be entirely presupposed in advance. Reference is also irreducibly *complex*, since it is shaped more by changing contexts and perspectives than by the (simpler) relations of signs with unique and static objects in the world.[18]

Peirce's interest in the dynamic nature of linguistic reference can be seen as epistemological, for his theoretical goal is to specify the cognitive contexts of signification. To identify and analyze such contexts, he thinks we need to go beyond foundationalist (specifically empiricist) visions of direct knowledge gained from unmediated observation: "With the exception of knowledge, in the present instant," he wrote in 1904, "of the contents of consciousness in that instant (the existence of which knowledge is open to doubt) all our thought and knowledge is by signs."[19] Thus for Peirce an explanation of the principles of linguistic and cultural signification is a necessary component of any account of scientific inquiry. He recognizes the possibility of (theoretical) error, of inadequate or incorrect explanations of phenomena, and the equally real possibility that such errors can be remedied. For him the import of a theory of signs, as of a theory of a "natural kind," is epistemic, since such theories can explain, in necessarily interdependent ways, aspects of the world in which we live: "What is the essential difference between a sign that is communicated to a mind, and one that is not so communicated? If the question were simply what we *do* mean by a sign, it might soon be resolved. But that is not the point. We are in the situation of a

18. Contrast my interpretation here with de Man's reading of Peirce, discussed in Chapter 1.

19. Letter to Lady Welby, October 12, 1904, in Charles Sanders Peirce, *Values in a Universe of Chance: Selected Writings of Charles S. Peirce*, ed. Philip P. Wiener (Stanford: Stanford University Press, 1958), p. 390.

zoologist who wants to know what ought to be the meaning of 'fish' in order to make fishes one of the great classes of vertebrates. It appears to me that the essential function of a sign is to render inefficient relations efficient. . . . [A] sign is *something by knowing which we know something more*" (pp. 389–90, second emphasis mine).[20]

Reference, Reality, and the Division of Linguistic Labor

The foregoing accounts of signification and reference have the virtue of providing us with an understanding of both the social determination of signs and the relative autonomy of language and signification in general, which are capable of producing new chains of meaning and significance. Unaddressed thus far, however, is the question of whether (and in what way) aspects of language might be more than merely conventional, might be referentially tied to the natural world. The holistic understanding of culture which Peirce's theory of semiosis presupposes leads to an interesting problem. If meanings are "culturally" determined and if this determination is seen as absolute (in the sense that these meanings do not require a relationship with anything outside the "culture"), then do meanings have no cross-cultural validity at all? Do cultural wholes "cut up" social meanings in such ways that a culture radically different from ours does not share any of our meanings but creates its own out of whole cloth? This is the most difficult question signaled by the term "reference." Are there *some* aspects of language at least that might refer to the same entity across languages and cultures, across the various conventional systems that produce meanings? In answering this question theoretically, we are led to a critique and correction of the kind of holism I have been talking about so far.

Let us take Umberto Eco's example discussed in the previous chapter. Eco declares that "dog" does not refer to any particular referent, that is, any individual dog, but to a "class," which is "culturally defined." His (Peircean) point is that reference is not an atomistic but a social enterprise, involving both arbitrariness and conventionality. Eco's example takes us as far as he wishes to take us with it, but it raises some interesting questions about the specific way in which reference works in a soci-

20. For an excellent discussion of Peirce's view of truth and the goals of scientific inquiry, see Christopher Hookway, *Peirce* (London: Routledge and Kegan Paul, 1985), esp. chaps. 2, 4, and 7.

ety. The reference of "dog," for instance, is not in fact fixed by *a* single cultural convention, since we might associate any number of properties with "dogness." It is (typically) a four-legged domestic pet to some members of the "culture," and an animal with the internal biological structure of a "mammal" (as opposed to, say, a reptile) to others. Not all these properties are equally significant in defining what "dog" refers to in this culture. Clearly, if you live in modern (let's say industrial) societies, the definition as "mammal" is more significant than the fact that it can be domesticated. In these societies, scientific knowledge about "dogs," once discovered and accepted by the scientific community, is accepted as essential to our definition of "dogness." Thus even though some members of the culture—perhaps a numerical majority— associate "dog" with "domesticated animal" and are, moreover, ignorant of its being a mammal, "domestication" is not considered the defining property of dogs. In this sense, the reference of "dog" is not fixed *simply* through a cultural convention. What we need to add to Eco's definition is an account of how, for some kinds of words and signs, conventionality and social constructedness are dependent on the hierarchically organized knowledge-gathering processes of a given society. There is a crucial vagueness in Eco's notion of the "cultural" determination of reference. If we are to believe philosophers such as Putnam and Kripke, on whose work I have been drawing, reference is in many instances a transcultural knowledge-gathering process and cannot be subsumed completely into a cultural convention. Putnam contends, for instance, that the reference of scientific terms relates us causally to the objective (mind- and culture-independent) real world. I think a materialist account of language and signification, of the kind I have been developing with the help of Bakhtin and Peirce, is incomplete without an account of what Putnam and the "causal" theorists seek to explain.[21]

One of the key questions concerning reference arises in debates within the philosophy of science. Developing some very rudimentary remarks by Engels, Putnam argues for the "realist" view that "concepts in different theories may refer to the same thing." The reference of scientific terms implies the complex social arrangement on which inquiry as a socially coordinated practice rests: "To have linguistic competence in connection with a term it is not sufficient, in general, to have the full battery of usual linguistic knowledge and skills; one must, in addi-

21. An excellent introduction to causal theories of reference is to be found in Michael Devitt and Kim Sterelny, *Language and Reality* (Cambridge: MIT Press, 1987), pt. II. See also Saul Kripke, *Naming and Necessity* (Cambridge: Harvard University Press, 1980).

tion, be in the right sort of relationship to certain distinguished situations (normally, though not necessarily, situations in which the *referent* of the term is present)."[22] It is not necessary, for example, that every speaker of a language (every member of a culture) know exactly what "electricity" is. The social division of linguistic labor ensures that once electricity is defined by experts, we all "know" the referent of the term electricity because we are related in a very specific socially organized way to the fixing of the reference of the term "electricity." This is true even for more familiar, less obviously "technical," terms. "Gold," another of Putnam's examples, is closer to my discussion of "dog." Putnam's description of the division of linguistic labor involved in the use of this term is worth quoting in some detail:

> Gold is important for many reasons: it is a precious metal, it is a monetary metal, it has symbolic value (it is important to most people that the "gold" wedding ring they wear *really* consist of gold and not just *look* gold), etc. Consider our community as a "factory": in this "factory" some people have the "job" of *wearing gold wedding rings*, other people have the "job" of *selling gold wedding rings*, still other people have the "job" of *telling whether or not something is really gold*. It is not at all necessary or efficient that everyone who wears a gold ring (or a gold cufflink, etc.), or discusses the "gold standard," etc., engage in buying and selling gold. Nor is it necessary or efficient that everyone who buys and sells gold be able to tell whether or not something is really gold in a society where this form of dishonesty is uncommon (selling fake gold) and in which one can easily consult an expert in case of doubt. And it is *certainly* not necessary or efficient that everyone who has occasion to buy or wear gold be able to tell with any reliability whether or not something is really gold.[23]

Thus this kind of argument would force us to specify, beyond the rather general claim that reference is fixed by a social convention, the ways in which different kinds of words or terms take on different kinds of reference through a division of epistemic labor. "Expert" members of our linguistic community recognize gold in our societies, but "the way of recognizing possessed by [them] is also, through them, possessed by the collective linguistic body, even though it is not possessed by each individual member of the body" (MM, p. 228). The conventionality of reference is related to the hierarchical structure of our socially based

22. Hilary Putnam, "Explanation and Reference," in *Mind, Language, and Reality*, vol. 2 of *Philosophical Papers* (Cambridge: Cambridge University Press, 1975), p. 199.
23. Hilary Putnam, "The Meaning of 'Meaning'," ibid., p. 227, hereafter cited as MM.

practices. As we shall see in Part Two, this issue is significant for our understanding of methodological holism, and for the implications of its various competing definitions.

It is not enough, then, to say that meanings are social conventions, for the conventionality of meanings itself needs to be specified further. Central to this task of specification will be an adequate social theory, plausible as an explanation not only of linguistic processes but of modern social forms and institutions as well. Accounting for meaning and reference involves theorization of a good deal of what is, by any definition, extralinguistic. An explanatory account of language involves auxilliary theories about cultural and social organization, which can be tested in relation to empirical data and alternative explanatory accounts.

But accepting this kind of thesis about the social nature of meaning and reference fixing is not, one could object, incompatible with relativism. Our experts tell us what gold is for us, and theirs tell us what "gold" is for them. Gold and "gold" are two different things, with no continuity of reference between them. Ultimately, notwithstanding the stratified nature of modern science and societies, one could argue that the reference of gold is determined by a cultural or social context (a whole) that has no point of contact with the way "gold" is defined and understood in the other culture or society. The implications of this relativist position are explored in a more general way and in greater depth in Chapter 5, where I challenge the claim that such a (methodological) stance leads to greater political tolerance and respect for the "other" society or culture. Without going into that question here, let me simply indicate exactly why Putnam's account of reference is antirelativist. Putnam would say (developing Saul Kripke's original work in crucial ways) that the reference of gold is ultimately fixed by its real nature, that is, by the modern scientific explanation of its microstructure. Once this is determined to the satisfaction of the scientific community, we would be able to say confidently that what, say, the Greek (expert) might have identified as "gold" is *in fact* "fool's gold"; that he confused real gold with something else. The extension of the term *gold* (that of which the term is true) is a part of the real world. Once we have discovered it scientifically, using criteria or proof and evidence that the best science today accepts (and it is definitely *not* the case that scientists have ever claimed to have discovered the real nature of everything, but there is in fact that kind of a consensus about gold), there is every reason to think that only what we now know to be gold was in fact the real gold in Attic society and culture. That their "gold" was a more inclusive term and included other kinds of bright yellow metal which we would now know are not gold might be of interest to the cultural or social historian but has no bearing on the reference of the term *gold*. Reference of "natural kind" terms such as *gold* or *dog* are not determined purely by convention, for their referents are parts of the natural world. We cannot define what gold "means" simply by referring to whatever "satisfies the *contemporary* 'operational definition' of *gold*" (MM, p. 235).

The reference of natural-kind terms alerts us also that such terms might have essential properties as opposed to inessential or less essential ones. Kripke gives the example of "yellowness" as such an inessential property of gold; it is an identifying mark that we might turn out to have been wrong about. If it turns out that gold is in fact blue and something contingent (such as an optical illusion) led us to err in our identification of the color of gold, that error would not make much difference once we know the microstructure of gold. There would no doubt be quite a story for newspapers to report and a good deal of readjustment of our cultural associations with the metal, but gold as a natural-kind term would remain essentially what it was. Similarly, if an animal that looked exactly like Umberto Eco's "dog" appeared in front of us and we were able to determine that it in fact had the internal structure of a reptile rather than a mammal, we would be justified in concluding that it is not a dog. If, for whatever accidental reason, we did not know about its internal structure and continued to think of it as a "dog," then a future group of humans who discovered the reptilic internal structure of Eco's "dog" would be perfectly right to conclude that we were, quite simply, wrong. That we were wrong, however, does not imply that they have the right to conclude that *everything* "we" (as a culture) believe about dogs and dogness is unjustified. That conclusion does not follow from this one error, and such cross-cultural judgments, though not in principle impossible, involve complex hermeneutical negotiations, processes of interpretation involving much more than just how "we" relate to "dogs" (the real ones and the reptilian imposters). This kind of interpretive practice involves a recognition of the holism of human language, culture, and society; a theory of meaning and reference of natural-kind terms does not provide us with an easy way of ignoring that. But such a theory (or the rudiments developed thus far in the work of Kripke and Putnam in particular) provides a natural complement to Bakhtin's and Peirce's specifications of the exact ways in which language is social.

In a more general way, they provide a valuable corrective to our current suspicions about "reference" as a necessarily reductive term, involving a naive conception of words or concepts as unproblematically mirroring the world. The "world," it would seem from the foregoing discussion, is not simply there, waiting for us to hold up a mirror to it or to give it a name. And neither is it *merely* a cultural and social convention. Language and the world hook up in interesting and complicated ways, and our analysis of reference depends at least in part on the open-ended discoveries of our various traditions of inquiry. On the general view I am defending, then, "reference" should be seen not as a static epistemic or representational relation but rather as a dynamic one, open, like knowledge itself, to error and its detection, to modification and "refinement." For as Hartry Field and Richard Boyd have noted, there are crucial instances of "partial" denotation, where terms in a particular (scientific) theory refer imprecisely to the world, but the imprecision is removed through advances in the science rather than through refinement of our purely linguistic habits and practices.[24] Boyd says that such instances should be seen as part of a more general process, "the ongoing project of continuous accommodation of language to the world in the light of new discoveries about [the world's] causal powers" (p. 523). Thus, for Boyd, reference is best seen as providing "epistemic access" to the world, and referential imprecision is tied to the current state of our knowledge about (an aspect of) the world. Hence the relevance of the basic methodological principle underlying all inquiry, a principle that Peirce would have championed as well: "Always inquire, in the light of the best available knowledge, in what ways your current beliefs about the world might plausibly be incomplete, inadequate, or false, and design observations or experiments with the aim of detecting and remedying such possible defects" (Boyd, p. 523).

Such a view of reference involves an account of the degrees of conventionality and social constructedness of linguistic meanings, but it sometimes also reveals how we in fact come to know things about the world, how we distinguish truth from error, fact from fiction. Reference does not guarantee meaning in a self-evident way, and not because of some unexplainable rhetorical property of language (as de Man suggests) but rather because words and the world, theories and things, hook up only in very mediated ways. This mediation would be cause for epistemic despair only if we were to assume what Nietzsche and a whole host of

24. See especially Hartry Field, "Theory Change and the Indeterminacy of Reference," *Journal of Philosophy* 70 (August 16, 1973), 462–81; Richard Boyd, "Metaphor and Theory Change: What Is 'Metaphor' a Metaphor For?" in *Metaphor and Thought*, 2d. ed., ed. Andrew Ortony (Cambridge: Cambridge University Press, 1993), pp. 481–532.

modern postpositivist thinkers say we should not: that knowledge is truly objective only when it is shorn of all perspectives, paradigms, and mediating theories. When we give up this (positivist) theoretical assumption about the nature of objective knowledge, we enable ourselves not only to recognize error but to diagnose its sources and its causes as well. The notion of reference, as I have been defining it in Chapters 1 and 2, is an aspect of a nonfoundationalist, socially based view of knowledge and language. I have also suggested that to evaluate a theory of language we need to examine more than its implications for readings of this or that "text" (literary or otherwise) and have tried to indicate why it would be seriously misleading to see our concerns with the autonomy of language as incompatible with our questions about the sociality of language.

3

THE LIMITS OF ALTHUSSER'S POSTSTRUCTURALIST MARXISM

My discussion thus far has indicated the need to understand how language use is related to social organization. We have seen in a more general way why an adequate theory of signification would depend on a detailed understanding of the social nature of both language and knowledge. In this chapter and the next, I turn to questions of ideology and "history," dealing directly with contemporary poststructuralist theorizations of textual interpretation and its social contexts. This chapter elaborates an understanding of ideology and examines its implications for contemporary critical debates. Louis Althusser's influential work in particular has made the discussion of ideology a major constituent of the interpretive and political problematic in which my discussion has been situated.[1] For a good theory of ideology grounds epistemological questions in practical contexts and explains how "truth" and "error" are lived and experienced by socially situated subjects. In fact such a theory can help explain the relevance of sound theoretical knowledge to everyday social struggles by exploring the links between subjective experience and objective knowledge, between "values" and "knowledge."

1. Louis Althusser, "Ideology and Ideological State Apparatuses (Notes towards an Investigation)," in *Lenin and Philosophy and Other Essays*, trans. Ben Brewster (New York: Monthly Review Press, 1971), pp. 127–86, hereafter cited parenthetically in the text as ISA. I shall also be quoting from *For Marx*, trans. Ben Brewster (London: New Left Books, 1977), cited as *FM*; *Essays in Self-Criticism*, trans. Grahame Lock (London: New Left Books, 1976), cited as *ESC*; and Louis Althusser and Etienne Balibar, *Reading "Capital,"* trans. Ben Brewster (London: New Left Books, 1970), cited as *RC*.

From the point of view of contemporary criticism, Althusser's most significant contribution to a theory of ideology and ideological processes is his simultaneous emphasis on ideology as text, as a readable system of representations, *and* as a practice serving to reproduce structures of power and the dominant relations of power. If we are to learn from Althusser, this double gesture must be formulated as a clear methodological challenge for criticism. Althusser, on the one hand, textualizes our understanding of ideology, enabling us to read particular ideologies with attention to their internal nuances and even inconsistencies. On the other hand, he makes it impossible for us to forget that hegemonic ideologies serve the needs of the dominant social order, implicated as they are in the larger processes of the reproduction of that order. Thus the cultural text, in this perspective, is not merely related to some backdrop that provides information; rather, it is symptomatic of a wider ideological and political process in which the functionings of power and domination become eminently visible. One major advantage of this reformulation is that we thus avoid the embarrassments of the simpler versions of the base-superstructure model, while also keeping at bay those ideologies of the text which would have us refine the macrofunctionings of power out of existence in their revolutions of word and syntax. In this chapter, I discuss this aspect of Althusser's theory of ideology by relating it to the relevant tradition within marxism and by grounding its claims in the context of the general poststructuralist (and postmodernist) critique of idealism and metaphysics. What I offer is not a survey of marxist theories of ideology; nor is it an exhaustive discussion of Althusser. But in examining Althusser's theory of ideology I would like to explore, more generally, the political and epistemological implications of different approaches to ideology. I would like to show exactly why Althusser's poststructuralist account of ideology is antiidealist and why it is useful for all radical cultural theory. I also intend to examine the limitations of Althusser's general antimetaphysical and antihumanist approach. I suggest why such an approach leads to an impoverished account of subjectivity and why it is itself based on an unjustified (almost positivist) suspicion that all normative claims are speculative and ultimately idealist. My critique is thus meant to introduce the fuller and more direct discussion of human agency and the epistemology of value in Part Two.

Ideology: The Traditional Account

The best way to discuss the Althusserian contribution to a theory of ideology, however, may not be to compare it to Marx's original views.

The reason is becoming more and more evident now that the Althusse-rian influence has subsided in contemporary theory, and we are begin-ning to get detailed readings of Marx's corpus which show exactly how complex a matter it is to read Marx. Althusser's achievement was cer-tainly to make the rereading of Marx's texts a respectable, indeed, a necessary project. Nevertheless, it is becoming increasingly apparent that his absolute division between an early and a late Marx (that is, a "humanist" and a "scientific" Marx) is no longer as useful as it once was. A second generation of readers and interpreters has now consoli-dated the insights of Althusser's readings, and another has arisen with equally viable and interesting readings of precisely those texts which Althusser seemed to want to discard because they were "pre-scientific." On the subject of ideology, for instance, it is possible to find both Al-thusserians and anti-Althusserians pointing to such texts as *The Ger-man Ideology* as examples of simplistic notions of false consciousness and "empiricist" notions of error. The notorious passages are easy to deconstruct: the metaphors of inversion, of ocularity (the famous cam-era obscura), and of pure illusion ("phantoms of the brain," mere "re-flexes," and so on) are certainly there when Marx and Engels attempt to discuss the relationship between the mystified consciousness and the political "reality" with which it is attempting to grapple. Yet it has been argued equally convincingly that texts written well before *The German Ideology* reveal a more complex notion of ideology, linking it not to a simple reflective consciousness but to a form of praxis, a mode of being in the world which cannot be dismissed as a mere *error* of cognition. Similarly, other studies have pointed out that even the notorious pas-sages need to be read in the context of their polemical occasion, and the metaphors need to be understood as responses to specific polemical opponents rather than as evidence of the dispensable metaphysical bag-gage of the early texts.[2] At any rate, what Derrida implicitly called for in *Positions*, that Marx's texts be submitted to "the protocol of reading," is

2. See, in particular, Louis Dupré, *Marx's Social Critique of Culture* (New Haven: Yale University Press, 1983), pp. 216–28. Dupré shows how *The German Ideology* is too com-plex to interpret as simply subscribing to the "false consciousness" notion of ideology. He admits that the "derogatory meaning" of ideology as "a basically false and deceptive mode of consciousness" appears in the book, but "the method of interpretation set up in the work no longer requires it" (p. 224). For a less equivocal criticism of the inadequacy of the theory of ideology in *The German Ideology*, see John Mepham, "The Theory of Ideology in *Capital*," in *Epistemology, Science, Ideology*, ed. Mepham and D.-H. Ruben, vol. 3 of *Is-sues in Marxist Philosophy* (New York: Humanities Press, 1979), pp. 141–73. Mepham con-trasts the more sophisticated view of ideology to be found in *Capital* with the simplistic one in the earlier text.

certainly being attempted now, and it may be confusing the issue in this context to appeal to the conflicted texts of Marx and Engels to evaluate to what extent a (post)Althusserian understanding of ideology is useful for contemporary criticism and theory.[3]

Instead, a better point of reference here would be the work of Georg Lukács.[4] Through a contrast with Lukács's understanding of ideology we may see that Althusser makes ideology a more textual matter, rendering visible elements and levels that we could appreciate earlier only as minor and subservient moments of a totalizing narrative. Lukács's useful analysis, which built on Marx's idea that consciousness is inherently practical, revealed how the limitations of bourgeois thought, for instance, arise from its class-determined passivity. The power of *History and Class Consciousness* as ideology critique consists in its ability to show how modern philosophy since Kant is limited and skewed because it unwittingly adopts a contemplative paradigm of knowledge.[5] Moreover, Lukács translates the specific content of each philosophical system into a formal dilemma, which can be resolved, he maintains, only when the contemplative mode is overcome. What his analysis acknowledges, thus, is the role of praxis, of purposeful human activity, in its capacity not only to change but also to interpret the world accurately. For Lukács (as for Marx), the possibility of a nonideological consciousness can be glimpsed at least since the birth of capitalism, inasmuch as it is potentially embodied in the historical agency and situation of the proletariat. Ideology is tied to class consciousness and is dependent on our situation in history and the social totality.

It would be important to recognize, then, that Lukács does not consider ideology to be a simple form of false or distorted consciousness. If bourgeois ideology is "false" at all for Lukács, it is not in the sense that the truth is available to members of the bourgeois class as a simple alternative, for he does not conceive of truth as a free floating and acon-

3. Jacques Derrida, *Positions*, trans. Alan Bass (Chicago: University of Chicago Press, 1981), see esp. pp. 62–68. Perhaps the most exciting development in recent decades has been a distinctively "analytical" marxism. See, in particular, G. A. Cohen, *Karl Marx's Theory of History* (Princeton: Princeton University Press, 1978); Cohen, *History, Labour, and Freedom: Themes from Marx* (Oxford: Clarendon Press, 1988); Jon Elster, *Making Sense of Marx* (Cambridge: Cambridge University Press, 1985); and Allen Wood, *Karl Marx* (London: Routledge and Kegan Paul, 1981). A useful anthology of writings in this tradition, with a good bibliography, is John Roemer, ed., *Analytical Marxism* (Cambridge: Cambridge University Press, 1986).

4. See especially Georg Lukács, *History and Class Consciousness*, trans. Rodney Livingstone (Cambridge: MIT Press, 1971), hereafter cited as *HCC*.

5. See especially Lukács, "Reification and the Consciousness of the Proletariat," ibid., pp. 83–222.

textual knowledge, graspable in the form of discrete philosophical propositions. Lukács's achievement was to have developed Marx's conception of ideology as a complex *relation* of the class (and the class subject) to its historical situation; it is for him an index of our general dependency on the world and our unavoidable implication in it.

> By relating consciousness to the whole of society it becomes possible to infer the thoughts and feelings which men would have in a particular situation if they were able to assess both it and the interests arising from it in their impact on immediate action and on the whole structure of society. . . .
> As the *Communist Manifesto* states: "Capital is a social force and not a personal one." But it is a social force whose movements are determined by the individual interests of the owners of capital—who cannot see and who are necessarily indifferent to all the social implications of their activities. Hence the social principle and the social function implicit in capital can only prevail unbeknown to them and, as it were, against their will and behind their backs. . . .
> Bourgeois thought observes economic life consistently and necessarily from the standpoint of the individual capitalist and this naturally produces a sharp confrontation between the individual and the overpowering supra-personal "law of nature" which propels all social phenomena. (*HCC*, pp. 51, 63)

This focus on the "social implications of [the agents'] activities" places Lukács in the long line of thinkers—from Condorcet and Destutt de Tracy to Marx—who have used the notion of ideology to question the innocence of ideas and to reveal their social moorings.[6] With Lukács (as with Marx) the political perspective of class struggle comes to the fore, and we also begin to understand ideology and the ideological relation in both practical and formal terms. Marx, in *The Eighteenth Brumaire*, sees the ideology of the French petite bourgeoisie as a structural limit it cannot go beyond, given its class position and interests.[7] Lukács

6. One of the best general introductions to the word *ideology* and its history is George Lichtheim's lead essay in his *Concept of Ideology and Other Essays* (New York: Random House, 1967), pp. 3–46.

7. Marx provides an analysis that would suggest the elements of a theory of ideology in general as the intersection of "interest" and the forms in which we imagine the real: "One must not take the narrow view that the petty bourgeoisie explicitly sets out to assert its egoistic class interests. It rather believes that the *particular* conditions of its liberation are the only *general* conditions within which modern society can be saved and the class struggle avoided. Nor indeed must one imagine that the democratic representatives are all *shopkeepers* or their enthusiastic supporters. They may well be poles apart from them in their education and their individual situation. What makes them representatives of the petty

generalizes this analysis and, taking the dominant history of post-Enlightenment philosophy as his focus, shows the structural limitations of both the problems and the solutions this philosophic tradition finds itself considering. At its most successful, Lukács's kind of analysis is a diagnostic reading that goes beyond mere textual exegesis or the "history of ideas" approach. His critique is in part internal, since it identifies the political logic inherent in the modern philosophical systems. His formal and structural analysis of philosophy is thus more successful as ideology critique than a purely external sociological approach would be.

Powerful as Lukács's ideological reinterpretation of philosophical texts is, it nonetheless reflects an understanding of philosophical discourse at only the most general level. Its emphasis on the formal or structural dimension of philosophical arguments is at first an enabling move, suspending for the moment the substance of philosophical arguments by transforming them into formal constructs, with their internal dynamic contradictoriness made available for analysis and evaluation. In literary criticism the advantage of such a move is best evident in Lukács's analogous emphasis on narrative as an act simultaneously of cognition and evaluation: for the critic, narrative becomes a subtextual form on which to map the writer's construction of social reality. As a characterization of certain realistic genres (the nineteenth-century European novel, for instance), this focus enables Lukács to reformulate the traditional dichotomy of form and content and draw attention to the social text that inheres in the constructs of fiction. This insight, however, does not work at the levels of language or the less visible details of narrativity. The generality of the focus yields large insights but prevents us from considering as ideologically significant other levels of textual process. Hence the notorious pronouncements on the modernist novel, for instance: whether it is Joyce or Woolf or Sartre, Lukács can see only a "carnivalization of interiority," and such techniques (unproblematically considered, that is) as "stream of consciousness" are seen as deriving unambiguously from an ideology of capitulation to the prevailing order, unable to muster the cognitive courage to rise above the

---

bourgeoisie is the fact that their minds are restricted by the same barriers which the petty bourgeoisie fails to overcome in real life, and that they are therefore driven in theory to the same problems and solutions to which material interest and social situation drive the latter in practice. This is the general relationship between the *political and literary representatives* of a class and the class which they represent." *The Eighteenth Brumaire of Louis Bonaparte*, in Marx, *Surveys from Exile*, ed. David Fernbach (New York: Vintage, 1974), pp. 176–77.

lure of the simply experimental.[8] The basis of all this, for Lukács, is the reified understanding of the social whole; he invokes a notion of totality as the image of the desired sociohistorical "truth" which can be grasped only through an active orientation of philosophy or artistic form.[9]

The weakness of *History and Class Consciousness* and Lukács's problematic in general, however, is that in considering the relation between the subject (the individual or class) and the world, Lukács sees ideology mainly in its larger forms, but its production, reproduction, and self-sustenance are largely considered in a relatively *disembodied* manner. In the case of literary modernism, for instance, Lukács can see the ideology of narrative form, as I mentioned, but he remains peculiarly blind to the signifying activity of the modernist novel at the level of the sentence or the word. (Susan Sontag was quite right to have complained, in exasperation, that Lukács could so adroitly transform content into form while remaining singularly impervious to the content implicit in the modernist forms themselves.) If Lukács conceives of ideology as text at all—and in giving it a form, a structure, he certainly does on one level—it is the produced text that he allows himself to analyze. Beneath the hypostases of the *énoncé*, the significance of enunciation, the necessary—and continuing—productivity of ideology, is systematically ignored.

Lukács's definition of ideology retains its epistemic component; ideology is opposed to knowledge as error—no matter how mediated—is to truth. But historical "knowledge" is always defined as the knowledge of a social whole, the kind of knowledge the Hegelian subject of history is capable of attaining. Ideology is always measured against such knowledge, the ideal knowledge of the subject-object of history—the proletariat. "The historical knowledge of the proletariat," Lukács declares, "begins with knowledge of the present, with the self-knowledge of its own social situation and with the elucidation of its necessity (its genesis)" (*HCC*, p. 159). Marx had made a claim in *Capital* (in the famous discussion "The Fetishism of the Commodity and its Secret") which is similar in some respects, but it was an empirical claim about the practi-

---

8. Georg Lukács, *Realism in Our Time*, trans. J. Mander and N. Mander (New York: Harper Torchbooks, 1974). Sartre's reply to Lukács's dismissal of existentialism as part of the general decay of modernism, in literature as well as philosophy, is well documented in *Search for a Method*, trans. Hazel Barnes (New York: Vintage, 1968).

9. For a reading of Lukács which stresses this aspect of his work, see Fredric Jameson, *Marxism and Form* (Princeton: Princeton University Press, 1971), pp. 160–205. For a useful general introduction, see Martin Jay, *Marxism and Totality* (Berkeley: University of California Press, 1984), pp. 81–127.

cal possibilities of social knowledge available to members of the proletariat.[10] Lukács suggests that here Marx sees "the whole self-knowledge of the proletariat . . . as the knowledge of capitalist society" (HCC, p. 170). But Marx's argument is in fact based not on the idealization of "self-knowledge" but on a social epistemology. It is not the worker as such, or the worker in the general context of labor, who is capable of removing the "veil . . . from the countenance of the social life-process" (Capital, p. 173), but workers who have formed an "association of free men, working with the means of production held in common, and expending their many different forms of labour-power in full self-awareness as one single social labour force" (p. 171). Rational and self-conscious collective agency, embodied in rational social organization (in which society comes under the "conscious and planned control" of free workers [p. 173]), is what Marx sees as the social basis of an accurate knowledge of society. Thus he emphasizes conscious political organizing of the working class, since it will facilitate the development of the proletariat's latent epistemological privilege, a privilege deriving partly from its structural position in the socioeconomic system.

For Lukács, on the other hand, the proletariat is a theoretical idealization: as a class, it has an *absolute* epistemological privilege in relation to capitalist society. Lukács is not interested in the critical consciousness of working people as they grasp in different ways their role in production and social exploitation; he is not interested in the everyday dimension of error, mystification, and the attempts of social agents to pierce through them. His focus is on the "worker" as the abstract subject of "the dialectical method": "When the worker knows himself as a commodity, his knowledge is practical" (HCC, p. 169); this knowledge cuts beneath the "quantitative exchange categories of capitalism" and the "fetish character of every commodity" to reveal the "qualitative, living core" of the social totality, "the relation between men, entering into the evolution of society" (p. 169). The knowledge of the worker is essentially a self-consciousness, and because it is, a self-conscious worker embodies the "essence of the dialectical method." This method "is distinguished from bourgeois thought not only by the fact that it alone can lead to a knowledge of totality; it is also significant that such knowledge is only attainable because the relationship between parts and whole has become fundamentally different from what it is in thought based on categories of reflection. In brief, from this point of view, the essence of the dialectical method lies in the fact that in every

10. Karl Marx, Capital, trans. Ben Fowkes (New York: Vintage, 1977), vol. 1.

aspect correctly grasped by the dialectic the whole totality is compre-
hended and that the whole method can be unravelled from every single
aspect" (*HCC*, pp. 169–70).

We can now understand why Althusser charges that Lukács relies on
an essentially idealist picture of history as an "expressive totality."[11]
Althusser's critique of such a model of totality is a critique of the idealizations involved in Lukács's understanding of historical and political
knowledge. Such an idealization, it can be argued, makes the definition
of both knowledge and ideology overly general. Lost in such definitions
is the crucial question about how ideologies are produced and reproduced, how they are practically effective in society; the form of ideology
may be contradictory, but its existence and functioning in the world
is relatively unproblematical and self-evident to the critic. This self-
evidence, this self-presence, also applies in Lukács's paradigm to historical periods, secure in the logic of their own identity. But Althusser's
alternative definition of ideology contains a thesis that problematizes
precisely this notion of identity and self-presence.

Beyond "Consciousness": Ideology as Text

Althusser's emphasis is on the textuality of ideology, and his notion
of textuality is linked in part to his attempt to appreciate the role of
ideology in the reproduction of the dominant relations of production.
Althusser provides an account of the way ideology is grounded less in
"ideas" or "consciousness" than in "practices." Practices are socially
determined in multiple ways, and they reveal how ideology is both necessarily "textual" (that is, discursively mediated rather than simple, homogeneous, and self-evident) and tied to social and political
institutions. One of Althusser's most far-reaching theses in "Ideology
and Ideological State Apparatuses" defends precisely this textualized
notion of ideology. Against the notion of ideology as consciousness, Althusser's first claim is the thesis that "an ideology always exists in an
apparatus, and its practice, or practices." "Ideology has a material existence" and can be understood only if approached in this way. Drawing
on Antonio Gramsci, who saw the significance of an analysis of institutions for an adequate understanding of ideological relations and the

11. Althusser's critique of Lukács is implicit in the section titled "Marxism Is Not a
Historicism," *RC*. Lukács is granted only the briefest mention in *For Marx*, mainly in two
footnotes.

workings of hegemony, Althusser goes on to provide a theory of its complex functioning in relation to state power. He directs our attention beyond the repressive apparatuses of the state (such as the police, the army, and so on), which classical marxism had identified as the primary basis of state power, to those institutional levels through which power is mediated in less transparent and more discursive ways. These institutions, which Althusser calls ideological state apparatuses, sustain the domination of the hegemonic class by legitimating its ideologies. Such institutions or apparatuses work, in the last instance, for the state, but their effectiveness depends on their appearance of neutrality. Thus, when Althusser declares that ideologies have a material existence, his point is that we need to locate them as practices in the larger context of the various relations of power, within institutions and apparatuses that normally sustain and reproduce such relations, and within the perspective of a struggle between different social groups (particularly classes) for power. It is essential to reconceive ideologies as practices that are always (already) situated in relation to other practices and to the institutions that sanction and organize such practices.

It is a central feature of Althusser's understanding of "practice" that it does not depend on our traditional notions of either "ideas" or "actions." According to "Ideology and Ideological State Apparatuses," ideology is embodied in material practices, but practices are not mere actions, conceived in the form of praxis, implying the subject of classical Hegelian marxism. Rather, actions are themselves to be understood as "inserted into *practices* . . . [and] these practices are governed by the *rituals* in which these practices are inscribed, within the *material existence of an ideological apparatus*" (ISA, p. 168). The "meaning" of a practice cannot be said to derive unproblematically from a reference to an authorizing human agent, a subject. Practices are, by definition, always decentered in relation to the subjective goals and intentions of human agents. The source of intelligibility of the practice lies not in the agent, or in the practice itself as an "act," but in the determined yet mobile (that is, changeable) social "rituals" of the ideological apparatus.

Speaking of the "ideas" of an "individual," Althusser maintains that their complexly determined nature is both "material" and mediated: "Where only a single subject (such and such an individual) is concerned, the existence of the ideas of his belief is material in that *his ideas are his material actions inserted into material practices governed by material rituals which are themselves defined by the material ideological apparatus from which derive the ideas of that subject*" (p. 169). "Ideas" are "actions"; they are produced by a causal chain that includes material practices, rituals, and ideological apparatuses. The individual agent's subjective reality is shaped, in a highly mediated way, by political forces. When, following the passage I have just quoted, Althusser goes on to discuss the different "modalities" of materiality, drawing attention to the complexity of discourses, he affirms the textual and always-already-interpreted form in which reality itself is available to us: "Naturally, the four inscriptions of the adjective 'material' in my proposition must be affected by different modalities: the materialities of a displacement for going to mass, of kneeling down, of the gesture of the sign of the cross, or the mea culpa, of a sentence, of a prayer, of an act of contrition, of a penitence, of a gaze, of a hand-shake, of an external verbal discourse or an 'internal' verbal discourse (consciousness), are not one and the same materiality" (p. 169). We are now quite far indeed from the self-conscious subject of history which Lukács idealized. What the different "modalities" of materiality are supposed to explain is how an individual's beliefs and actions are socially determined on a number of levels. Althusser's argument is that the individual subject is shaped by ideology in all these complex ways, and thus ideology cannot be reduced to "error"—practical or theoretical. The glossary prepared under Althusser's supervision for the English edition of *Pour Marx* explains that ideology is not to be distinguished from science because of its "falsity" (*FM*, p. 252); rather, it is the lived relation of humans to their social world. This relation is mediated by the "materiality" of representations and discourses, narratives and theories. It is this thesis about the complex materiality or the causal effectivity of discursive and "theoretical" phenomena which Althusser thinks is the antiidealist kernel of his definition of ideology.

Indeed, there is a basic continuity between this account of the "textuality" of the material world and the general anti-Hegelian problematic Althusser had developed in his earlier readings of the Hegel-Marx relationship. As early as 1962, in the important essay Contradiction and Overdetermination," there is a criticism of Hegelian historiography which in crucial respects anticipates Derrida's critique of metaphysics.[12] Althusser says that despite the ritual invocation of history, Hegel's model of "contradiction" as the key to events and historical periods is essentialist and thus inadequately historical in that it reduces the complex causal relations that constitute a society to one "internal principle" (of contradiction). In the *Philosophy of History*, Althusser points out, Hegel sees Rome as an "organic totality" that "is *reflected in a*

12. Compare, also, the explicit statements in *RC*, esp. pp. 16–17, 62–63, and 186–89, with those in Derrida's *Positions*, esp. pp. 56–60.

unique internal principle, which is *the truth* of all those concrete determinations" (*FM*, p. 102). It is worth quoting Althusser at some length here, for his own emphasis draws our attention to the underlying images that shape Hegel's historical method:

> Thus Rome: its mighty history, its institutions, its crises and ventures, are nothing but the temporal manifestation of the internal principle of the *abstract legal personality*, and then its destruction. Of course, this internal principle contains as echoes the principle of each of the historical formations it has superseded, but *as echoes* of itself— that is why, too, it only has one centre, the centre of all the past worlds conserved in its memory; that is why *it is simple*. And its own *contradiction* appears in this very simplicity: in Rome, *the Stoic consciousness*, as consciousness of the contradiction inherent in the concept of the abstract legal personality, which *aims* for the concrete world of *subjectivity*, but *misses it*. This is the contradiction which will bring down Rome and produce its future: *the image of subjectivity* in medieval Christianity. So all Rome's complexity fails to overdetermine the contradiction in the simple Roman principle, which is merely the internal essence of this infinite historical wealth. (*FM*, p. 102)

The "abstract legal personality" of Rome has, as its mere "echoes," all its past; it is "simple" because it has "one centre." Thus, the "contradiction" Hegel finds is formulated as the explanatory principle of an essentially centered text, and despite the "complexity" that it intends to analyze and explain, the model based on this "contradiction" fails to account for historical and social complexity as anything but mere epiphenomena expressing the transcendental reality of this "internal essence." For Hegel (and for Lukács) a particular society is a totality that "expresses" an essence. Once identified, such an essence forecloses analysis of the complexly organized causal relations that are not already seen as part of the center. Essentialist thinking distorts by idealizing, Althusser would argue, and it reduces historical analysis to a search for the logos. His own theory of ideology suggests that historical explanations must be more open to the "inaudible" and the "illegible": "The truth of history cannot be read in its manifest discourse," he says in *Reading "Capital,"* "because the text of history is not a text in which a voice (the Logos) speaks, but the inaudible and illegible notation of the effect of structure of structures" (p. 17). Essences function as myths of origins, which make genuine historical analysis impossible. Indeed, such myths are convenient because they suppress what cannot be thought in order to make the reductive idealization seem natural and self-evident: "The function of the concept of origin, as in original sin, is to summarize in one word what has not to be thought in order to be able to think what one wants to think" (*RC*, p. 63).

The Althusserian notion of social "overdetermination" should thus be seen as a critique of the reductive essentialism he thinks is typical of all idealist historiography. The language of consciousness, as source and center, is always tied to this atextual—that is, idealist— problematic.

> Because the past is never more than the internal essence (in-itself) of the future it encloses, this presence of the past is the presence to consciousness of consciousness itself, *and no true external determination. A circle of circles, consciousness has only one centre*, which solely determines it; it would need circles *with another center than itself—decentered circles*—for it to be affected at its centre by their effectivity, in short for its essence to be overdetermined by them. But that is not the case. (*FM*, p. 102)

"Decentered circles"—this is the image that the Althusserian redefinition of ideology suggests. The "essence" is always in fact "overdetermined" for Althusser, and the image of "decentered circles" with overlapping and multiple sources of causal influence and pressure is meant to point to an antifoundationalist epistemology (see *RC*, pp. 16–17, in particular). When Althusser defines ideology as a "system (with its own logic and rigour) of representations" (*FM*, p. 231), he insists, I have been suggesting, on an understanding of *representations* as themselves causally effective. For he sees them as tied to the irreducible plurality of practices through which individuals imagine and live their relations to their social world.

Althusser's argument is thus implicitly anti-Lukácsian; he thinks that "ideology" cannot be defined as cognitive or epistemic failure because it is coextensive with subjectivity. "What is represented in ideology is therefore not the system of the real relations which govern the existence of individuals, but the imaginary relation of those individuals to the real relations in which they live" (ISA, p. 165). Naturally, the representations of ideology do not "belong" to the individual. They constitute the repertoire of the individual's "imaginary relation" to the real conditions of existence, through a process that is controlled from out-side the sphere of the individual's consciousness.

Althusser also links his critique of idealism to a much stronger thesis, however. The subject is for him a mere "effect" of society: "The subject acts insofar as he is acted by the following system (set out in the order of its real determination): ideology existing in a material ideological apparatus, prescribing material practices governed by a material ritual, which practices exist in the material actions of a subject acting in all consciousness according to his belief" (p. 170). This thesis about the subject is crucial because it is here that the new understanding of ideology as both coextensive with subjectivity and an index of social relations of power and domination becomes evident. The Althusserian subject is formed at—and as—the intersection of the discourses of the social institutions. Thus, it is possible to see in the lived unity of the subject the projected coherence of the dominant social form. Althusser's claim is that these unities are always constituted in advance, in the social domain, and at one level the illusory unity of the subject is the political reality of this "subjection." Althusser's notion of the "interpellation" of subjects is a valuable general reminder that "reality" is in great measure a "social construction." Power should be understood through the processes by which it informs our inner selves, that is, through its embodiment in structures and relations of the personal. The analysis of language as social interaction, for instance, or of classroom behavior in, say, a primary school can provide a useful and accurate account of the intangible yet material processes of power related to the formation of subjectivities. In fact, following Althusser's suggestions, some of the most valuable research into power and ideology has focused on the microprocesses of classroom behavior in order to understand schooling as an ideological process, emphasizing the construction of subjects by the hidden curricula of class and gender.[13]

Subjectivity without Agency or "Human Nature"

An appreciation of the strengths of Althusser's thesis about the inter-pellation of the subject needs to be qualified by an understanding of its formal reductionism. For corresponding to the assertion in "Ideology and Ideological State Apparatuses" that the subject's "unity" is an

13. See, in particular, the seminal work of Basil Bernstein on the sociology of education: *Class, Codes, and Control* (London: Routledge and Kegan Paul, 1973–77).

index of its ideological nature is the suggestion that processes of ideology can be understood purely in terms of a unity-disunity opposition. The major source of Althusser's understanding of subject formation is Lacanian psychoanalytic theory. Specifically, Althusser is indebted to Lacan's insistence on the constitutive function of the mirror stage, which installs the "imaginary" in the form of a gestalt of oneness and unity which is available to the presubjective infant. For Lacan, the theoretical function of the mirror stage is to make possible an understanding of the construction of a purely specular unity:

> The total form of the body by which the subject anticipates in a mirage the maturation of his power is given to him only as *Gestalt*, that is to say, an exteriority . . . in contrast with the turbulent movements that the subject feels are animating him.
> This form would have to be called the Ideal-I . . . under which term I would place the functions of a libidinal normalization. But the important point is that this form situates the agency of the ego, before its social determination, in a fictional direction, which will always remain irreducible for the individual alone.[14]

In Lacan's theory, the "total form of the body" is the ideal image into which the complexity of presubjective experience is reduced. It provides "in an exemplary situation, the symbolic matrix in which the I is precipitated" (*Ecrits*, p. 2). The mirror stage explains not only the process but also the principle by which the ego is constructed, a principle that determines the (later oedipal) construction of the subject. The first decisive moment in this account of human development is the ineluctable reduction of the child's "turbulent movements" into a "specular image" (p. 2). The image is derived from the Other (the image in the mirror, the mother, or another body) with whom the child comes to identify. The ego, then, is constructed in and as a fiction, later to permit accession to the symbolic realm through language and the oedipal structure of the family. Anika Lemaire, commenting on Lacan's theory of the mirror stage, points also to the "alienating narcissism" that constitutes the paradox of the first stage of subject formation: "The mirror stage is the advent of coenaesthetic subjectivity preceded by the feeling that one's own body is in pieces. The reflection of the body is, then, salutary in that it is unitary and localized in time and space. But the mirror

14. Jacques Lacan, *Ecrits: A Selection*, trans. Alan Sheridan (New York: Norton, 1977), p. 2.

stage is also the stage of alienating narcissistic identification (primary identification); the subject *is* his own double more than himself."[15]

This is *exactly* the form in which Althusser conceives the social and ideological process of the interpellation of subjects. For the specular unity in Lacanian theory, he transposes the unified imperative of the institutional discourse.

> Ideology "acts" or "functions" in such a way that it "recruits" subjects among the individuals (it recruits them all), or "transforms" the individuals into subjects (it transforms them all) by that very precise operation which I have called *interpellation* or hailing, and which can be imagined along the lines of the most commonplace everyday police (or other) hailing: "Hey, you there!"
>
> Assuming that the theoretical scene I have imagined takes place in the street, the hailed individual will turn round. By this mere one-hundred-and-eighty-degree physical conversion, he becomes a *subject*. Why? Because he has recognized that the hail was "really" addressed to him, and that "it was *really him* who was hailed" (and not someone else). (ISA, p. 174)

Thus the subject becomes a cipher, or at best an *instrument* of the discourses of power. Both power and the subject remain defined in narrowly functionalist terms, precisely because in this account the articulation of resistance to the dominating discourse is rendered unintelligible. The subject is not conceived as a space of contestation and productivity; power defines, rules, and obliterates. In rejecting idealist appeals to consciousness, Althusser produces a conception of subjectivity that is itself radically impoverished. Creativity, resistance, and the capacity for action are all explained by the dominant relations of power. The individual subject is never more than a "structure of structures" (*RC*, p. 17).

Why is it that the Althusserian theory of ideology contains two such divergent possibilities of development? On the one hand, it makes possible a textualization of ideology, grounding it in the multiply determined practices of individual agents. It makes possible an understanding of cultural texts as representative instances of power relations. On the other hand, however, especially in the centrality ascribed in the theory to a purely formal notion of the subject, Althusser's view of ideology robs the individual subject of any genuine agency, any capacity to

15. Anika Lemaire, *Jacques Lacan*, trans. David Macey (London: Routledge and Kegan Paul, 1977), p. 81.

resist and fight. Thus the theory of ideology ultimately remains informed by a notion of power that is reified and unidimensional; the subject of Althusserian ideology remains an element of an absolute structure.

I think the reason for the failure of Althusserian theory to provide an adequate account of subjectivity and agency is a deep one. Althusser dismissed all talk of human nature as ideological, contending that any appeal to a philosophical anthropology, with its account of human needs and capacities, is idealist and "humanistic." Thus, a genuine marxism has no need for an account of human nature. Indeed, he thought that it was "insufficient theory" that produced the need for the ideological comfort of "humanism." In the absence of good theory, "philosophical humanism . . . is destined to give certain Marxist ideologues the *feeling* of the theory that they lack" (*FM*, p. 241). What, then, is genuine theory? It is the scientific knowledge of the relations of production, the "real stage directors of history, [which] should not be reduced to mere *human relations*" (*RC*, p. 140).

> It must be said that the union of humanism and historicism represents the gravest temptation, for it procures the greatest theoretical advantages, at least in appearance. In the reduction of all knowledge to the historical social relations a second underhand reduction can be introduced, by treating the *relations of production* as mere *human relations*. This second reduction depends on something "obvious": is not history a "human" phenomenon through and through, and did not Marx, quoting Vico, declare that men can know it since they have "*made*" all of it? But this "obviousness" depends on a remarkable presupposition: that the "actors" of history are the authors of its text, the subjects of its production. But this presupposition too has all the force of the "obvious," since, as opposed to what the theatre suggests, concrete men are, in history, the actors of roles of which they are the authors, too. Once the stage director has been spirited away, the author-actor becomes the twin-brother of Aristotle's old dream: the doctor-who-cures-himself; and the *relations of production*, although they are the real stage-directors of history, are reduced to mere *human relations*. (*RC*, pp. 139–40)

Althusser's thesis is presented surreptitiously, in the form of a polemic against what we are supposed to consider an idealist account of human agency. In contrast to such idealism, Althusserian science explains how the "relations of production" are the sole determinants of history, its sole "authors." Human agents who are capable of acting and reflecting on their actions, of holding beliefs and examining these beliefs in a critical light, are then mere reflexes of the relations of production—interpellated by its discourses. Belief in the capacity for reflection and rational agency is in fact scoffed at (compare the "doctor-who-cures-himself"); in Althusser's view "science" has nothing to gain by considering such illusory notions. In "Marxism and Humanism" we are told that "during the eighteenth century, the 'rising class,' the bourgeoisie, developed a humanist ideology of equality, freedom, and reason" (FM, p. 234), and Althusser never pauses to ask if there could, instead, be a "scientific" account of such concepts. Fleeing from idealism, Althusser ends up being skeptical about *all* claims about human nature. He does not even allow for the possibility that empirical inquiry can tell us anything of substance about the tenability of such claims. Part of the problem he faces is that with such a radically constructivist approach to human nature, he would have no way of justifying his own implicit visions of social justice—except, that is, in relativist and conventional terms. He would, for instance, have no convincing answer to a claim that since human nature is completely malleable we ought to be fighting for a society where everyone's material comfort is guaranteed but at the expense of, say, his or her political freedom. The claim that the right to self-determination is a necessary feature of just societies is based at least in part on the (metaphysical) view that the capacity for rational agency is a fundamental human capacity and that it defines what humans are like—across social and historical differences. This is (part of) a view about human subjects as such, but Althusser's extreme and unqualified antihumanism makes even such a basic view untenable. He is ultimately opposed to any kind of philosophical anthropology. He sees even a nonspeculative account of human needs and capacities as both unnecessary and dangerous, because there are no such things as human needs, grounded in a general human nature. "Needs" are always specific to the socioeconomic system that produces them (see esp. RC, pp. 167, 161–64). So one could not argue for the human need for self-determination or political freedom, since they are normative concepts and hence have no place in a marxist science of society and history.

The underlying reason for Althusser's extreme constructivism about human nature is that he shares with the positivist a distrust of all normative notions and concepts. He sees all normative concepts as essentially ideological (in the pejorative sense), sharply opposed to science and knowledge. Althusser retained this essentially positivist attitude toward the normative even in his later writings, where he criticized his earlier "theoreticist" tendencies. He recognizes in Essays in Self-

Criticism, for instance, that scientific inquiry is itself a socially situated activity of human agents, whose political commitments affect what they come to see. Thus, he ascribes what he had earlier called Marx's "epistemological break" to Marx's own political activism and experience: "It was by moving to take up absolutely new, proletarian class positions that Marx realized the possibilities of the theoretical conjunction from which the science was born" (p. 157). Because of his "ever deeper engagement in the political struggles of the proletariat," Marx's "treatment of his object, Political Economy, takes on a radically new character: breaking with all ideological conceptions to lay down and develop the principles of the science of History" (p. 160). This insight could provide the basis for a genuinely social and political epistemology, but Althusser is unable to develop it. His account remains purely descriptive; it isn't clear exactly why Marx's political experience played the crucial epistemic role that it did. The conjunction of politics and knowledge is asserted as a conjunction—no more.

Since Althusser is wary of all accounts of personal agency and subjective experience, he can sketch only the most general and abstract explanation: "It was indeed politics which allowed [the young Marx] to move from one object to another (schematically: from Press Laws to the State, then to Political Economy), but this move was realized and expressed each time in the form of a new philosophical position. On the one hand the philosophical position appears to be the theoretical expression of the political (and ideological) class position. On the other hand this translation of the political position into theory (in the form of a philosophical position) appears to be the condition of the theoretical relation to the object of thought" (p. 158). In all this talk of "expression" and "translation" a basic question is never asked: What is it about the proletarian class position—and ideology—that made it scientifically illuminating? Or in other words, why is one ideology better than another? This is Lukács's question about the standpoint of the proletariat, but my way of putting the question does away with the idealized subject-object of history, focusing instead on the practical consciousness of situated human agents. It points to a host of further questions that inevitably arise from Althusser's own account of the political conditions that enabled Marx's scientific discovery: Are some subjective experiences more epistemically illuminating than others? Are some evaluations more "scientific" than others? Can "values" and "knowledge," ideology and science, form a continuum? These questions could have taken Althusser out of his essentially positivist conception of value and, I would argue, enabled him to articulate a more adequate theory of the social basis of knowledge. But he remains adamantly blind to the fact that some normative positions and views may be not only tolerable but also epistemically productive and illuminating. In "Is It Simple to Be a Marxist in Philosophy?" he continues to present an almost incoherent position on the status of the normative. He maintains that all known revolutions have either been "premature" or have "miscarried," but he wants to express this view without any implicit claim about what it might mean for a revolution to *succeed*. Thus he wishes for a "theory" that "dispenses with the normative notions of prematurity and of mis-carriage, that is, with a normative standpoint" altogether! (*ESC*, p. 187). This conception of "theory" is based on the positivist fantasy of pure description, with objective knowledge conceived as simply an inductive generalization from the facts.[16]

Ultimately, I suspect, it is this positivist suspicion of the normative which makes it impossible for Althusser to articulate a vision of social change. The analysis of social reproduction as it is presented in the Al-thusserian theory of ideology needs to be informed by an analysis of the historical conditions of the emergence of the radically new, of social formations that can, in their real or potential existence, articulate a cri-tique of that which exists. A radical social and political theory should do more than just "diagnose confusions"; it should also "suggest new directions."[17] To do so, it needs to provide a richer and more nuanced epistemology than Althusser's, especially of moral terms. It also needs to go beyond blanket dismissals of "humanism" in order to produce empirically grounded conjectures about such concepts as "freedom," "equality," and "social justice" which draw on a reasonable and nonide-alist account of human nature. I try to show in Part Two what such conjectures and accounts might look like, arguing that a nonfounda-tionalist naturalist epistemology would better serve radical political projects such as Althusser's than his own skeptical attitude toward all normative questions. I argue in effect that such an epistemology, grounded in a postpositivist realist conception of human nature, of both science and value, would be the best way to realize and complete Al-thusser's antiidealist project.

16. On this and related points, I am indebted to Roy Edgley, "Marx's Revolutionary Science," in *Epistemology, Science, Ideology*, pp. 5–26. On the epistemic status of evalua-tive terms, see Chapters 6 (esp. the concluding section) and 7.

17. See Richard Miller, *Analyzing Marx* (Princeton: Princeton University Press, 1984), pp. 129–36.

4

JAMESON'S MARXIST HERMENEUTICS
AND THE NEED FOR
AN ADEQUATE EPISTEMOLOGY

Althusser's theory of ideology, as we saw, is only partly successful in its attempt to link the political power of institutions with the material practices of everyday life. Its failure lies in its inability to provide a convincing account of subjectivity as multidimensional, and this inability derives from Althusser's unqualified skepticism toward all statements about human needs and capacities, that is, about human nature and welfare. Such skepticism, I suggested, may be based in part on Althusser's suspicion of all normative claims as necessarily tied to an idealist and reductive historical teleology. All these issues are related, of course, and it is in the context of a specifically marxist cultural criticism that the relations among them become clear, for these issues are central to any project of textual interpretation which also attempts to provide a unified account of the social and historical dimensions of texts. In this chapter I choose as my focus the one marxist cultural critic in the United States whose work represents both a systematic hermeneutical project and a theoretical concern with the claims of interpretation. Fredric Jameson's criticism covers a wide range of subjects and texts, from films and popular culture to literary "high" modernism, but central to his theoretical writings has been a concern with the poststructuralist challenge to traditional marxist hermeneutics. I proceed by examining Jameson's synthesis of key poststructuralist insights with marxist hermeneutics.[1] After discussing why Jameson's defense of in-

1. My main focus, then, is on Jameson, *Marxism and Form* (Princeton: Princeton Uni-

terpretation remains exemplary for contemporary criticism, in the final section of this chapter I turn to a crucial theoretical absence in his work, the lack of an adequate materialist account of the social bases of reason and knowledge. Jameson's defense of the hermeneutical project is based on a useful rewriting of Althusser's critique of essentialist and idealist historiography, but he also uncritically adopts some of the central aspects of the poststructuralist (specifically Althusserian) view of reference and knowledge. He combines such an epistemology with a Lukácsian faith in the idealized subject-object of history and thus produces a rather odd theoretical synthesis. Both the strengths of Jameson's theoretical work on the nature of cultural interpretation and the weaknesses that arise from inadequate attention to a materialist epistemology pose urgent questions for radical literary and cultural studies. My analysis of Jameson's critical theory builds on the discussion (in Chapter 3) of the antiidealist basis of Althusser's work, and my critique, especially in the final section of this chapter, is intended to serve as an introduction to the discussion of epistemological, metaethical, and metaphysical issues in Part Two.

Jameson's first theoretical book, *Marxism and Form*, was published in 1971; *The Political Unconscious: Narrative as a Socially Symbolic Act* came out in 1981—that is, almost exactly ten years later. The theoretical space between these two books registers some of the most challenging questions that have ever been raised in Anglo-American criticism. For a cultural marxism, in particular, these years saw one of the most fruitful debates between an older tradition (Lukács, Sartre, the larger tradition of Hegelianism) and the thoroughgoing critique of it mounted by the Althusserians. The Althusserian critique was specifically poststructuralist, and it identified some of the idealist tendencies in the Hegelian tradition in marxism. But at the same time, this critique brought with it unresolved questions about the nature of interpretation and explanation and a radically impoverished account of subjectivity and agency. The value of Jameson's theoretical work lies, at the most basic level, in its powerful rewriting of this debate, for he refocuses and elaborates some of the key issues any contemporary marxism must nec-

---

versity Press, 1971), and *The Political Unconscious: Narrative as a Socially Symbolic Act* (Ithaca: Cornell University Press, 1981), hereafter referred to as *MF* and *PU* in the body of the text. The other major theoretical books by Jameson I draw on are *The Prison-House of Language* (Princeton: Princeton University Press, 1972), cited as *PHL*; *The Ideologies of Theory: Essays* (Minneapolis: University of Minnesota Press, 1988), vols. 1 and 2; *Late Marxism* (London: Verso, 1990); and *Postmodernism, or The Cultural Logic of Late Capitalism* (Durham, N.C.: Duke University Press, 1991).

essarily face. At the same time, through particular textual analyses, he proposes a number of valuable and sometimes radical theses about critical activity in general.

In all Jameson's work, we see thematized two key questions central to contemporary theory. The first is the metacritical question of the politics of interpretation, that is, the validity and motivations of interpretive activity, along with the essential metaphors that emerge from it. The second is the equally crucial question about the representation of history. With contemporary theory's examination of the complex nature of representation, this latter issue increasingly seems to be a dark, unthought region in classical marxism. Nevertheless, for Jameson, as it must for every contemporary marxist critic or philosopher, this issue provides the underlying challenge in the effort to work out an account of how history is available to critical discourse.

The Fate of Interpretation

Let me first address the problem of interpretation, to which the long theoretical chapter of *The Political Unconscious* is explicitly devoted.[2] The poststructuralist critique of the idea of interpretation essentially takes the form of deconstructing the basic hermeneutical metaphors that have traditionally been used. For the most part, these have been images of excavation or search, of essence and depth, of center and periphery, of inside and outside. These metaphors, as various writers have convincingly shown, imply a model of texts which undermines the specificity of discourses or the unsynthesizable heterogeneities of language and textuality by relegating them to the ultimately inessential level of the "surface." In light of this powerful critique, Jameson sees his first goal as metacritical: as the theoretical defense of interpretation as such, of the possibility of legitimate hermeneutical analysis. As we saw in Chapter 2, the notion of levels is crucial for marxism, if not in a simple deterministic model of base and superstructure, then at least in some hierarchical form that would render explanation and diagnostic analyses possible. The issue at stake, then, is a major one for contemporary marxism. It must come to terms with the metaphors it lives by, and a hermeneutical marxism must survive the interrogation of what Althusser would call its idealist and homogenizing tendencies.

Now in one way, *Marxism and Form* and *The Political Unconscious*

2. Jameson, "On Interpretation: Literature as a Socially Symbolic Act," pp. 17–102.

subscribe to the same depth model of the text and, hence, of the interpretive act. In the latter book, especially in the more polemical passages, the assertion is made explicitly. Almost as if with a vengeance, to retain for marxism its critical, hermeneutic function, Jameson makes the image even more explicit. Reacting strongly to the antihermeneutic thesis latent in poststructuralism, he talks of the necessity of "restoring to the surface of the text the repressed and buried reality of . . . history" (*PU*, p. 20). This dominant metaphor is at work with less force, but also with less self-consciousness, in *Marxism and Form*:

> Dialectical critique therefore involves a leap from the purely conceptual to the historical level, from idea to that corresponding lived experience which is then "judged" insofar as it is put in historical perspective for us. This is, indeed, the hermeneutic dimension of dialectical thinking, which is called upon to restore to the abstract cultural fact, isolated on the level of the superstructure, its concrete context or situation; the latter has, of course, vanished when we have to do with cultural objects from the past. But when we have to do with products of contemporary culture, this concrete situation becomes the object of repression to the degree that we wish to ignore the socio-economic situation in which we are really involved. (*MF*, p. 348)

Yet even in this earlier book, the issue is not as simple as a cursory reading of the images would suggest. Indeed, one of the central theses of *Marxism and Form* is that "inside" and "outside" are themselves historically created categories, specific to a culture that divides reality into the private and the public, making it then necessary for the critic to rejoin history with the text, the social with the individual. For Jameson, this hermeneutical operation remains fundamentally a process of "laying bare," for history is inscribed, as "inner form," in the text itself, and thus "all events [and texts] carry their own logic, their own 'interpretations,' within themselves: an interpretation which we can articulate into a logical succession" (*MF*, p. 345).

Jameson's defense of interpretation is based on the rejection of a naive positivistic conception of textual interpretation as access to a prediscursive and unmediated "meaning." As a marxist critic, Jameson is naturally firmly committed to the idea that, since texts are socially produced and consumed, textual meanings are subject to historical change and hence are mobile and unstable. But he is also sympathetic to the more radical view of semiotic theory that meanings are purely intradiscursive. Thus, Jameson can (with approbation) quote Greimas, who sees signification as "nothing but . . . transposition from one level of language to another, from one language to a different language," and "meaning" as "nothing but the possibility of such transcoding" (*PHL*, pp. 215–16). Jameson's own critical practice thus attempts to redefine textual meaning, in good structuralist fashion, as meaning-effect. Behind this new view of meaning is in fact the extreme constructivist claim of semiotics about the "infinite regress from signifier to signified, from linguistic object to metalanguage" (p. 215). This claim, Jameson argues, requires us to bracket "truth" and the "object" to draw attention to the *semiosis* of the meaning process. It isn't quite clear how far Jameson believes the "infinite regress" goes. In particular, it isn't clear—at least not in *The Prison-House of Language*—to what extent the truth of what *Marxism and Form* calls "lived experience" (p. 348) would need to be bracketed. In employing such a purely semiotized notion of textual meaning, however, Jameson's critical practice engages the kinds of constructivist theoretical claims I discussed in Chapter 1, but it also participates in a more general trend in modern philosophy. In at least the broad outlines, there is a similarity between such a move and the shift in Anglo-American philosophy from "meanings" to "sentences." As Ian Hacking has suggested, the analytical emphasis of philosophers as different as Quine and Feyerabend on sentences and their interrelationships is also best appreciated as a rejection of the notion of a prediscursive meaning.[3]

The poststructuralist (Derridean and Althusserian) attack on essentialism and the identity principle—in the sense that a moment (or an event, a text, and so on) is ever completely present to itself in its fullness of meaning—is, as we saw in Chapter 3, a powerful critique of the positivist and idealist notions of history and, as such, important for marxist cultural studies. The poststructuralist claim is that the ontological basis of "history" needs to be rethought through the specificity of our readings. Rather than consider an event (or a text) an unproblematical given, says Jameson, we must learn to recognize the constitutive nature of interpretive activity: history is available only in textual form. Compare this claim to an even more explicit argument by Hayden White, a philosopher of history:

Common opinion has it that the plot of a narrative imposes a meaning on the events that comprise its story level by revealing at the end a

3. Ian Hacking, *Why Does Language Matter to Philosophy?* (Cambridge: Cambridge University Press, 1975), pp. 115–87.

structure that was immanent in the events all along. What I am trying to establish is the nature of this immanence in any narrative account of real events, the kind of events that are offered as the proper content of historical discourse. The reality of these events does not consist in the fact that they occurred, but that, first of all, they were remembered and, second, that they are capable of finding a place in a chronologically ordered narrative.[4]

Here is the constructivist thesis in historiography stated in a stronger form. This thesis about the narrative and discursive construction of historical events, of facts, of "texts" in the ordinary sense, is a corollary of the notion of meaning identified earlier. Together, they detheologize history and text, opening them up—as Bakhtin and Peirce do with linguistic phenomena—to the heterogeneous play of interpretation which mediates our access to them. For a marxian literary criticism, such a radical constructivism banishes the myths of secure meaning, radicalizing our perception of the text as an intertextual phenomenon. At a more local level (within literary criticism), it problematizes the idea of authorial intention, joining other methods that reveal the "author" to be yet another text to be deconstructed. Thus, Jameson says, it is impossible for marxism to posit history as a prehermeneutical center, the living source that would restore meaning to dead texts. History cannot *mean* anything in a prediscursive way; the object is to open up both history and text to their own radical semiosis. For Jameson, at least in *The Political Unconscious*, such an opening up would be tantamount to reactivating their equally rich *semantic* heterogeneity. Jameson argues implicitly for a Bakhtinian view of history and textuality: the semiotic heterogeneity we identify is indeed already there, in history. For both Jameson and Bakhtin, the constructivist thesis simply makes richer, more accurate historical analysis possible.

So when Jameson argues for the priority of the marxian methods in literary and cultural criticism on grounds of their "semantic richness," he is claiming that a good marxist analysis reactivates the hidden semiotic dimension of historical events. Thus, his chapter on George Gissing in *The Political Unconscious* suggests how such an analysis might proceed by way of a bracketing of the obvious social "facts," the referent of naturalist fiction. Gissing's novel *The Nether World* is, according to Jameson, "best read not for its documentary information on the conditions of Victorian slum life, but as testimony about the narrative para-

4. Hayden White, "The Value of Narrativity in the Representation of Reality," *Critical Inquiry* 7 (Autumn 1980), 23.

digms that organize middle-class fantasies about those slums and about 'solutions' that might resolve, manage, or repress the evident class anxieties aroused by the existence of an industrial working class and an urban lumpen-proletariat" (*PU*, p. 186). History is seen as the general referent here, and it is seen in its infinite mediations through inherited paradigms Jameson calls "ideologemes." Ideologemes are the ideologically charged raw material upon which Gissing's narrative art works— seeking to articulate and work through the deeper contradictions by the complex process of generating new narrative details. But the ideologeme is never itself a simple *given:* "The sign or ideologeme . . . exists nowhere as such: part of the 'objective spirit' or the cultural Symbolic order of experience, it vanishes into the past along with the latter, leaving only its traces—material signifiers, lexemes, enigmatic words and phrases—behind it" (*PU*, p. 201).[5]

Thus Jameson brackets the obvious referent of this high naturalist narrative—that is, the documentary notion of social reality as observable facts. He does so, however, in order to reconstruct the full semiotic/semantic richness of the way Gissing's narrative works on received ideological (and intertextual) material: the twin plot structures of the melodramatic and the sentimental as they derive from, among other sources, Dickens's influential narrative models. Such a refocusing facilitates our understanding of the generation of characters as new types as well as new ideological positions to be filled in this structural *combinatoire* (see, for example, Jameson's discussion of Gissing's alienated intellectual, who would be less a "character" in his own right than a structural position, fulfilling a complex function in the larger narrative machinery). The process of Gissing's narrative production is specified in its details, its nuances, its hesitations, seen in its always-already mediated form. History is invoked to explain and illuminate Gissing's narrative art, but it is seen as a text—not as static referent or unproblematical source of meaning but as this continual semiosis of ideologemes. Textual meaning is not simply discovered; it is *produced*

5. Here is how ideologemes are defined: "When we . . . find that the semantic horizon within which we grasp a cultural object has widened to include the social order, we will find that the very object of our analysis has itself been thereby dialectically transformed, and that it is no longer construed as an individual 'text' or work in the narrow sense, but has been reconstituted in the form of the great collective and class discourses of which the text is little more than an individual *parole* or utterance. Within this new horizon, then, our object of study will prove to be the *ideologeme*, that is, the smallest intelligible unit of the essentially antagonistic discourses of social classes" (*PU*, p. 76). The ideologeme is called an "amphibious formation," since it can manifest itself both as "a conceptual or belief system" and as a "protonarrative" (p. 87).

in a mediated way. Interpretation is, for Jameson, not an allegorizing of texts or a search for things past but an opening up of the text to the winds of history.

The Role of "Mediating" Categories

Jameson's representation of history as text and narrative is thus a self-conscious figuration of what essentially resists appropriation into a single figure. Jameson proposes the following solution: if history is a narrative, it is one without any real beginning or end, a battle in which memories of past skirmishes collide endlessly with emerging conflicts and where no one confrontation ever takes place in a single-minded unity of purpose. At the same time, there are embattled groups—and the struggles of life and death. The image that emerges in the work of both Jameson and Bakhtin is a politicization of Jacques Derrida's concept of the "trace"—each moment a layering of past and future, "residual" and "emergent" (to use Raymond Williams's terms), never completely accessible in its pristine purity. "Revolutions," Jameson says, are only the open nerves of such narrative process:

> Just as overt revolution is no punctual event . . . but brings to the surface the innumerable daily struggles and forms of class polarization which are at work in the whole course of social life that precedes it, and which are therefore latent and implicit in "pre-revolutionary" social experience, made visible as the latter's deep structure only in such "moments of truth"—so also the overtly transitional moments of cultural revolution are themselves but the passage of a permanent process in human societies, of a permanent struggle between the various co-existing modes of production. The triumphant moment in which a new systemic dominant gains ascendency is therefore only the diachronic manifestation of a constant struggle for the perpetuation and reproduction of its dominance, a struggle which must continue throughout its life course, accompanied at all moments by the systemic or structural antagonism of these older and newer modes of production that resist assimilation or seek deliverance from it. The task of cultural and social analysis thus construed will then clearly be the rewriting of its materials in such a way that this perpetual cultural revolution can be apprehended and read as the deeper and more permanent constitutive structure in which the empirical textual objects know intelligibility. (PU, p. 97)

The image is a layered one, with a clear causal hierarchy. A good explanation will reveal the underlying causal forces, "the innumerable daily struggles" that are the "the more permanent constitutive structure" of social life.

If cultural analysis is ultimately a form of social and historical explanation, connecting the different layers or levels of social experience, then one of its key concepts would be what Lukács called "mediation": those analytical categories that make buried historical and ideological phenomena visible. But as students of Althusser would remember, Althusser, in *Reading "Capital,"* saw the very concept of mediation as tied to the idealism of Lukács's "genetic" method. Mediations were supposed to facilitate our access to some absolute origin, to some "original unity undivided between *subject* and *object*, between the real and its knowledge."[6] Jameson quite perceptively sees the Althusserian critique of mediation as a critique of an idealist and "expressive" model of history, that is, a local, strategic assault on the reductive allegorizing tendency of some historical interpretations. Such a critique, Jameson maintains, is best understood in the context of the work of someone such as Lucien Goldmann, who solves the problem of the ultimate determination of superstructure by base by merely positing homologies between the two levels. Such a relationship may be valid in some instances, but as social theory it remains inadequate precisely because it is not dialectical enough. In other words, Goldmannian homology is merely a variant of the old reflection theory and, as such, constitutes a short-circuiting of the complex process whereby text and context, infrastructure and superstructure, can be said to articulate with each other.

One of the main contributions of *The Political Unconscious* to marxist literary and cultural studies is its substantive theory of narrative as a mediational category. Jameson sees mediation as an explanatory category, necessary whenever we attempt to understand a new text or a new historical phenomenon; we must perforce invent a set of terms that "can be used to analyze and articulate two quite distinct types of objects or 'texts,' or two very different structural levels of reality" (*PU*, p. 40). Mediation is thus the process of conferring meaning, the universal activity of "transcoding." In this sense—a much more general sense than Althusser would allow—choice of the right mediating term or concept becomes for Jameson synonymous with the self-reflexiveness of dialectical thinking. And an elaboration of a theory of mediation and social explanation becomes one of the challenges for any cultural marxism.

6. Louis Althusser and Etienne Balibar, *Reading "Capital,"* trans. Ben Brewster (London: New Left Books, 1970), p. 63.

Narrative, "Transcoding," and
Textual Interpretation

Narrative is the supreme mediatory concept for Jameson, and it enables him to desubstantialize our understanding of meaning and focus on its production. Behind this idea is a conception of the text not as something "out there," but as something available only through our translations and transcodings. Jameson conceives of interpretation as engagement in a continual polemic where the truth-value of our readings resides in their strength as critical translations. The only way to dislodge an interpretation is to provide a stronger one. And one of the more explicit claims of Jameson's theoretical work is that marxist interpretations are more powerful than others precisely in their explanatory comprehensiveness and their metacritical sophistication—or their ability to subsume and complete the partial interpretations of other methodologies.

For Jameson, the advantage of narrative as a mediating concept is that it provides a critical comprehensiveness without reducing either text or history to idealized fictions. In the three critical studies where Jameson best demonstrates its use (the essays on Balzac and Conrad in *The Political Unconscious* and the book on Wyndham Lewis, *Fables of Aggression*), narrative as category proves to be a supple instrument of cultural analysis. The attention to the narrative structuration of desire and ideology, to history available only as such a structured—narrated—system of openings and closures, of possibilities and "nightmares," enables us to understand the complex ideological drama of cultural production. Significantly, in all three instances, Jameson uses "narrative" to show how literary works provide complex resolutions—in the realm of the ideological or the symbolic—to the more basic contradictions on the level of the political or the socioeconomic.

Jameson's chapter on Balzac shows how a literary text provides a symbolic resolution to deeper ideological dilemmas and conflicts. An important underlying question in this essay is one that Balzac—given the transitional nature of the time he lived in—best makes available for us: the specific processes of the constitution of the modern subject. Jameson finds Balzac's novella *La Vieille Fille* exemplary for the way it registers the shifting modalities of the construction of subjectivity, revealed in the polyvalence through which the text structures, organizes, and "invests" the author's profoundest desires. Such desires are inescapably political, entwined as they are with Balzac's royalism and the obviously "social" subject matter of the Balzacian corpus. In themselves (pure, uncathected, as it were), these desires are rarely available to us, however. Hence the inherent interest of the "narrative apparatus" of Balzac, which mediates and realizes them, acting as "libidinal investment or authorial wish-fulfillment, a form of symbolic satisfaction in which the working distinction between biographical subject, Implied Author, reader, and characters is virtually effaced" (*PU*, p. 155). An examination of the details of this narrative machinery, then, as well as a study of its larger structures, opens up the specific, mediatory ways in which Balzac's texts explore, articulate, and resolve the determinate contradictions that form their subtextual level.

In Jameson's analysis the primary motor force of the narrative is a utopian impulse, suggested both in the initial description of Mme Cormon's townhouse as the object of an ideal, a-subjective desire and in the personification of this desire in the Mademoiselle, "comic, grotesque and desirable all at once" (*PU*, p. 158). Together, in terms of the larger narrative, these twin figures of desire suggest the objective correlatives of a longing to go beyond the immediate closures and historical contradictions of what the narrative will later thematize. Thus, the utopian nature of the desire, incorporating the author, the characters, and the reader all at once, floating at a more general level perhaps, consists in the way these figures realize for us "the longing for landed retreat and personal fulfillment as well as for the resolution of social and historical contradictions" (p. 158). Even the farcical narrative involving Mme Cormon and her suitors exists at this utopian level, offering a detached comic perspective on the "vicissitudes of carnal desire" (p. 158). All the elementary features of the text, then, are seen in their allegorical dimension, since they express deeper social elements and desires. But "farce" is not the only level at which the plot of *La Vieille Fille* can be read. The simplicity of the farcical contrasts with the deeper level where a system of characters—allegorical, again, in the preceding sense—is generated. Here the struggle for Mme Cormon's hand seems to suggest the class struggle between the bourgeoisie and the aristocracy for control over France itself. The two main suitors are, then, obviously Lukácsian "types," the bourgeois Du Bousquier and the aristocrat Chevalier. The text foregrounds this allegorical dimension, shuttling the reader between some "pure sexual farce" and the larger, representative narrative. The character system is complicated, Jameson points out, by the fact that the brusque swashbuckling Du Bousquier turns out to be sexually impotent. Nevertheless, Chevalier the aristocrat, effeminate, "cultured," but sexually potent, loses (true to history, as Lukács would have said) the struggle for the lady's (France's) hand.

If this were the extent of the reading, however, we would not be very far from a Lukácsian reading, in which Balzac's text would be seen as articulating a greater historical truth than the author's royalist sympathies might allow for. The specific insight of Jameson's analysis, however, consists in the recovery of a more complex mediation: the mosaic of narratives works out (by generating a scheme of characters, a certain suspension of the narrative's inexorable movement) a symbolic *act* that constitutes the text. The Balzacian antinomy between the undesirable (impotent) energy and the ineffective (languorous, passive) cultural values needs to be resolved, Jameson argues, in narrative form. It is here that the mediating level of the political unconscious enters, articulating the deepest tensions that inform the text. Faced with real historical contradiction, "the political unconscious nonetheless seeks by logical permutations and combinations to find a way out of its intolerable closure and to produce a 'solution' " (*PU*, p. 167). This notion of a political unconscious constitutes one of the radical innovations of Jameson's work. It has considerable potential as a mediating category for any cultural marxism, for it can cut across the convenient (ideological) boundaries between our monadic sense of ourselves as subjects and the properly historicopolitical. Jameson's term draws on both a more textual notion of the "political"—it is not fully conscious, "out there" in a fully realized form—and a radicalizing of the Freudo-Lacanian doctrine of the essential *form* of the unconscious (Lacan: "The unconscious is structured like a language"). The idea of a political unconscious provides us with a mediation that has the advantage of shifting back and forth between levels, suspending preconceived notions of the subject, desire, and textual form. It draws on Gilles Deleuze and Félix Guattari's suggestion that all desire is fundamentally social, involving an investment of heterogeneous elements that cannot be compartmentalized only to be "related" later on. And the more immediate debt to Jean-François Lyotard's notion of the *dispositifs pulsionnels* as the form of the production and organization of desire is also apparent. The advantage, in short, consists in the articulation of desire with the social, an analysis of the political that inheres in aesthetic forms and choices.

Faced with determinate historical contradictions, the text's political unconscious must, in the form of the narrative, seek out some ideal resolution. For what is inherent in this metanarrative drama is the symbolic articulation and solution of what is in reality a subtextual problem. Jameson sees the "modal" shift of Balzacian narrative as crucial. Registering the dilemma, it would at the same time seek to nullify its historical inevitability by switching from the purely indicative mode of conventional realism to the conditional. The narrative turns into an object lesson, the apparent didacticism consisting in the bracketing of the real movement of the narrative's logic of content by showing it in the less binding form of the conditional "as if." The only real, and here impossible, suitor—the solution!—that emerges is the character generated merely to fill this structural gap: the Comte de Troisville. But the Count does not belong to any realistic narrative, or to any empirical or probable history. Rather, he is the ideological alternative that the narrative, of its own necessity, generates. His presence symbolically reformulates history by positing another one "in which some genuine Restoration would still be possible, provided the aristocracy would learn this particular object-lesson, namely, that it needs a strong man [like the Count] who combines aristocratic values with Napoleonic energy" (PU, p. 168).

But then what about Balzac, the biographical author or the historical figure? In this analysis, the recourse to a biographical extratextual determinant is naturally suspended. "Balzac" becomes this nexus of conflicting currents of desire, history, and narrative, the mediating but unsynthesized level where the production and ideological organization of narrative is rendered intelligible. Like the text, the author is seen as a node of interaction, as the crisscrossings of ideology, desire, and the intransigence of history (history seen as necessity). The political unconscious as this intermeshing of levels becomes a way to open the text to history in its semic "lived" richness as desire and closure, utopia and ideology. The detailed analyses of Balzac's text, or of Wyndham Lewis's in *Fables of Aggression*, restore the multivalent dynamics of aesthetic production as both a real complex of desires and a register of the determinate contradictions and closures of ideology and history. In the book on Lewis, for instance, Jameson mediates between the molecular level of Lewis's sentence production—an aesthetic event in its own right— and the larger drama at the narrative level. What emerges is a specific account of Lewis's aesthetic "act" in its political "situation," striving to resolve the antinomies of political desire in the face of a "nightmarish" historical conjuncture. Thus the problem of Lewis's fascism, his particular brand of expressionism, the historical subtext of between-the-wars Europe, can all be articulated together, registered on a single dense semantic/semiotic medium that would be as sensitive to desire and fantasy, on the one hand, as it would be to the exigencies of the real, on the other.

History as the real—the Lacanian term is rewritten in Jameson's work. What was for Lacan the purely unthematizable algebraic term, is now interpreted as the supreme horizon that is never quite visible except as pure limit. The real continues to elude representation. Indeed, if it is available, it is only as an unassimilable figure. Invoking neither a simplistic teleology nor the lure of a prediscursive meaning, history emerges in Jameson's later work as, finally, an asymptote, that ever-receding horizon that yet lends perspective and coherence to political and cultural analysis. Our explanations and the real do not coincide, as Althusser would also have said. The real (history) always remains an absolute other of discourse. "In terms of language," Jameson writes in one of his most important essays, "we must distinguish between our own narrative of history—whether psychoanalytic or political—and the Real itself, which our narratives can only approximate in asymptotic fashion and which 'resists symbolization absolutely.' "[7] At the limits of a contemporary marxist cultural analysis lies this tantalizingly brief account of language and reference and, underlying it, some unexamined questions regarding materialist epistemology. The rest of this chapter develops some of these questions, and the second part of the book addresses these issues more directly, on their own terms.

If Jameson's work is consistent in its emphasis on the cognitive dimensions of criticism and literature, why does he remain ambivalent about the claim that we may gain objective knowledge about what he calls history? Why, for instance, does an explanation of, say, what he called in *The Political Unconscious* the "innumerable daily struggles and forms of class polarization" or the "deeper and more permanent constitutive structure" that underlies cultural texts *not* constitute objective knowledge, the knowledge of what history in fact is? Poststructuralist critics have accused Jameson of retaining too theological a notion of history in his work. I would point to the deep inconsistency between his genuinely cognitivist approach to social explanation and his rather skeptical formulation of history as the absolutely unthematizable horizon of human experience. The skeptical position, if it is to be sufficiently clear, needs to answer the following questions: What would it mean to symbolize history "absolutely"? What kind of explanation would that be? It can only be something like what is suggested by the image of an idealized epistemological subject grasping history in its

7. Jameson, "Imaginary and Symbolic in Lacan," in *Ideologies of Theory*, 1:107.

very essence, the image that lies behind Lukács's project. If that is the case, however, Jameson is not saying anything new in arguing against such idealism. The real question for Jameson's position is how objective our knowledge of history can be, given the limited epistemic creatures that we in fact are. To what extent are objectivity and error tied to our practical efforts to gain control over the social conditions of our lives? How can we go about seeking deeper, more accurate, historical knowledge?

I think his formulation of history as the real—as, that is, the unthematizable horizon for the individual's experience—is Jameson's response to the poststructuralist denial of reference and his answer to the account of proliferating meanings and signifiers. Thus history is in Jameson's theory the limit of signification, for it defines the absolute boundaries of the play of meaning. But since he does not have a developed account of signification in his work, particularly an account of the relation between meaning and reference (of the kind discussed in Chapter 2) as a complex social process, he ends up accepting the poststructuralist thesis about the reference of individual words and signs as essentially reductive. Jameson's solution is to go elsewhere. Abandoning the attempt to theorize language in historical materialist terms, he turns to the theme of interpretation. The problem, however, is that he does so by accepting at face value the poststructuralist theory of language. Within its bounds, "history" becomes the general "referent" of an interpretive discourse, and "materialism," strangely enough, becomes "a set of propositions about language." We cannot gain "objective knowledge" about either language or history, since each is very sharply contrasted with the "lived experience" of the individual subject. Both Jameson's view of knowledge and his conception of "history" betray the limitations of the terms set by the debate between phenomenology (or, more generally, the idealist tradition) and poststructuralism. These limits are most clearly evident in passages such as this:

> The chief defect of all hitherto existing materialism is that it has been conceived as a series of propositions about matter—and in particular the relationship of matter to consciousness, which is to say of the natural sciences to the so-called human sciences—rather than as a set of propositions about language. A materialist philosophy of language is not a semanticism, naive or otherwise, because its fundamental tenet is a rigorous distinction between the signified—the realm to semantics proper, of interpretation, of the study of the text's ostensible meaning—and the referent. The study of the referent, however, is the

study, not of the meaning of the text, but of the limits of its meanings and of their historical preconditions, and of what is and must remain incommensurable with individual expression. In our present terms, this means that a relationship to objective knowledge (in other words, to what is of such a different order of magnitude and organization from the individual subject that it can never be adequately "represented" within the latter's lived experience save as a term limit) is conceivable only for a thought able to do justice to radical discontinuities, not only between the Lacanian "orders," but within language itself, between its various types of propositions as they entertain wholly different relations with the subject.[8]

There are many question-begging formulations and claims in this passage, but perhaps the crucial question is why "objective knowledge" has to be defined negatively as that which cannot be represented within the subject's "lived experience." Most contemporary sciences define objectivity in terms of their own protocols of reasonable argument and evidence, and it is hard to imagine why we need such an extremely subject-centered formulation of the claims of objectivity. Also, it is difficult to see why "objectivity" is tied to the representation of "discontinuity," especially a discontinuity between the various kinds of "propositions" that the individual subject "entertains." On this view objective knowledge seems to have very little to do with *justification*, which is fundamentally a social affair. Instead, it is seen as an essentially individual matter and a question of mental or psychic *representation*. It is with such an individualist epistemology that Jameson ends up, and basic questions about the nature of objectivity as a socially realizable ideal remain foreclosed.

It becomes clearer in Jameson's later study of cultural postmodernism that he takes over without much interrogation Althusser's view of epistemology, in particular the dubious sundering of experience from knowledge, ideology from science.[9] Jameson accepts the central Althus-

---

8. Ibid., p. 108.
9. Jameson, "The Cultural Logic of Late Capitalism," in *Postmodernism*, pp. 52–54. This is the best place to clarify what may already be obvious to my readers: what Jameson calls "postmodernism" has almost nothing to do with what has been my focus in these chapters, that is, a distinct epistemological view characterized by relativism and skepticism, even when it is presented indirectly as a cultural or political claim. Thus, I have identified and analyzed the arguments that Lyotard, Spivak, Felman, and Culler articulate with some clarity. In many cases, their formulations are useful because they are clear, but the arguments themselves represent a more general intellectual culture that is not only antifoundationalist but also radically skeptical. What Jameson calls postmodernism is an aesthetic and cultural phenomenon, "the cultural dominant of the logic of late capitalism" (*Post-*

serian claim that the individual subject cannot ever completely "know" objective reality, which is the realm of abstraction and scientific truth. Objectivity and error, knowledge and mystification, are seen as necessary concepts for historical materialism, but instead of being conceived as dialectically related to each other—thus admitting of differences in degree—they are subsumed into Althusser's absolute opposition between science and ideology.

> Althusser . . . remobilizes an older and henceforth classical Marxian distinction between science and ideology that is not without value for us even today. The existential—the positioning of the individual subject, the experience of daily life, the monadic "point of view" on the world to which we are necessarily, as biological subjects, restricted—is in Althusser's formula implicitly opposed to the realm of abstract knowledge, a realm which, as Lacan reminds us, is never

modernism, p. 46). Jameson is characterizing a general cultural phenomenon, and I am describing (and criticizing) a distinct intellectual position. His "postmodernism" cannot easily be reduced to a series of propositions; mine can—or at least that is what I attempt to show. Jameson does attempt to distinguish between cultural postmodernism and what he calls "postmodernism theory" (see pp. xx-xxii), but he is not terribly sanguine about the explanatory power of such theory. Thus he is not even sure that his own account of cultural postmodernism, with its clear diagnosis that as a phenomenon it is "only the reflex and concomitant of yet another systemic modification of capitalism" (p. xii), is itself sound as an explanation. The argument is that postmodern culture is a new historical phenomenon that may, in some historically unique way, prove recalcitrant to explanation: " 'Culture,' in the sense of what cleaves almost too close to the skin of the economic to be stripped off and inspected in its own right, is itself a postmodern development. . . . Unfortunately, therefore, the infrastructural description [of postmodern culture] I seem to be calling for here is necessarily itself already cultural and a version of postmodernism theory in advance" (p. xv). These claims are suggested but not fully developed, and I am not quite sure if Jameson means to give up the strong cognitivist, diagnostic, and (what I would call) "realist" account of postmodern culture as "a reflex" of a new stage of capitalism. But it ought at least to be clear why what I call "postmodernism" in this book is a narrower phenomenon, and what I am examining are the intellectual claims I identify and elucidate. My goals are much more modest and circumscribed. I say nothing about the possible relation between what Jameson calls cultural "postmodernism" and the epistemological position I identify as "postmodernist" because I am not sure there is any relation whatsoever. In my opinion, if we were to attempt a sociological explanation of postmodernist epistemology, it would need to deal less with "late capitalism" and more with the power of the Western academy over intellectual discourse, with its power—through its structure of recognition and rewards—to discourage critical examination of one of its most fashionable theories. This kind of institutional analysis would certainly not be enough to produce an adequate explanation, but it would at least make clear to what extent postmodernist theory (of the kind I am examining here) is—to put it crudely—a creation of the market, rather than a genuine intellectual development. It is my feeling that without such basic sociological analyses, more general explanations of the historical determinants of postmodernist epistemology will be speculative and impressionistic.

positioned in or actualized by any concrete subject but rather by that structural void called le sujet supposé savoir (the subject supposed to know), a subject-place of knowledge. What is affirmed is not that we cannot know the world and its totality in some abstract or "scientific" way. Marxian "science" provides just such a way of knowing and conceptualizing the world abstractly, in the sense in which, for example, Mandel's great book [*Late Capitalism*] offers a rich and elaborated knowledge of the global world system, of which it has never been said here that it was unknowable but merely that it was unrepresentable, which is a very different matter. The Althusserian formula, in other words, designates a gap, a rift, between existential experience and scientific knowledge. Ideology has then the function of somehow inventing a way of articulating those two distinct dimensions with each other. (p. 53)

Before we accept this metatheoretical distinction between science and experience as even remotely plausible, however, it would seem that we need to understand something more fundamental about the way human cognition works: how beliefs (compare the "propositions" of the earlier passage) are formed, for instance, and the socially coordinated ways in which variously positioned social creatures not only hold these beliefs but analyze and evaluate them as well. Thus we need to also understand more about reason as a practical capacity. To be able to pose our questions well, we need to understand more than the psychological processes through which an individual comes to change her beliefs, for we have to take into account the different ways in which "beliefs" are related in any given society to "knowledge," which is by definition a socially determined and defined phenomenon. Individual beliefs are not simply "ideological"; they exist in a continuum that includes not only our subjective experiences as individuals but also our hierarchically organized social practices, including our sciences, our specific divisions of linguistic, technical, and epistemological labor. This is in fact what we saw in the basic account of reference discussed in Chapter 2.

As philosophers such as Putnam demonstrate, neither a theoretical account of reference nor a theory of meaning can be elaborated without an adequate understanding of how we organize inquiry through various social institutions and practices. Epistemology is necessarily a social, not an individual matter, and this is the major lesson that the "causal" theory of reference in particular holds for cultural marxism. This lesson suggests that Jameson needs an understanding of reference, as well as a theory of meaning and signification, which would attempt to explain more than does the semiotic account of "transcoding" on which he relies. That notion is only the beginning of an antiidealist account of meaning; it is primarily a negative gesture, the denial of textual "presence." A marxist cultural theory needs to be able to explain two issues discussed in Chapters 1 and 2: the epistemic component of reference and the unavoidably social basis of epistemology. The theoretical questions about socially coordinated meaning production and the fixing of reference cannot be investigated without a sophisticated understanding of how we (in contemporary societies, for instance) *collectively* justify our beliefs and produce reliable knowledge. Such an understanding, together with a general theory of the practical rationality of which human agents are capable in different social conditions, would enable us to develop a more reasonable notion of objective knowledge. What we mean by objectivity depends on our understanding of the social bases of justification and reliable knowledge; it should not be imagined—in almost eschatological terms—as the "science" that only some future subject of history will adequately "represent" to himself.

This idealist conception of the identical subject-object of history is what makes Jameson's interesting conception of "cognitive mapping" so impossibly utopian instead of useful in the shaping of a viable cultural politics. In Jameson's book on Adorno, for instance, "dialectical reason" is invoked to settle conclusively an all-too-brief discussion of the current debates over the status of reason. But it is envisioned as a fully formed epistemological agent waiting in the wings of history: it "*corresponds to* a social organization that does not yet exist, has not yet come into being in any hegemonic form."[10] This conception of reason as a socially embodied ideal was common to Kant and Marx, but they were also deeply interested in reason as a practical capacity, representing an epistemic and political virtue of individual agents. The interest in practical reason led both radical thinkers to formulate an understanding of the necessary pedagogical value of democratic politics and the epistemic component of everyday social struggles. This practical orientation grounds reason (an epistemic ideal) in a social space, and makes our understanding of it implicitly historical. Given his Lukácsian commitment to the abstract achievements of the dialectic, however, Jameson is not able to focus on practical reason. Rather, cultural politics is seen exclusively as a matter of an ideal representation, the representation of the whole. The pedagogical role of the social relations of struggle disappears from this picture of politics and culture. The individual subject—socially undifferentiated, unmarked, for instance, by either class or gender—waits for a "breakthrough."

10. Jameson, *Late Marxism*, p. 236, emphasis added.

The following passage from the conclusion of "The Cultural Logic of Late Capitalism" suggests quite clearly what I am pointing to: "An aesthetic of cognitive mapping—a pedagogical political culture which seeks to endow the individual subject with some new heightened sense of its place in the global system—will . . . have to hold to the truth of postmodernism, that is to say, to its fundamental object—the world space of multinational capital—at the same time at which it achieves a breakthrough to some as yet unimaginable new mode of representing this last, in which we may again begin to grasp our positioning as individual and collective subjects and regain a capacity to act and struggle" (p. 54). It seems to me that this vision of political struggle is abstract and impoverished to the extent that it relies on such a "breakthrough," on the dialectic to appear as a fully realized representation. I am not denying that a radically new form of art or culture might in fact be invented, for radical cultural novelty, though rare, is not unheard of in history. What I am questioning is the view that art or culture, with its "as yet unimaginable new mode of representing," will arrive in this eschatological form, in which the dialectic will answer our epistemological questions and, with the same wave of the wand, resolve all our existential and ethical dilemmas, breathing life and spirit into us. What is inadequately examined in such images is the way the dialectic evolves and is justified as a guiding procedure for inquiry, the way reason is a historically—and politically—produced epistemic norm, based on the social struggles of human agents. What is missing, in short, is an account of the social and historical bases of knowledge and of the continuity between "theory" and subjective experience, between science and value.[11]

I think it is this inadequacy in Jameson's understanding of the social basis of epistemology which explains what may be identified as the idealist core in his historiography, a Hegelian desire to find allegories and essences in historical periods and national cultures. It is this desire that underlies his reductive and overly general conception of "third-world literature" as "necessarily . . . allegorical": "Third-world texts, even those which are seemingly private and invested with a properly libidinal dynamic—necessarily project a political dimension in the form of a national allegory: *the story of the private individual destiny is always an allegory of the embattled situation of the public third-world culture*

11. For a discussion of the relation between subjective experience and objective knowledge, see my realist account of cultural identity (and a related interpretation of Toni Morrison's *Beloved*) in Chapter 7. My "realist" theory of experience and identity is based on a "naturalized" conception of epistemology as social practice.

and society."[12] Such claims have been widely criticized, most notably by Aijaz Ahmad, who pointed out at the end of his response to Jameson that a key problem with the latter's account is the reductive allegory. Jameson thinks, Ahmad argues convincingly, that "the heart of all . . . [historical or cultural] analytic procedures . . . is a search for a . . . unitary determination which can be identified."[13] That Ahmad is right about so much of Jameson's later work is indeed ironic, for as my analysis of his earlier writings from *Marxism and Form* through *The Political Unconscious* and *Fables of Aggression* shows, his work, more than that of other marxist critics, has demonstrated that texts are complexly mediated products rather than "expressions" of "essences." Why, then, is Jameson so quick to see either third-world cultures or the form of future social formations in such reductively utopian or abstract terms? I think the reason is the weakness in his epistemological view (most evident in the later work, especially after *The Political Unconscious*), for it cannot account for the complex variety of relations between objectivity and error, since all such variety is subsumed into the Althusserian opposition between science and ideology. And as we have seen, this Althusserian distinction arises out of a desire to build an entire epistemology on the poststructuralist claim that individual subjects can never attain objectivity because they can never "represent" scientific knowledge in the terms provided by their subjective "experience." What neither Jameson nor Althusser questions is the legitimacy of this move to define objectivity exclusively in terms of the individual's "representations," rather than through the socially coordinated practices of reasoning and justification.

Theses about absolute "rifts" and "gaps" between the individual's experience and scientific knowledge are theoretically appealing only to the extent that we begin by making impossible demands of objectivity and knowledge. Such poststructuralist views about the relation between experience and knowledge in fact turn out to be mirror images of the idealist figure they were meant to dislodge—the fully transparent subject of knowledge. Neither the poststructuralist nor the idealist is sufficiently attentive to the complex social bases of error—how it arises in different kinds of social practice, what its sources are, and how an understanding of the causes of error can strengthen our attempts to gain greater objectivity. Both Althusserian science and Lukácsian dialectic

12. Jameson, "Third-World Literature in the Era of Multinational Capitalism," *Social Text* (Fall 1986), 69.

13. Aijaz Ahmad, "Jameson's Rhetoric of Otherness and the 'National Allegory,' " in *In Theory* (London: Verso, 1992), p. 119.

are idealizations that assume that the agent of knowledge is an unlimited, ideally rational being for whom cognitive success would consist in the attainment of truth. But human subjects are cognitively limited creatures, with (precisely because of their limitedness) the capacity for cognitive failure as well as success; for human epistemic agents, thus, the need to examine the practical sources and causes of error is urgent because that becomes the only way to overcome error and to attain greater objectivity. Jameson ends up implicitly accepting this idealized image of the epistemic agent common to Althusser's and Lukács's theories. Jameson's lapses into an overly abstract historiography are explainable in terms of his inattention to this question about how objectivity and error might be socially and methodologically related. Without an adequate epistemology, what he works with is at most a sociology of knowledge, which is only interested in how beliefs reflect or refract their social contexts. Questions of justification are left out as either irrelevant or settled on a different theoretical level.[14]

In Part Two, I continue this discussion of justification and knowledge, explaining why it is both important and urgent that political critics face epistemological questions directly. In Chapter 5, I focus on one ironic consequence of postmodernism's skepticism about knowledge, especially knowledge of cultural or historical others. Such skepticism— and the relativism it entails—does not ensure tolerance of difference; indeed, as I hope to show, its logic leads more easily to indifference. I outline an alternative to relativism in the final section of the chapter, before directly addressing some of the central epistemological issues I have discussed so far. My argument in Chapters 6 and 7 is that the radical political project Jameson and Althusser share would be better

14. I make this criticism from the perspective of a naturalist-realist epistemology, the strongest contemporary alternative to idealism. Philip Kitcher's comment is directly relevant to the point I am making against the Althusserian and Lukácsian visions of the epistemic agent: "Attributions of justification and rationality stem from the idea that the epistemic performances of subjects may be appraised whether or not the beliefs they acquire are true. For unlimited beings such attributions would be pointless: epistemic performance would simply be assessed by the attainment of truth (more exactly, the epistemic good). Cognitively limited beings, however, can do well or badly in trying to overcome their limitations. We cannot think of them as limited only with respect to 'matters of fact'; their perspective on how to proceed in forming their beliefs may also be limited." Kitcher, "The Naturalists Return," in "Philosophy in Review: Essays on Contemporary Philosophy," special issue of *Philosophical Review* 101 (January 1992), 67. My implicit argument in this book (and especially in Chapters 6 and 7) is that radical cultural critics and social scientists, if they wish to develop an adequate materialist epistemology, need to focus on the cognitive successes and failures of finite—as opposed to ideal—epistemic agents. That focus will yield a more nuanced social and political epistemology than the general skepticism that characterizes poststructuralist or postmodernist theory.

served by a naturalist-realist conception of human knowledge than by a poststructuralist one. In fact, as I hope to demonstrate, central to such a conception would be a thesis about the continuity between experience and knowledge, between ideology and science, where both are understood in fundamentally social rather than individualist terms.

Part Two

5

POLITICAL CRITICISM AND THE

CHALLENGE OF OTHERNESS

In a context in which the relations between our knowledge of and participation in the external world and such criteria as truth, objectivity, and rationality are being reexamined, the claims of a specifically political criticism come to occupy the center of the intellectual stage. Whether inspired by social and intellectual movements such as feminism, marxism, and antiimperialist nationalisms or by interdisciplinary academic developments such as deconstruction and, more generally, postmodernism, political criticism can be identified by at least a common desire to expose the social interests at work in the reading and writing of literature. It may not always be tied to larger programs or alternative models of cultural practice, but criticism is political to the extent that it defines as one of its goals the interrogation of the *uses* to which literary works are put, exploring the connections between social institutions and literary texts, between groups of people understood collectively in terms of gender, sexuality, race, and class, on the one hand, and discourses about cultural meanings and values, on the other. This chapter is an attempt to identify, define, and criticize what I see as an unexamined philosophical position latent in contemporary political-critical practice—cultural or historical relativism. Relativism appears less as an explicit claim than as a practical and theoretical bias and leads to historical simplification and political naiveté.

My specific contention is that a relativist position does not allow for a complex understanding of social and cultural phenomena since the vagueness of its definition of rationality precludes a serious analysis of historical agency. In outlining the claims of two versions of relativism, an extreme and a more sophisticated kind, I intend to show why we need a more precise definition of rationality than either offers. It would be seriously debilitating for critical analysis to confuse a minimal notion of rationality as a cognitive and practical human capacity with the grand a priori foundational structure that has traditionally been called reason. Indeed, as we seek now to understand the colonial encounters that have shaped our historical modernity and to extend or radically revise our current notions of philosophical and cultural "conversation,"[1] the task of elaborating a positive but nonidealized conception of the "human" can be seen as tied to this specification of a minimal rationality. I suggest that political criticism must face the need for a basic definition of human agency and the conception of practical rationality it implies, and I shall outline the context in which this and related issues might be analyzed. After providing preliminary definitions of political criticism and relativism and delineating some of the relevant contexts in which they can be discussed, I turn in the next section to a more specific account of a debate within social anthropology to show the complexity of political motives, alignments, and positions involved in any topic-specific consideration of relativism. In the third section I outline the primary arguments against relativist positions considered generally, suggesting why they will not serve as useful bases for political criticism. In the last two sections I develop my reasons for considering human agency and rationality urgent issues for contemporary criticism and suggest how such issues can be addressed.

1. The allusion is not so much specifically to Richard Rorty, who has advocated a model of philosophy as an aspect of the continuing "conversation of mankind," as it is more generally to the liberal pluralist politics that might accompany so-called antifoundationalist positions in cultural criticism. While Rorty makes a convincing case against the dominant self-image of academic philosophy as a relentless search for a truth that would be the foundation for all other forms of knowledge and social practice (*Philosophy and the Mirror of Nature* [Princeton: Princeton University Press, 1979]), he would probably be quite willing to grant that his own alternative account of philosophy engaged in "the conversation of the West" (p. 394) invites political interrogation. If the forms and protocols of this conversation have developed historically—as they must have, given Rorty's arguments—we would need to be more attentive to the work of those feminist, antiimperialist, and otherwise radical scholars who have been focusing on the exclusions that have shaped this conversation. In this context, my point is simply this: the arguments against foundationalism in philosophy notwithstanding, an appreciation of these exclusions is possible only through a great deal of historical specification, and such specification can be done poorly and inadequately if we adopt the basic position of cultural or historical relativism. Indeed, the antifoundationalist position in contemporary philosophy does not *entail* the kind of cultural or historical relativism I discuss in this chapter, even though in practice, as *attitudes*, the two might seem to go together. (I discuss Rorty in more detail in the next chapter.)

But it would be useful, first, to indicate the intellectual context in which relativism originated to clarify both its value as a political gesture and its limits as a concept for the analysis of literature and culture. Even though it took definite shape in the course of the nineteenth century, relativism has its origins in the late eighteenth-century reaction to the universalist claims of Enlightenment thought. Stressing not merely the presence of historical variety but also the constitutional differences evident in human languages, communities, and societies, writers such as J. G. Herder urged that we recognize the changeability of "human nature." Their arguments pointed up the inability of any single faculty, such as what the Enlightenment thinkers called reason, to comprehend the diverse manifestations of human culture and history. Herder emphasized the creativity of the human mind and argued that we understand its individual creations only by situating them in their particular social and cultural contexts. The development of relativism as a powerful intellectual presence, as Patrick Gardiner has shown in a useful essay, is best seen as a post-Herderian phenomenon which draws on nineteenth-century German idealist philosophy, and on such thinkers as Fichte, Hegel, and Dilthey.[2] Very generally understood, this development underscored the need to define the claims of difference over identity, historical novelty and variety over methodological monism. Against the Enlightenment's emphasis on a singular rationality underlying and comprehending all human activities, relativism pursued the possibilities of change, variety, and difference, and began thereby to pose the question of otherness.

It is this question that becomes a basic political gesture in the context of contemporary literary theory and criticism. To situate and illustrate this politics, let me quote from three fairly influential and representative sources that suggest both the dominant political-critical climate these days and a possible basis for relativist arguments.

[The] epistemological mutation of history is not yet complete. But it is not of recent origin either, since its first phase can no doubt be

2. Patrick Gardiner, "German Philosophy and the Rise of Relativism," *Monist* 64 (April 1981), 138–54. The literature on relativism is voluminous and is probably best approached in terms of specific topics or disciplines. Useful discussions as well as bibliographic leads can be found in Martin Hollis and Steven Lukes, eds., *Rationality and Relativism* (Cambridge: MIT Press, 1982), and Michael Kranz and Jack Meiland, eds., *Relativism: Cognitive and Moral* (Notre Dame, Ind.: University of Notre Dame Press, 1982).

traced back to Marx. But it took a long time to have much effect. Even now—and this is especially true in the case of the history of thought—it has been neither registered nor reflected upon, while other, more recent transformations—those of linguistics, for example—have been. It is as if it was particularly difficult, in the history in which men retrace their own ideas and their own knowledge, to formulate a general theory of discontinuity, of series, of limits, unities, specific orders, and differentiated autonomies and dependences. As if, in that field where we had become used to seeking origins, to pushing back further and further the line of antecedents, to reconstituting traditions, to following evolutive curves, to projecting teleologies, and to having constant recourse to metaphors of life, we felt a particular repugnance to conceiving of difference, to describing separations and dispersions, to dissociating the reassuring form of the identical. . . . As if we were afraid to conceive of the *Other* in the time of our own thought.[3]

In the beginning are our differences. The new love dares for the other, wants the other, makes dizzying, precipitous flights between knowledge and invention. The woman arriving over and over again does not stand still; she's everywhere, she exchanges, she is the desire-that-gives. . . . Wherever history still unfolds as the history of death, she does not tread. Opposition, hierarchizing exchange, the struggle for mastery . . . —all that comes from a period in time governed by phallocentric values. The fact that this period extends into the present doesn't prevent woman from starting the history of life somewhere else. Elsewhere, she gives. . . . This is an "economy" that can no longer be put in economic terms. Wherever she loves, all the old concepts of management are left behind. At the end of a more or less conscious computation, she finds not her sum but her differences. . . . When I write, it's everything that we don't know we can be that is written out of me. . . . Heterogeneous, yes . . . the erotogeneity of the heterogeneous.[4]

What is now in crisis is a whole conception of socialism which rests upon the ontological centrality of the working class, upon the role of Revolution, with a capital "r," as the founding moment in the transition from one type of society to another, and upon the illusory prospect of a perfectly unitary and homogeneous collective will that will render pointless the moment of politics. The plural and multifarious character of contemporary social struggles has finally dissolved the

3. Michel Foucault, *The Archaelogy of Knowledge*, trans. A. M. Sheridan Smith (New York: Harper and Row, 1972), pp. 11–12.
4. Hélène Cixous, "The Laugh of the Medusa," in *New French Feminisms*, ed. Elaine Marks and Isabelle de Courtivron (New York: Schocken, 1981), pp. 263–64; 260.

in scholarly literature for anyone interested in looking) but primarily because of uncritical application and extension of the very ideas with which the West has defined its enlightenment and its modernity—reason, progress, civilization.[7]

In this general context—so general that it would be impossible to understand developments in most of the social sciences and the humanistic disciplines without it—the relativist thesis initially becomes a valuable political weapon. Opposing the imperial arrogance of the scholar who interprets aspects of other cultures in terms of the inflexible norms and categories of the scholar's own, the relativist insists on the fundamentally sound antipositivist idea that individual elements of a given culture must be interpreted primarily in terms of that culture, relative, that is, to its own unique system of meanings and values. Thus relativism teaches a clear political lesson: it cautions us against ethnocentrist explanations of other communities and cultures. Drawing on the example of ethnology, the relativist tells us that texts (or events or values) can be significantly *misunderstood* if they are not seen in relation to their particular contexts. The relativist warns against reductionist explanations that use the terms of the familiar culture to appropriate the terms of the unfamiliar one. The central challenge is to the practices of interpretation and the unconscious evaluations embedded in them, for relativism teaches us that interpretation and understanding have historically been tied to political activities and that "strong" and "meaningful" interpretations have often been acts of discursive domination. Instead, relativism urges care and attentiveness to the specificities of context; it emphasizes the differences between and among us rather than pointing to shared spaces. What is hoped is that we will, one day, learn to share; that is relativism's utopia.

Anthropology: An Instructive Exchange

From this very general account it is possible to see the great attraction the relativist position can hold for contemporary political criticism. Problems begin to appear when we go beyond this general formulation and examine the position a little more closely, articulating its deeper

7. The best representative of the overly optimistic strand of the Enlightenment which emphasized universalism and progress as the march of reason and the conquest of superstition is Condorcet. I briefly critique this tradition within the Enlightenment in Chapter 7, distinguishing it from others that are much more relevant for contemporary progressive social struggles.

implications and presuppositions. I shall be arguing in a moment that relativism is an untenable—and indeed rather dangerous—philosophical ally for political criticism. But let me first identify the larger scope and potential ambiguity of the issues involved by focusing on two essays, one by Ernest Gellner and the other by Talal Asad. Gellner's classic essay was first published in 1951 and canonized by its inclusion in undergraduate textbooks in Britain to this day; Asad's critique appeared in a 1986 collection of essays by anthropologists critical of the politics of their own inherited tradition.[8] Gellner attacks the relativist thesis in anthropological theory, associating it with a confused and "excessively charitable" intellectual and political attitude. Asad, in his critique of Gellner's essay, does not defend relativism so much as outline one serious misconception in Gellner's attack. In Asad's view, the emphasis should be placed on the anthropological practices and institutions of "cultural translation," which exist in a matrix of unequal languages and asymmetrical access to the institutions of discourse and power. I would like to outline some of these arguments briefly to indicate the instructive complexity of the issues involved in this debate; then, I would like to show why, despite the cogency of Asad's critique—which is particularly trenchant when it identifies the sloppy arguments underlying Gellner's imperious tone—the problems surrounding the issue of relativism need to be explored more thoroughly.

One of the main points Gellner wishes to make in his essay concerns our attitude toward what we might consider "illogical" or "incoherent" ideas in the culture being studied. If the relativist claim is that all cultural ideas are to be adequately understood only in their own contexts, that is, only in terms of the systematic beliefs, practices, and values of the culture being studied, is the interpreter necessarily always committed to finding meaning and coherence and giving up all capacity to judge ideas in other cultures as incoherent and meaningless? The contextualist relativist, says Gellner, errs in adopting this attitude of unwarranted "charity." For often in fact we *need* to grasp the internal incoherence of ideas as they operate within a culture in order to understand their precise function adequately. Thus, even though the contextual interpretation claims to be giving us the "real" interpretation of something by situating it in its surrounding world of beliefs and practices, Gellner

8. Ernest Gellner, "Concepts and Society," in *Rationality*, ed. Bryan R. Wilson (New York: Harper and Row, 1971), pp. 18–49; Talal Asad, "The Concept of Cultural Translation in British Social Anthropology," in *Writing Culture: The Poetics and Politics of Ethnography*, ed. James Clifford and George E. Marcus (Berkeley: University of California Press, 1986), pp. 141–64.

would argue that in many cases the acontextual—isolated—evaluation of it (that is, of a statement, proposition, or belief) is necessary if we are to provide deeper accounts of it as a cultural phenomenon. What Gellner calls interpretive "charity" is thus more a kind of sentimental liberalism: it dehistoricizes in the name of contextual analysis and ends up ignoring the deep-structural bases of the other culture.

After identifying the extreme form of the contextualist position, which would hold that all ideas are to be interpreted solely in terms internal to the context in which they are produced and used, Gellner insists on the need for a strong evaluative interpretation. Instead of arguing for abandoning the subjective dimension in interpreting others Gellner wishes to assert the need for applying criteria that do not derive simply from the object itself but are shared by the anthropologist's own culture. The following passage contains what may be the most succinct statement of his methodological thesis:

> Professor Raymond Firth has remarked in *Problem and Assumption in an Anthropological Study of Religion:* "From my own experience, I am impressed by the ease with which it is possible to add one's own personal dimension to the interpretation of an alien religious ideology, to raise the generalizations to a higher power than the empirical content of the material warrants." My point is, really, that it is more than a matter of *ease*—it is a matter of necessity: for interpretation cannot be determinate without assumptions concerning the success or failure of the interpreted communication, and the criteria of such success are not manifest in the "content of the material" itself. One has to work them out as best one can, and it will *not* do to take the short cut of reading them off the material by assuming that the material is always successful, i.e. that the statements investigated do satisfy and exemplify criteria of coherence, and hence that interpretation is not successful until this coherence has been made manifest in the translations. The logical *assessment* of an assertion, and the identification of its nearest equivalent in our language, are intimately linked and inseparable. (pp. 33–34)

Building on his claim that "sympathetic, positive interpretations of indigenous assertions are not the result of a sophisticated appreciation of context" and that in fact it may be that "the manner in which the context is invoked, the amount and kind of context and the way the context itself is interpreted, depends on prior tacit determination concerning the kind of interpretation one wishes to find" (p. 33), Gellner introduces a series of more specific claims. Let me reemphasize the crucial ones:

The "logical assessment" of an idea we have identified in the other culture is absolutely necessary for interpretation of the idea; an adequate interpretation of an idea in an unfamiliar culture involves a close translation into the "language" of the familiar—that is, the anthropologist's—culture.[9] Charity is less crucial here than we might think; indeed, it might be a conceptual and analytical straitjacket. If Gellner is right, we need to worry more about the internal coherence or logic of the idea in isolation *before* we begin to determine what the appropriate context for interpreting it might be.

Gellner himself makes this last point elsewhere in the essay. We evaluate an idea encountered in another culture by apprehending it as an "assertion," for which we then seek an equivalent assertion in our own language. And just as we judge assertions in our own language as either "good" or "bad" (Gellner's deliberately schematic terms to cover such polar attributes as true and false, meaningful and absurd, sensible and silly), we need also to evaluate the assertion/idea in the other culture. The "tolerance-engendering contextual interpretation" evades this rigorous "logical assessment," however, by assuming in advance that all assertions we encounter in the other culture are "good," that is, meaningful and coherent, especially when we understand their own contextual terms and functions. For Gellner, this assumption makes a mockery of the interpretive process, which must build on the logical assessment of (isolated) assertions (pp. 24–32).

The crucial assumption here is that "logical assessment" of assertions can be made only to the extent that we define them in isolation, and we isolate assertions in their (unfamiliar) language exactly the way we do in our (familiar) one. It would seem that for Gellner the identification of an assertion—its definition in isolation from whatever we consider its context—is an unproblematical activity. It is this naive atomism, difficult enough to sustain when we are studying elements within our own culture and obviously more complicated and arrogant when we are approaching another, on which Gellner's argument seems to be based. Despite the occasional appearance of terms such as "interpretation" and "hermeneutics," the essay exists in the bliss of prehermeneutical empiricist confidence. Gellner's terms of analysis, derived

9. That the passage I have just quoted begs basic questions is worth mentioning, especially to highlight the contrast with Gellner's imperious tone. How determinate, for instance, does an interpretation have to be? Or how absolute a conception of success or failure (of "the interpreted communication") do we need to have? Gellner presumes the answers are self-evident, but they seem to me to raise the most crucial hermeneutical issues involved in anthropological—or any textual—interpretation.

from his essentially positivist framework, obscure significant issues involved in anthropological interpretation. Talal Asad identifies one of these quite well; I would like to provide a selective account of his critique before I discuss the inadequacy of Gellner's treatment of relativism. In doing that, however, I will need, first, to develop our understanding of the relativist position by adding another level of complexity to the issues involved; and second, to make Gellner's case against relativism with entirely different terms, challenging the liberal relativists he attacks not for their excessive charity and tolerance but for the political apathy entailed by their philosophical position.

Since Asad's critique of Gellner might have some bearing on contemporary literary-critical theory and practice, it would be instructive to look at it in some detail. The most basic consideration Asad wishes to introduce into the discussion is simply the context of anthropological interpretation itself—not just the interpretation of, say, the Nuers and the Berbers but of Anglophone white anthropologists writing in the middle of the twentieth century within intellectually and politically sanctioned hierarchies and codifications of knowledge. For what Gellner is able to ignore in his entire essay is the existence of institutionally sanctioned power relations between interpreter and interpreted which determine the politics of meaning in the first place. That the following reminder is necessary is itself embarrassing, and it might indeed point up the ambiguity of any critique of relativism, including the one I am making in this chapter. Asad is not interested in defending the version of contextual relativism Gellner attacks; rather, he is at pains to lay out the basic contextual terms with which any anthropological interpretive practice that sees itself as performing "cultural translation" must engage:

> The relevant question . . . is not how tolerant an *attitude* the translator ought to display toward the original author (an abstract ethical dilemma), but how she can test the tolerance of her own language for assuming unaccustomed forms. . . . [T]he matter is largely something the translator cannot determine by individual activity (any more than the individual speaker can affect the evolution of his or her language)—that is governed by institutionally defined power relations between the languages/modes of life concerned. To put it crudely: because the languages of Third World societies—including, of course, the societies that social anthropologists have traditionally studied—are "weaker" in relation to Western languages . . ., they are more likely to submit to forcible transformation in the translation process than the other way around. The reason for this is, first, that in their

political-economic relations with Third World countries, Western nations have the greater ability to manipulate. . . . And, second, Western languages produce and deploy *desired* knowledge more readily than Third World languages do. (pp. 157–58)

Asad raises two closely related questions here to contest Gellner's abstract approach. The first wonders about the adequacy of Gellner's formulation of the problem of interpretation in terms of logical "charity" or "tolerance," and we shall see in a moment how Asad would extend the meaning of the terms by restoring their practical context to them. The second question deals with the basic model of "translation" itself. Gellner's formulation of anthropological interpretation in terms of "charity" is a convenient abstraction that obscures the practice of Western anthropologists studying other—that is, non-Western—cultures, particularly in colonial and postcolonial contexts, since it ignores the basic hermeneutic question about the adequacy of the anthropologist's own cultural language (its capacity for "tolerance" of new and unfamiliar meanings). Gellner's account of the interpretive process ignores the *possibility* that the interpreter and her analytical apparatus might be fundamentally challenged and changed by the material she (and it) are attempting to "assess." Whether this account and others like it are naively positivist or whether they trail clouds of ideology and a specifiable political motive needs more detailed local analysis.

But the general point is this: in our obsessive fear that the typical Western anthropologist might be guilty of excessive interpretive charity, we ignore the more significant fact that in our particular historical contexts the anthropologist, in order to be able to interpret at all, needs to educate himself through cultural and political "sympathy." Indeed, if we deepen the analysis we realize that the model of cultural translation is itself misleading: "The anthropologist's translation is not merely a matter of matching sentences in the abstract, but of *learning to live another form of life*," notes Asad (p. 149). The echo of Wittgenstein raises the important question about the limits of the conception of anthropological interpretation as a translation from one language to another. It suggests that "languages" are not merely "texts," if by that we mean that "translations" can be considered "*essentially* a matter of verbal representation" (p. 160). Anthropological interpretation can be conceived as translation only if we recognize that a successful translation may change our own language, for the success of the translation of a significant text depends on our ability to transform our language—

that is, our modes and habits of thought and action.[10] By extension, these modes and habits include our institutional contexts of interpretation, our "disciplines" and their regimes of truth and scientificity, and the organization of power relations within the global system. An adequate anthropological interpretation must then include not only "translation" but also an account of "how power enters into the process of 'cultural translation' [which must be] seen both as a discursive and as a non-discursive practice" (p. 163). An instance of this *discursive* power—and the nondiscursive power it banks on—is Gellner's very influential formulation of the interpretive process. The model of language and writing here serves to blind us to an entire history that is embedded in the processes of "logical assessment" and decoding meaning. Gellner arrogates to himself the "privileged position" of the neutral interpreter to the extent that he wishes, as anthropologist, not to interrogate his very real control of the entire operation of this translation, "from field notes to printed ethnography." His "is the privileged position of someone who does not, and can afford not to, engage in a genuine dialogue with those he or she once lived with and now *writes* about" (p. 155).

Gellner's "privileged position" is both theoretically and historically specifiable. The Whiggish tone of the essay betrays more than a simple emotional attitude; it in fact points to a philosophical confidence in a narrowly defined reason to lay bare the world, a deeply entrenched belief in the adequacy of his "logical assessment" of the "assertion" of the other culture to comprehend its underlying social function. Gellner's "logic" encompasses the entire space of the globe and its meanings; complexity of contextual function and meaning in every conceivable other space is granted only a limited autonomy since its central terms remain formulated by the terms of Gellner's discursive world.[11] Asad points out that this view is historically convenient since it blinds the social anthropologist to the contexts of power she or he inhabits; a sophisticated relativist would add an account of the ways in which Gellner significantly misunderstands the complexity of his object of study by reducing them to translatable "assertions."

10. This point is made very well in Walter Benjamin, "The Task of the Translator," in *Illuminations*, trans. Harry Zohn (New York: Schocken, 1968), pp. 69–82, esp. 80–81.

11. This is the prehermeneutical and instrumental notion of logic and rationality which Adorno and Horkheimer criticize in *The Dialectic of Enlightenment* (trans. John Cumming [New York: Continuum, 1993])—see my account of their critique in the Introduction, and the alternative conception of reason developed here and in Chapters 6 and 7, esp. the concluding pages of Chapter 7.

The Political Implications of Relativism

It is important to note, notwithstanding the critique of Gellner's reduction of complex cultural objects to "assertions," that his claim that the "incoherences" of a given culture can indeed be "socially functional" (p. 42) is basically sound. What Gellner fails to recognize, however, is that this is an issue entirely different from the presence of varying criteria of "rational" judgment in different cultures. In other words, the fact that assertions or beliefs may be incoherent in a significant way does not diminish the interpretive complexity of the anthropologist's task in determining the specific terms with which they must be evaluated. And the issue raised by the sophisticated relativist is simply that these terms, these criteria of rationality, may vary to a significant degree from culture to culture. Before I provide my explanation of this position, it might be best to see what *extreme* relativism involves and why it is problematical.

Now, the most extreme relativist formulation of the problem would be that there are no common terms between and among different cultures, and their models of rationality, since the spaces different cultures define are entirely different from one another. Reacting sharply to the ahistorical vision underlying Gellner's Whiggish universalism, the extreme relativist would point to the necessity of restoring to our critical perspective the presence of a plurality of spaces and values, the plurality of criteria of judgment and rationality implicit in the different cultural and historical contexts. Gellner's narrow conception of rationality, it would be easy to argue, is predicated on a false and reductive view of modern history as unproblematically unitary. Guided by reason, obeying the logic of progress and modernization, Gellner's model of history should belong to the prehistory of a critical anthropology, for in our "postmodern" world, history is no longer feasible; what we need to talk about, to pay attention to, are histories—in the plural. This position builds on the pervasive feeling in the human sciences these days that this grand narrative of history seems a little embarrassing; what we need to reclaim instead, as is often pointed out in cultural criticism and theory, is the plurality of our heterogeneous lives, the darker and unspoken meanings that are lived, fought, and imagined as various communities and peoples seek to retrace and reweave the historical text. In the history of criticism, encountering for the first time the challenge of alternative canons defined by feminist, black, third-world scholars and others, this is initially not only a valuable critical idea but also the basis for an energizing critical-political project. After all, we have just been learning to speak of feminisms, instead of the singular form which implicitly hid the variety of women's struggles along different racial and class vectors under the hegemonic self-image of the heterosexual white middle-class movement; we have learned to write "marxism" without capitalizing the "m," thereby pointing to the need to reconceive the relationship to some unitary originary source; we have, in effect, taught ourselves that if history was available to us, it was always as a *text* to be read and reread dialogically and to be rewritten in a form other than the monologue, no matter how consoling or noble its tone or import.

Plurality is thus a political ideal as much as a methodological slogan. But the issue of different rationalities raises a nagging question: How do we negotiate between my history and yours? How would it be possible for us to recover our commonality, not the ambiguous imperial-humanist myth of those shared human (and indeed almost divine) attributes that are supposed to distinguish us absolutely from animals but, more significant, the imbrication of our various pasts and presents, the ineluctable relationships of shared and contested meanings, values, material resources? It is necessary to assert our dense particularities, our lived and imagined differences; but can we afford to leave untheorized the question of how our differences are intertwined and, indeed, hierarchically organized? Could we, in other words, afford to have *entirely* different histories, to see ourselves as living—and having lived—in entirely heterogeneous and discrete spaces?

It will not do, then, to formulate the question about why criteria of rationality vary in the rather simplistic terms of merely different rationalities and histories. The extreme relativist position, despite its initial attraction, seems to be philosophically and politically confused. Every philosophy textbook will tell us that this kind of relativism is easily refutable. In fact, some philosophers will declare a little contemptuously, such a relativism is *self-refuting*. The argument can be summed up rather neatly: If the relativist position is that there can be nothing other than context-specific truth-claims, that the "truth" of every cultural or historical text is purely immanent to its immediate context, then on what grounds should I believe the relativist? If the relativist says that everything is entirely context-specific, that we cannot adjudicate among contexts or texts on the basis of larger—that is, more general—evaluative or interpretative criteria, then why should I bother to take seriously *that very claim?* The point is that one cannot both claim to hold the relativist position and expect to convince anyone who does not already believe; there is no serious way in which the relativist can ask me to take him seriously—insofar as he wishes to be consistent. Self-refutation is built into the argument, and it renders relativism less a significant philosophical position than a pious—though not ineffectual—political wish.

The problem is, however, that a refutation of this sort is not quite relevant for the way relativist ideas operate in literary critical circles. It is rarely as an explicit and reasoned position that relativism appears; instead, as I have suggested, it is embedded in our critical gestures, in the kinds of questions we ask or refuse to ask.[12] The more significant challenge would be to see whether there are political implications of the relativist position which the relativist would be interested in *not* including in his baggage. And I think there is at least one rather serious problem in what relativism entails: To believe that you have your space and I mine; to believe, further, that there can be no responsible way in which I can adjudicate between your space—cultural and historical— and mine by developing a set of general criteria that can have interpretive validity in both contexts (because there can be no interpretation that is not simultaneously an evaluation)—to believe both these things is also to assert something quite large. Quite simply, it is to assert that *all spaces are equivalent,* that they have equal value, that since the lowest common principle of evaluation is all that I can invoke, I cannot—and consequently need not—think about how your space impinges on mine or how my history is defined together with yours. If that is the case, I may have started by declaring a pious political wish, but I end by denying that I need to take you seriously. Plurality instead of a single homogeneous space, yes. But also, unfortunately, debilitatingly insular spaces. Thus this extreme relativist position—and extreme especially when its implications remain inadequately thought out—is in no way a feasible theoretical basis of politically motivated criticism. It is in fact a dangerous philosophical ally, since it is built on, at best, naive and sentimental reasoning. To the extent that our initial interest in relativism was motivated by a political respect for other selves, other spaces, other contexts, relativism seems now to be an unacceptable theoretical position. For it might encourage a greater sensitivity to the contexts of production of cultural ideas, but it will not, given the terms of its formulation, enable what Talal Asad calls for—a "genuine dialogue" between anthropologist and native, the ex-colonizer and the ex-colonized.

12. Cf. the discussion of Lyotard in the final section of this chapter.

The sophisticated relativist would deny Gellner's claim that the West's rationality can unproblematically evaluate the beliefs and practices of the other culture, and would also wish to distance himself from the extreme relativism that commits us all to radically separate and insular spaces. A genuine dialogue of the kind Asad envisions would become possible only when we admit that crucial aspects of the non-Western culture may have a great degree of coherence as part of a larger web of ideas, beliefs, and practices, and moreover that *some* of these aspects may be untranslatable into the language of the Western anthropologist's culture because of its historically sedimented and institutionally determined practices of knowing. The classic example encountered by anthropologists in this context is the practice of "magic" and ritual. From the point of view of the modern West these practices might be seen as coherent and of a piece with an entire form of life, but interpreted more rigorously they could reveal a "primitive" system of belief and an "irrational" practice. Magical rites are patently "unscientific" when the primitive culture pursues them despite the lack of observable or tabulatable evidence that they do have the effects they are supposed to have. Rituals surrounding the planting of crops, for instance, may be practiced because of the belief that they bring about the right kind of weather, and if this were observed to be true, the practice of such rituals would have at least *an* intelligible basis in reason. But what if, as an outsider may well note in instance after instance, the practice of this ritual continues despite the absence of any correlation between it and the weather? In that case should the practitioners not be considered irrational in their practice of at least this ritual, and quite possibly unscientific in their use of magic and ritual generally?

The philosopher Peter Winch contends in his famous essay "Understanding a Primitive Society" that it would be wrong to come to even this conclusion.[13] Disagreeing with Alasdair MacIntyre, Winch points out how important it is to specify the details of the context with greater care. It may be that the Zande practice of magic and ritual can go hand in hand with a clear working distinction between practices and knowledges that are technical and those that are magical. In this case—and indeed this is the case according to the anthropological account of the Azande by Evans-Pritchard, which both Winch and MacIntyre are discussing—Zande magic cannot be subsumed into the Western category of the "unscientific." Since Zande practices exist in a larger web, which

13. Peter Winch, "Understanding a Primitive Society," in *Rationality*, ed. Wilson, pp. 78–111. The essay originally appeared in 1964 in the *American Philosophical Quarterly*.

is constituted in part by the magical-technical opposition, Zande magic could be considered (merely) unscientific only if the Azande *confused* it with their technical practices. In the case where a clear distinction exists between magical and technical practices, a one-to-one translation across cultures that ignores the intention of the practitioners becomes either misleading or at least grossly reductionist.

According to Winch, the significant hermeneutical problem in this context can be raised through a kind of dialogue between the Western web of beliefs and practices and the Zande one. Thus he considers it important to recognize "that *we* do not initially have a category that looks at all like the Zande category of magic" (p. 102). This is the source of the difficulty but also the beginning of an answer: "Since it is we who want to understand the Zande category, it appears that the onus is on us to extend our understanding so as to make room for the Zande category, rather than to insist on seeing it in terms of our own ready-made distinction between science and non-science" (p. 102). The reason this would constitute the beginning of a *dialogue* is that "we" are forced to extend our understanding by interrogating its limits in terms of Zande categories of self-understanding. This dialogue, as Asad might have pointed out, marks the true hermeneutical moment, which in turn ought to frame and guide what Gellner calls the "logical assessment" of a discursive object. Two systems of understanding encounter each other to just the extent that both are contextualized as forms of life; this encounter leaves open the possibility of a fundamental change in both. If we recall the basic issues raised by the passages I quoted at the beginning of this chapter, it will be clear how this kind of hermeneutical encounter provides at least one solution to the problem posed by the Other.

Winch's achievement consists in showing us that we need to respect other cultures not as insular and impenetrable wholes but rather as complex webs of beliefs and actions. He points out that notions of rationality cannot be unproblematically applied across cultures precisely because there are different—and *competing*—rationalities, and one must acknowledge that there are in order to appreciate the specific modalities of actions and beliefs in a given culture. The relation between cause and effect in cultural practices, for instance, can be understood at different levels. The Zande magical rites performed during the planting of crops need not necessarily be understood by the Azande themselves as leading to (having the effect of) a certain change in the weather. It would clearly be an improper interpretation, then, to consider these rites as unscientific or irrational, since the Azande have other purely technical practices that are meant to influence conditions related to the planting of crops and the harvest; it would be wrong, in short, to see these magical rites as "misguided" technical practice. The distinction between technical practices and magical ones should alert us that magic may serve functions of a different *order* altogether. Here is the way Winch explains the idea of different orders, different levels of human practice:

> A man's sense of the importance of something to him shows itself in all sorts of ways; not merely in precautions to safeguard that thing. He may want to come to terms with its importance to him in quite a different way: to contemplate it, to gain some sense of his life in relation to it. He may wish thereby, in a certain sense, to *free* himself from dependence on it. I do not mean by making sure that it does not let him down, because the point is that, *whatever* he does, he may still be let down. The important thing is that he should understand *that* and come to terms with it. Of course, merely to understand that is not to come to terms with it, though perhaps it is a necessary condition for so doing, for a man may equally well be transfixed and terrorized by the contemplation of such a possibility. He must see that he can still go on even if he is let down by what is vitally important to him; and he must so order his life that he still *can* go on in such circumstances. (pp. 103–4)

The terms with which Winch formulates the discussion in this rich passage make clear that to conceive magical rites as complex practices not reducible to the rational-irrational or scientific-unscientific polarities of the West involves a deeper conception of human practices in general—that is, in all societies—as complex in their modalities of intention and meaning. As suggested earlier, the notion of cause and effect itself needs to be interpreted according to its specific modalities. Even within the anthropologist's culture one recognizes the quite different conceptions of causal influence when one speaks of "what made Jones get married" as opposed to, say, "what made the airplane crash" (p. 103). Not to acknowledge these differences is simply—as we say in contemporary criticism—to "read" badly. Thus, the most useful lesson the sophisticated relativist teaches us is that we cannot understand complex cultural acts by hastily reducing them to their propositional content; indeed, such a reduction often involves basic kinds of misreading and misidentification. And to the extent that we define "rationality" on the basis of such terms as logical consistency or the pragmatic choice of means for our technical ends, Winch's arguments as I have presented them would challenge this most basic of our concepts.

The key question is, of course, whether there can be more to the idea of rationality—or culture—than this. For even though he discusses the ways in which different cultures can learn from one another, Winch does not quite face up to the question inherent in his own idea of *competing* rationalities. Winch is right to emphasize that difference teaches us not merely new technical possibilities but also new and possible forms of life. Criteria of rationality are connected to what we call "culture," the larger moral and imaginative patterns through which we deal with our world. Content as he is, however, with definitions of rationality and cultural practices at the most general level, Winch, in seeing cultures only as coherent systems, underestimates the complexity of evaluative comparison among these rationalities and cultures. (The absence of emphasis on evaluative comparison is, we recall, what makes a theoretical position ultimately a relativist one.) But such a comparison should be more rigorously interpretive than Winch imagines, involving specification of the various elements and levels that constitute cultures as *articulated* wholes. Winch's cross-cultural comparison of "forms of life" is pitched at such a high level of generality that his versions of human culture and rationality cannot register and include significant moral and imaginative practices and choices. If it is to constitute a relevant political interrogation, I would argue, the dialogue across cultures which we envision anthropological interpretation at its best to be conducting must in principle be able to include the levels of ordinary, everyday activity. For such inclusion to be possible, we need—at least—a minimal conception of rationality that can help us understand human activities, both grand and humble, as the actions of agents. Let me explain what I mean.

The Subject of Culture

For Peter Winch, the common point of all human cultures is the presence of a few "limiting notions," fundamental ideas that determine the "ethical space" of the culture, "within which the possibilities of good and evil . . . can be exercised" (p. 107). The three such notions Winch specifies are birth, sexuality, and death. Together they map the limits of possibility which define our lives for us and, consequently, outline our ethical universe. According to Winch, then, it is in this universe that rationality has its moorings. I wonder, however, if we do not lose as much as we gain if we pitch the issues on this high a level. We are, according to Winch, rational creatures able to engage in a dialogue with those who are significantly different from us, but this difference is negotiated at such a level of generality that significant aspects of human life, such as, for instance, the conditions in which we work, our struggles to forge political communities, or our varying conceptions of cultural identity and selfhood, remain unarticulated and indeed invisible.

Winch's human cultures are individually rational, and they are capable of communicating with one another in a process of hermeneutical self-critique and interrogation. But the "rationality" they share is not defined in terms specific enough to register and include a great deal of what we usually consider to be our significant practices and beliefs. It is defined merely as the overall *coherence* of the *whole*, the most general systematicity revealed in the way a culture's actions, beliefs, and intellectual judgments all hang together. Given such a broad definition, *most* of what constitutes our historical life, our humbler acts as social agents and thinkers, remains closed to transcultural dialogue, to the very extent that these acts are not ultimately subsu[...]le to birth, death, and sexuality, not registered in the systematic[...] of the whole. Winch's version of rationality as inevitably tied in th[...] ay to the large cultural schemes by which we define and live our [...] has gained in moral suppleness over the positivist or the ethno[...]ric ones, but it seems to have forfeited much of its capacity to j[...] and interpret; it may have gained in amplitude, but it has also bec[...], as it were, tone-deaf. And in matters of cultural interpretation, [...]uch, of course, depends on the *tone* of things.

A more specific commonality than the one [...]ch's definition would posit for all human cultures and societies is t[...]e implicit in the very definition of "culture" as social practice. Th[...]rspective of "practice," as it has been proposed in several developn[...]s in social theory across disciplines and methodological approach[...]does not necessarily involve the notion of a unitary and self-suf[...]nt subject as the author of

14. R. W. Connell's book *Gender and Power:[...]ty, the Person, and Sexual Politics* (Stanford: Stanford University Press, 1987) provi[...]n excellent summary of these developments and discusses quite lucidly the implic[...]s of this emphasis for social theory in general. The most original and ambitious wo[...]th this focus is Pierre Bourdieu's. See especially *Outline of a Theory of Practice*, trans. Richard Nice (Cambridge: Cambridge University Press, 1977), and, for a more succinct formulation of his theory, chaps. 2–4 of *Distinction: A Social Critique of the Judgement of Taste*, trans. Richard Nice (Cambridge: Harvard University Press, 1984). The idea that social actions are necessarily "recursive," i.e., never entirely original and always a revision of existing social meanings, practices, and institutions, is explained quite well by Anthony Giddens in *The Constitution of Society: Outline of the Theory of Structuration* (Cambridge: Polity Press, 1984).

its actions. The basic claims would include the following: humans make their world; they make their world in conditions they inherit, which are not all within their control; theoretically, understanding this "making" involves redefining social structures and cultural institutions as not simply given but *constituted* and, hence, as containing the possibility of being changed. Moreover, in this conception, humans are seen as individual and collective *agents* in their world, and their practices can be specified for analysis without a necessary reduction to their subjective beliefs and intentions. Of course, the agents' intentions and beliefs about their practices are not irrelevant (since agents can be aware of their purposes and actions), but these beliefs cannot be considered the sole determinant of the meaning of the practice. "Culture" is thus best understood as defining the realm of human choices in (potentially) definable contexts, choices of individuals and collectives as potentially self-aware agents. It is in effect a field of practices, a field constituted in part by the assumptions, values, and beliefs that accompany the actions of social agents. It is the significance of such agency which Winch's related definitions of culture and rationality fail to register adequately. What enables him to hold the relativist position, with its overly general definitions of rationality and culture as large (imaginative and conceptual) schemes, is the absence in his account of any further specification of the "human" which would make comparative interpretation and evaluation of ordinary human activity possible. One specification we need to make in literary and cultural criticism, I believe, is that (rational) *agency* is a basic capacity shared by all humans *across cultures.* And in understanding the divide between "us" and "them," it is this common space we all share that needs to be elaborated and defined.

In terms of the problematics of modern social theory, Winch remains, if by default and underspecification, on the side of those who privilege the role of structure and system at the expense of human agency in their interpretations of social phenomena. In literary and cultural criticism, developments associated with structuralism and poststructuralism have made us aware of the way language and cultural and semiotic systems, seen as systems, determine both meanings and subject positions. The political agendas of these movements have been tied to a genealogical analysis of European humanism, and a great deal of attention has been paid to the deconstruction of one of the hallmarks of modern European history—the subject, an effect of specific discursive and institutional forces masquerading as universal man. In this archaeological critical climate, instances of positive elaboration of the human have been noticeably absent. This absence is, we recognize at first, due to a salutary caution. We are all familiar with accounts of "the human" which are patently speculative and serve sexist, racist, and imperialist programs. We are also aware of how historical knowledge can be used selectively to construct such accounts, and how these definitions can be made to serve dangerous political ends. But the larger question that a philosophical anthropology pursues (regarding the capacities, tasks, and limits that might make up a specifically human existence) will not go away, quite simply because our analyses of social and cultural phenomena often involve acknowledged or implicit answers to this and related questions. To the extent that criticism deals with "culture"— that is, engages in the interpretation of texts and contexts in the light of what people, individually and collectively, do, think, and make of their lives—these questions regarding the *subject* of cultural practices will remain to be dealt with explicitly. A thoroughgoing deconstruction of idealist humanism and its self-authorizing subject should be seen as clearing the ground for reconsideration of the problems involved.

It is in the context of political criticism, with its specific concern with other values, texts, and cultures, that the need for a minimal account of the human, defining a commonality we all share, becomes immediate and clear. Donald Davidson has shown how an interpretation of the Other is dependent on an acknowledgment of common ground. Arguing against the general idea of radical untranslatability (between conceptual schemes, cultures, rationalities, and so on) which extreme relativism assumes, Davidson has stressed that we appreciate differences to precisely the extent that we acknowledge our pool of shared words, thoughts, and ideas.[15] Indeed, "we improve the clarity and bite of declarations of difference . . . by enlarging the basis of shared (translatable) language or of shared opinion" (p. 197). Davidson concludes the famous essay in which he makes this argument by saying that there is no "intelligible" basis for the view that all cultures, rationalities, and languages are so radically different that we cannot translate any portion of one to the other at all; at the same time, the fond belief that all humankind shares "a common scheme and ontology" (p. 198) is not— yet—convincing either. Winch's "rationalities" are homologous to what Davidson calls "schemes" here, and I think it would be important to recognize how the competition among rationalities must be conceived, beyond Winch's own account, by specifying and elaborating shared terms, ideas, and spaces. The shared ground helps us situate and

15. Donald Davidson, "On the Very Idea of a Conceptual Scheme," in *Inquiries into Truth and Interpretation* (Oxford: Clarendon Press, 1984), pp. 183–98.

specify difference, understand where its deepest resonances might originate. If (as I argued against the relativist position earlier) we are to deal seriously with other cultures and not reduce them to insignificance or irrelevance, we need to begin by positing the following minimal commonality between us and them: the capacity to act purposefully. We must acknowledge that the human being is in principle capable of agency and basic rationality.

But what exactly does a specifically *human* agency imply? It is not limited to doing things, such as fetching a bone or building a nest. Animals and birds are capable of such things, but we do not attribute to them the kind of agency which is so crucial to defining practices and, collectively, cultures. It is not even that our actions are purposive and theirs are not, since animals do in fact act purposefully with an end in view and with varying degrees of organizational economy. But what, by our most careful contemporary philosophical accounts, distinguishes us from animals is that we possess the capacity for a certain kind of second-degree thought, that is, not merely the capacity to act purposefully but also to reflect on our actions, to *evaluate* actions and purposes in terms of larger ideas we might hold about, say, our political and moral world or our sense of beauty or form. This capacity underlies the distinction some philosophers make between the vague generic definition we might have of a member of the human species and a fuller concept of the human "person": the former is a conceptually unspecific, purely descriptive term, whereas the latter begins to define the terms and categories with which we act and learn, participate in a community and are held accountable.[16] It is this capacity for a second-order understanding and evaluation, this ability to be critically and cumulatively self-aware in relation to our actions, which defines human agency and makes possible the sociality and historicality of human existence. It is this theoretical ability in effect to possess a meaningful history which we cannot afford to deny to the cultural Other if we are to interpret it.

To go back to the example of the Azande, we would need to specify that their magical rituals, which do not make sense to "us," are at the very least the actions of agents in the sense I have just outlined. They cannot, in theory, be unintelligible and meaningless, not merely because they accord with the larger cultural and rational pattern whereby the Azande organize their lives and their values (as Winch would point

16. See especially Harry Frankfurt, "Freedom of the Will and the Concept of a Person," *Journal of Philosophy* 68 (1971), pp. 5–20; and Charles Taylor's essay "Rationality," in *Philosophy and the Human Sciences*, vol. 2 of *Philosophical Papers* (Cambridge: Cambridge University Press, 1985), pp. 134–51. The general idea is a Kantian one.

out) but also because of the more specific point that the rituals are the practices of human agents, open to us for analysis (and comparative evaluation) in terms of motives, meanings, and larger goals. But in analyzing rituals as practices, we also understand that the agents do not themselves need to be fully conscious of purpose, direction, and meaning. Indeed, rituals are a specific kind of social practice in which the role of human agency needs to be appreciated in its historically sedimented and collective dimension: most of the practitioners of the Zande ritual may well be unaware of the original intention and purpose of these activities now, which may have become dense and inscrutable in relation to contemporary individual or collective motivations. Nevertheless, no matter how apparently bizarre their manifestations, these rituals, as social and cultural phenomena, can be understood to the extent that we see them as practices which "they," the practitioners, can in principle themselves understand. In a word, "we" have no way of understanding "them" until we allow them a history, that is, grant to their actions the minimum basis of intelligibility that, in principle, human agents have of their actions. Needless to say, this principle would hold true for their values, their texts, and their languages.

Evaluating Otherness

To return to my discussion of relativism, then, it should now be clear why it is important to go beyond a simple recognition of differences across cultures. "They" ultimately do what "we" do, since they share with us a capacity for self-aware historical agency. If their terms, categories, and solutions are fundamentally different from ours, we have identified not merely a difference but what Charles Taylor calls an "incommensurability." Incommensurable activities are different, according to Taylor's useful distinction, but "they somehow occupy the same space." "The real challenge is to see the incommensurability, to come to understand how their range of possible activities, that is, the way in which they identify and distinguish activities, differs from ours."[17] The "range of possible activities" outlines the space of "cul-

17. Taylor, "Rationality," p. 145. Taylor considers our capacity for "articulation," or laying things out "in perspicuous order," the basic component of human rationality. There is a good account of the issues involved in conceiving a postpositivist rationality in Hilary Putnam, *Reason, Truth, and History* (Cambridge: Cambridge University Press, 1981); and Putnam, "Beyond Historicism," in *Realism and Reason*, vol. 3 of *Philosophical Papers* (Cambridge: Cambridge University Press, 1983), pp. 284–303. I develop this discussion of agency and rationality in the next two chapters.

ture," but in this definition culture is grounded in a specific and important common feature. The centrality of practice in this understanding of culture, emphasizing the social actions of individuals and collectives in definable situations, enriches our notion of difference by historicizing it.

Only when we have defined our commonality in this way can the why question, about the reason underlying different practices and different choices, become not only intelligible but also *necessary*. For given this essential common space, otherness appears not as insular or merely contiguous but as a complex historical phenomenon, available to us only through hermeneutical comparison and specification. Mere difference leads, as I said earlier, to a sentimental charity, for there is nothing in its logic which necessitates our attention to the other. Winch's sophisticated relativism emphasizes the ethical dimension, but to the extent that it, too, remains underspecified in its conception of rationality, its political implications are at best vague. The rationality that a political-cultural criticism cannot afford to ignore is implicit in the very definition of human agency I have sketched, the practical capacity that all human "persons" and "cultures" in principle possess to understand their actions and evaluate them in terms of their (social and historical) significance for them. It is this issue that relativism, in both the extreme and the sophisticated formulations I have discussed, obscures.

I do not see how political criticism (poststructuralist or otherwise) can afford to deny this minimal rationality that is implicit in human agency or avoid theorizing what it entails. Consideration of the question of rationality is unnecessarily complicated if we confuse the kinds of basic definitional issues I have been outlining here with the philosophical search for large schemes that have traditionally been called reason. The search for reason, understood as the grand foundational structure that would subtend (and hence explain) all human capacities and ground all knowledge, is now probably best seen as a noble but failed dream. But that does not mean that there is no rational component to human actions or, more crucial, that we can afford to ignore this rationality (philosophically). Drawing on cognitive psychological theory, Christopher Cherniak has argued against Cartesian attempts to define the ideal epistemic agent, since "the fact that a person's actions fall short of ideal rationality need not make them in any way less intelligible to us." Often, he continues, "we have a simple explanation of why the person cannot accomplish all inferences that are apparently appropriate for him—namely, that he has finite cognitive resources."[18] But recognizing that human agency can be defined only in the context of this unavoidable finitude need not be cause for despair, according to Cherniak; rather, it is an essential precondition for understanding the rationality of agenthood and for orienting our search toward a "context-sensitive" rather than a "highly idealized" reason. Since for political criticism the concern with agency must be crucial, it would be debilitating at the present moment to confuse the claims of an ideal and comprehensive reason with the basic capacities we can identify and define in terms of the different kinds of rationality they involve.[19]

Moreover, once we understand that human rationality need not be simply a formal matter, as positivists (like Gellner) insist, but is instead a fundamental capacity for reflection and articulation which underlies our social actions and enables us to be historical creatures, we can begin to realize what else is at stake in all this for political criticism. So long as we base our political analyses of culture on relativist grounds, avoiding the challenge posed by the competing claims of various (cultural) rationalities, we will surrender complex historical knowledge of Others to sentimental ethical gestures in their direction. We might remain wary of ethnocentric evaluation of alterity, but there is a basic evaluation involved in positing connections, perceiving similarities and differences, organizing complex bodies of information into provisionally intelligible wholes. Central to this process of evaluative judgment, with its minimal tasks of ordering and creating hierarchies of significance, is the understanding of humans across cultural and historical divides as capable of the minimal rationality implicit in agency. This cross-cultural commonality is one limit our contemporary political notions of difference and otherness need to acknowledge and theorize.

Relativism and Literary Theory

Why are so many scholars working in literary and cultural theory drawn to relativism? Are there any cogent intellectual reasons, apart from the political ones I have been discussing? My view is that for many literary theorists cultural relativism of some sort is sanctioned by a deeper epistemological relativism or skepticism. And such an epistemological view (or attitude) is supposed to derive from the genuine antipos-

18. Christopher Cherniak, *Minimal Rationality* (Cambridge: MIT Press, 1986), p. 20.
19. For an elaboration of this claim, see Chapter 7.

itivist insight of modern thought that all knowledge is contextual and mediated by theories and paradigms. Such a link between the contextual and theory-laden nature of knowledge, on the one hand, and epistemological skepticism or relativism, on the other, may have originally been suggested by Nietzsche's assertion that there are no facts, "only interpretations."[20] Nietzsche was cautioning against a purely positivist view of inquiry and an impossibly abstract and asocial account of "objective" knowledge, for he wished to draw attention to his own naturalistic account of "interpretations." They ultimately serve our "needs," he said, our "drives and their For and Against" (p. 267). Neitzsche's postmodernist followers often try to develop a progressive, anticolonialist politics on the basis of his epistemological perspectivism. They argue in effect that since old colonizing habits die hard, we need an extreme form of cultural relativism in order to avoid imposing our "needs and drives" on the (cultural) other. In his influential book *The Postmodern Condition*, for instance, Lyotard provides an idealized account of cross-cultural contact between unequal "traditional" and "modern" cultures.[21] Traditional cultures, says Lyotard, rely on narratives to cement "the social bond"; narrative is the preeminent form through which they formulate "their knowledge." Modern, "scientific" cultures, on the other hand, rely both on "proof[s]" and on a "metaphysical" view that "the same referent cannot supply a plurality of contradictory or inconsistent proofs" (p. 24). Scientific knowledge and narrative knowledge are, moreover, systematic and coherent on their own terms and also entirely incommensurable: "Both are composed of sets of statements; the statements are 'moves' made by the players within the framework of generally applicable rules; these rules are specific to each particular kind of knowledge, and the 'moves' judged to be 'good' in one cannot be of the same type as those judged 'good' in another" (p. 26). There is no overlapping space here, no possibility of a common world to which the different cultures could refer in different and partial ways. "It is . . . impossible to judge the existence or validity of narrative knowledge on the basis of scientific knowledge and vice versa: the relevant criteria are different. All we can do is gaze in wonderment at the diversity of discursive species" (p. 26).

This kind of relativism is based on the conjunction of a certain (dubious) anthropological account (the exclusive reliance of traditional cul-

20. Friedrich Nietzsche, *The Will to Power*, trans. Walter Kaufmann and R. J. Hollingdale, ed. Kaufmann (New York: Vintage, 1968), p. 267.
21. Jean-François Lyotard, *The Postmodern Condition*, trans. Geoff Bennington and Brian Massumi (Minneapolis: University of Minnesota Press, 1984), p. 24.

tures on the "narrative form") and a particular view of knowledge (the primacy of the culture-specific "rules" of the knowledge game, the impossibility of seeking a common, cross-cultural referent, and so on).[22] The goal is to overcome ethnocentrism and to promote tolerance, to "gaze in wonderment" at the other, unwilling to judge, hastily or otherwise. But this kind of tolerance, as we have seen, is won at a great cost. Whether or not relativism is underwritten by the epistemological view Lyotard and other postmodernists hold, cultural relativism of any kind is unlikely to be of help in engaging another culture in a noncolonizing dialogue. If "we" decide that "they" are so different from "us" that we and they have no common "criteria" (Lyotard's term) by which to evaluate (and, necessarily, even to interpret) each other, we may avoid making ethnocentric errors, but we have also, by the same logic, precluded the possibility that they will ever have anything to teach us. Moreover, we may gain only an overly general and abstract kind of tolerance, divorced from an understanding of the other culture. Given the relativist view of pure difference, difference can never represent genuine cross-cultural disagreement about the way the world is or about the right course of action in a particular situation. There is simply no need to worry about the other culture's views; they provide no reason to make us question our own views or principles. We are equal but irredeemably separate.

The lure of epistemological relativism is especially strong when the justified and reasonable caution about ethnocentric idealizations of rationality and a narrow view of objectivity is inflated to a vague and undifferentiated skepticism toward knowledge. This specifically postmodernist attitude is as theoretically underjustified as it is debilitating for cross-cultural inquiry. It coexists, however, with a language of respect for otherness and what Lyotard calls "the desire for the unknown" (p. 67). Gayatri Spivak, who draws heavily on a postmodernist epistemology, asserts that all explanations are suspect because they always "marginal[ize]."[23] Similarly, Jonathan Culler identifies as the "defining feature of post-structuralism" an epistemological claim concerning "the breakdown of the distinction between language and metalanguage."[24] The objectivity of metalanguage, the language of explanation,

22. For a critique of Lyotard's conception of reason, see Seyla Benhabib, "Epistemologies of Postmodernism: A Rejoinder to Jean-François Lyotard," in Feminism/Postmodernism, ed. Linda Nicholson (New York: Routledge, 1990), pp. 113–16.

23. Gayatri Chakravorty Spivak, "Explanation and Culture: Marginalia," in In Other Worlds (New York: Methuen, 1987), p. 113, and cf. 105–6.

24. Jonathan Culler, Framing the Sign (Norman: University of Oklahoma Press, 1988), p. 139.

is compromised by the very nature of language or discourse. Thus we are suspicious not only of the grand narratives Lyotard cautions against but also of every account that claims to explain something objectively: "Notions of realism, of rationality, of mastery, of explanation" all "belong to [a] phallocentric" view of the world.[25] In all these gestures and claims, what emerges is an overly generalized and unqualified suspicion of objectivity and explanation. In those cases where such skepticism is conjoined with a relativism of some kind (as, say, for Lyotard), we are left in the uncomfortable position of seeking a noncolonizing relationship with the other culture but accepting a theoretical premise that makes anything that can be called a relationship impossible. Neither agreement nor disagreement is possible in a cross-cultural encounter where otherness provokes nothing but "wonderment" as a cognitive stance. If we adopt this stance or accept the skeptical or relativist premises on which it is based, it is difficult to make decolonization a meaningful project involving cross-cultural contact and dialogue. And it is equally difficult to imagine any kind of multiculturalist project that requires learning from others.

We can learn from others only if we take them seriously enough to imagine situations in which they might in fact be wrong about some things, in ways that we can specify and understand. The version of multiculturalism that demands a suspension of judgment on purely a priori grounds offers us at best a weak pluralist image of noninterference and peaceful coexistence which is based on the abstract notion that everything about the other culture is (equally) valuable. Given the lack of understanding or knowledge of the other, however, the ascription of value (and of equality among cultures) is either meaningless or patronizing. Genuine respect depends on a judgment based on understanding, arrived at through difficult epistemic and ethical negotiations. Charles Taylor, for instance, agrees with "the presumption . . . that all human cultures that have animated whole societies over some considerable stretch of time have something important to say to all human beings." But this, he cautions, is only "a starting hypothesis with which we ought to approach the study of any other culture. The validity of the claim has to be demonstrated concretely in the actual study of the culture."[26] That this "actual study" is complexly mediated by our own culture's biases, ideologies, and theoretical paradigms makes cross-cul-

25. Jonathan Culler, On Deconstruction (Ithaca: Cornell University Press, 1982), p. 62.
26. Charles Taylor, "The Politics of Recognition," in Multiculturalism and the Politics of Recognition: An Essay by Charles Taylor, ed. Amy Gutmann (Princeton: Princeton University Press, 1992), pp. 66–67.

tural encounters of any kind unavoidably difficult, but a retreat into either a positivist view of objective knowledge or the kind of skepticism or relativism I have identified cannot provide a way out of this difficulty.

What is required for this "actual study" and for the sort of cross-cultural dialogue it enables is the belief that "getting it right" is often important, for both "us" and "them." Nicholas Sturgeon, a philosopher who has written insightfully about the inadequacies of moral relativism, explains why we should be wary of hastily presuming that this or that cross-cultural disagreement is in principle "unsettleable."

> Disagreement is a challenge to our views and a stimulus to inquiry, for we care that our views be correct. . . . To be sure, we are not equally challenged by disagreement with just anyone: we are intellectually most disconcerted when challenged by people who seem competent, thoughtful, knowledgeable in ways relevant to the issue, and so on. But, of course, our adversaries in the moral disagreements to which relativists apply their doctrine will tend to include people with such qualifications: if that were not so, the disagreements would have little chance of looking unsettleable to us. To be told that these disagreements are not genuine, therefore, and that we and the other parties are merely talking past one another, is to be deprived of an important motive for trying to understand the opposing viewpoint, seek common intellectual ground, and in other ways learn from one another. . . . Listening carefully to opposing views, regarding them as a challenge to one's own and attempting to appropriate their insights is, among other things, a mark of mutual respect that can provide a bond even across considerable disagreement.[27]

Contrary to relativists, who emphasize almost exclusively the extent to which cultures are distinct, different, and radically incommensurable (see Lyotard's division between the traditional and the modern), many nonrelativists say that we can understand both differences and commonalities adequately only when we approach particular cross-cultural disputes in an open-ended way. Thus, a basic question to ask about particular disagreements is whether—and to what extent—they refer to the same things, the same features of the world. This question cannot be settled a priori; it must be part of the "actual study" of cultures, the evolving empirical inquiry that should accompany and inform any

27. Nicholas L. Sturgeon, "Moral Disagreement and Moral Relativism," in *Cultural Pluralism and Moral Knowledge*, ed. Ellen Frankel Paul, Fred D. Miller Jr., and Jeffrey Paul (Cambridge: Cambridge University Press, 1994), pp. 112–13.

theoretical cross-cultural negotiation. Where no common reference is found, there is no disagreement. Where, notwithstanding the differences in language or conceptual framework, there is at least a partial overlap, however, there exists the possibility of genuine dialogue based on a critical understanding. Vital cross-cultural interchange depends on the belief that there is a "world" that we share (no matter how partially) with the other culture, a world whose causal relevance is not purely intracultural. It is possible, on this view, to provide more—or less—accurate accounts of these causal features. Claims about the "accuracy" of such accounts are themselves partly the product of intercultural negotiations, based on various epistemological considerations and criteria; these claims cannot be justified through an exclusive reference to a transcendental—unmediated—world. The process of developing this shared epistemic and social space, however, is hardly peculiar to cross-cultural encounters. Indeed, it characterizes the everyday practices of cooperative inquiry within the most homogeneous of social groups. Wherever intellectual disagreements appear and need to be resolved, when "we care that our views be correct," as Sturgeon puts it, and not exclusively that we achieve consensus (which could be done, on purely pragmatic grounds, through subtle coercion or manipulation), inquiry is simultaneously theoretical and empirical, a complex form of cooperative social practice open to revision and change.

What emerges as an alternative to relativism and skepticism is thus a postpositivist conception of objectivity as a goal of inquiry which includes the possibility of error, self-correction, and improvement. On this view, objectivity is a social achievement rather than an impossible dream of purity and transcendence; it is based on our evolving understanding of the sources and causes of various kinds of error. Proponents of postmodernist epistemology are in fact often wary of objectivity to the very extent that they have an undifferentiated view of error as ubiquitous and inevitable. The alternative epistemological position I am sketching in this book—that of a postpositivist "realism"—offers a less extreme view of knowledge, for it proposes that theoretical accounts of objectivity depend on explanatory accounts of error and distortion. Both kinds of accounts base understanding—as well as its limits—in social practice.[28]

28. For a contrasting account in contemporary literary theory, see Barbara Herrnstein Smith, "Belief and Resistance: A Symmetrical Account," *Critical Inquiry* 18 (Autumn 1991), 125–39. The best survey of these general issues is provided by Philip Kitcher, who shows (among other things) how the rejection of apriorism in epistemology can lead to a more "naturalistic" understanding of "the social dimensions of human knowl-

This general discussion might help make clear, then, why in order to understand the social bases of knowledge we need to understand exactly how our social location has *epistemic* consequences. For we can be right or wrong (in different ways, in varying degrees) about the way our social locations enable or inhibit certain kinds of understanding. Our methodological and moral scruples refer beyond ourselves and our immediate relationships to the social world; in fact, they are part of its fabric, its essential furniture. Relativism blurs the outlines of this world, substituting a hazy vision of cultural equality for accurate knowledge and genuine engagement. The next two chapters are an attempt to sketch the rudimentary outlines of a realist theory of knowledge, culture, and society which would make such an engagement possible.

edge." Kitcher, "The Naturalists Return," in "Philosophy in Review: Essays on Contemporary Philosophy," special issue of *Philosophical Review* 101 (January 1992), 113. According to this understanding, "the ideal of [epistemology as] a meliorative project" is "preserve[d]" in a revised form (p. 114). Richard Boyd, "How to Be a Moral Realist," in *Essays on Moral Realism*, ed. Geoffrey Sayre-McCord (Ithaca: Cornell University Press, 1988), pp. 181–228, is an important discussion of the relationship between scientific and moral epistemology; my understanding of these issues owes a great deal to it, as well as to many conversations with Boyd.

6

ON SITUATING OBJECTIVE KNOWLEDGE

The various poststructuralist theses I have examined in the preceding chapters and the general positions (such as cultural relativism or liberal pluralism) that are seen as vaguely implied or entailed by them constitute one strand of contemporary postmodernism. The other is the version of pragmatism Richard Rorty has developed and popularized. Rorty's postmodernist pragmatism is seen as complementing the poststructuralists' positions because it originates in a thorough critique of epistemological foundationalism, and because it rejects the image of philosophy as an ahistorical discipline that searches for the absolute ground of all human knowledge.

This chapter examines the sources of antifoundationalism in modern thought and shows what critiques of foundationalism tell us about one of the issues I have been discussing in these pages from the beginning—the "social situatedness" of knowledge. If knowledge is seen not as grounded in ahistorical truths but as socially situated, that is because the *justification* of knowledge is understood as a social affair. The rejection of foundationalism does not necessarily lead to postmodernist positions such as relativism or skepticism about objectivity, however. Indeed, as I show in this chapter, the strongest position to which a thoroughgoing antifoundationalism leads is postpositivist realism, not any version of postmodernism.

First, I identify the key components of the case against foundationalism, and by following part of the trajectory of Rorty's impressive account in *Philosophy and the Mirror of Nature*, I show how they do not necessarily lead to postmodernism.[1] At key points in the argument I part company with Rorty, however, since I think there are many reasons why his pragmatist conclusions are not the best ones to derive from the critique of foundationalism. Central to Rorty's critique of traditional conceptions of philosophy is the antipositivist insight that can be identified as epistemological holism, which is the thesis that we justify knowledge (for example, "confirm" scientific hypotheses) not by holding up isolated claims to see how they "fit" with "the world" but rather by examining their coherence with everything else we know. In literary theory and cultural studies we acknowledge this kind of holism when we point to hermeneutic circularity, for instance, and to the kind of theory dependence it implies. Epistemological holism thus suggests why positivist conceptions of pure observation in science or disinterested interpretation in social inquiry are limited and impoverished. My major goal in what is roughly the second half of this chapter is to show that a politically useful realist conception of objectivity can be developed by making holism and antifoundationalism much more concrete and specific. This specificity will explain the deeper basis of many postmodernist arguments, and it can also suggest what form a postpositivist realist alternative can take.

The first section is thus devoted to a discussion of Rorty's arguments, outlining the main components of his case against foundationalism and examining the pragmatist conclusions he derives from them. I focus on the intellectual sources of epistemological holism, especially in the philosophy of science, and explain the implications for historical inquiry and cultural interpretation of the ideas of key thinkers such as Quine and Kuhn. In the next section I develop this discussion of historical inquiry by defining such key concepts as explanation and causation, which help outline the differences between postmodernism and realism. In particular, I compare the notion of causation implied in the Derridean critique of Western metaphysics with the naturalistic, antispeculative view of causation which postpositivist realists advocate. This view I develop as part of a more comprehensive account of human knowledge, of both the natural and the social sciences and the relations among them.

The Social Justification of Knowledge

The primary reason Rorty is seen as a philosophical friend of literary and cultural theorists is that he has provided in the second part of his

1. Richard Rorty, *Philosophy and the Mirror of Nature* (Princeton: Princeton University Press, 1979), hereafter cited in the text as *PMN*.

justly famous *Philosophy and the Mirror of Nature* a devastating critique of the traditional image of epistemology based on truth and its accurate representation in the mind. In some ways this critique is parallel to the poststructuralist analysis of the problematic of representation, in particular the Heideggerian and Derridean view that ocularity and unmediated presence are the constitutive epistemological metaphors of Western metaphysics. This parallel between the two traditions is not accidental; Heidegger is one of the heroic antifoundationalists in Rorty's account, although the critique in part 2 does not draw directly on either Heidegger or his followers. The primary focus is on the history and self-image of modern philosophy in the Cartesian-Kantian mold and the critiques of this tradition which have been formulated within Anglo-American philosophy by such thinkers as Quine and Donald Davidson, Wilfrid Sellars and Kuhn.

Let me begin with a basic sketch of Rorty's arguments. The traditional image of philosophy, with a foundationalist epistemology at its center, seeks from mental representations an increasingly accurate picture of the world-as-it-is. This kind of philosophy, Rorty says, is flawed at its very core. Truth is not a matter of correspondence to a stable and singular world outside, for there is no such world.[2] Nor can truth be sought by aprioristic reasoning and refinement of the "mirrors" that we see as the "privileged representations" of reality. Instead of seeking epistemological foundations on which all other kinds of knowledge can be based, we need to recognize that knowledge is a matter of social practice, constructed historically by humans, and is thus always subject to revision and change. "Truth" is made, not found. It cannot be that bedrock of nonempirical necessity which, once discovered, will guide us once and for all in organizing all our knowledge. It is defined by our practices of justification and thus tied to human communities, situated in history.

Now this is a very bare summary, but it must be easy to see even in this account that Rorty raises important issues for contemporary literary and cultural theory, especially a theory concerned with examining postmodernist claims. For one thing, the most general relation between theory and its object, that which the theory seeks to explain, is thrown into relief. What implications can one see in this account for our explanations and interpretations of social and historical phenomena? Are our

2. This view about the existence of a mind-independent "world" makes Rorty seem a clear-cut "irrealist," but in fact his position is a little more complicated. Michael Devitt has shown convincingly that Rorty may in fact be a closet realist. See Devitt, "Rorty's Mirrorless World," *Midwest Studies in Philosophy* 12 (1988), 157–77.

various explanations in fact just alternative "descriptions"? What is the status of (social and historical) explanation? Does the critique of epistemological foundationalism amount to a rejection of all notions of objective knowledge? Dealing directly with Rorty's arguments and the kind of arguments he is summarizing will help us specify what exactly it is that literary theorists need to learn from contemporary philosophy, in what ways it complements and questions related developments in what we call poststructuralism, and what kinds of social and political-theoretical implications these ideas have.

I hope to show that Rorty's critique of the epistemology-centered philosophical project that has determined the self-image of Western academic culture as a whole is accurate and useful for our purposes, but the critique of foundationalism needs to be understood precisely so that we do not see it as endorsing relativism. For cultural criticism as well as contemporary philosophy, to the extent that they seek to analyze and explain social phenomena, the question of truth is not settled in quite the way Rorty sometimes suggests. Rorty is weakest at the very point where he slides from the critique of epistemology to social and political theory. The work of philosophers such as Quine, on which Rorty's critique of foundationalism is based, shows that the justification of knowledge is essentially a holistic matter and thus quite unlike what the atomistic epistemology of the empiricist program assumes. Quine points to the inevitable need for "theory" in the most basic confirmatory practices of science, since even "observation" is profoundly mediated by conscious or unacknowledged presuppositions about the world. This general point is akin to the hermeneutical position of Heidegger and Gadamer, and it should lead (according to Quine) not to relativism but to a rejection of the conception of epistemology as an a priori enterprise requiring purely "rational reconstruction" of the discoveries of science. Epistemic norms are themselves to be empirically investigated, to be examined in the same way we examine other features of the natural world. From the perspective of such a "naturalized" antifoundationalist epistemology, "objectivity" is seen as essentially mediated, socially and theoretically situated. Objective knowledge is gained not by rejecting all forms of "bias" (that is not possible) but rather by examining the epistemic consequences of our various biases, social and theoretical. Quine and other naturalists maintain that we should conceive of epistemology as a meliorative enterprise, one that tells us about the deeper (theory-mediated) reasons for our cognitive successes and failures. The goal is to understand how we epistemically limited creatures might go about producing a good "structured account" of the world, that is, a corrigible but reliable causal explanation of how nature and society work.

From Skepticism to Foundationalism

Descartes is generally credited with founding modern philosophy, in part because of the antispeculative method he outlined for philosophical inquiry, a method based on the analysis of clear and distinct ideas that survive our most rigorous skepticism about the external world. But the "problem of the external world," as Rorty points out, is tied to a problematic that involves the creation of the mental as a distinct realm, "carving out inner space" (PMN, p. 139), for the external world is defined in a particular way once we assume the mental as our primary space. The problem then becomes one of getting from the inner to the outer, from mind to world. The centrality of epistemology to modern philosophy is dependent on this kind of "skeptical" problematic, this set of assumptions about inner and outer, for it generates the further (closely related) issues of mirroring, accurate representation, and the search for certainty. Rorty explains: "The idea of a discipline devoted to 'the nature, origin, and limits of human knowledge'—the textbook definition of 'epistemology'—required a field of study called 'the human mind,' and that field of study was what Descartes had created. The Cartesian mind simultaneously made possible veil-of-ideas skepticism and a discipline devoted to circumventing such skepticism" (p. 140). The crucial point is that these different Cartesian ideas and assumptions together constitute a problematic; that is, these assumptions and ideas, and the questions they imply, are interrelated and interdependent in a specific way.

The Cartesian problematic was not in itself sufficient to bring about the new image of epistemology in seventeenth-century Europe, however. A crucial assumption that complemented this problematic was the general empiricist confusion (emblematized in Locke's writings) between "knowledge of" (for example, some thing) and "knowledge that" (for example, some proposition is or is not true). Perceptual "knowledge," says Rorty, drawing on T. H. Green's analysis of Locke, cannot be confused with knowledge as communities of human inquirers use it when they talk of knowledge as "justified belief" (p. 141); knowledge in the latter sense cannot be reduced to or exclusively underwritten by the "proper functioning of our organism" (p. 141). We justify propositions in a more complex way, in part by explaining their relations to other propositions. Locke and other seventeenth-century thinkers, Rorty maintains,

> simply did *not* think of knowledge as justified true belief. This was because they did not think of knowledge as a relation between a person and a proposition. *We* find it natural to think of "what S knows" as the collection of propositions completing true statements by S which begin "I know that. . . ." When we realize that the blank may be filled by such various material as "this is red," "e = mc²," "my Redeemer liveth," and "I shall marry Jane," we are rightly skeptical of the notion of "the nature, origin, and limits of human knowledge," and of a department of thought devoted to this topic. But Locke did not think of "knowledge that" as the primary form of knowledge. He thought, as had Aristotle, of "knowledge of" as prior to "knowledge that," and thus of knowledge as a relation between persons and objects rather than persons and propositions. Given that picture, the notion of an examination of our "faculty of understanding" makes sense, as does the notion that it is fitted to deal with some sorts of objects and not with others. It makes even more sense if one is convinced that this faculty is something like a wax tablet upon which objects make *impressions*, and one thinks of "having an impression" as in itself a *knowing* rather than a causal antecedent of knowing. (pp. 141–42)

Locke and the empiricists "shuffle," as Rorty points out, between the conception of knowledge as the mind's "having an idea" (in the sense of having it impressed upon it as sense data are upon a tablet) and the conception of knowledge as "that which results from forming justified judgments" (p. 146). Indeed, there is a surreptitious claim that the two are the same, that the description of a succession of apprehensions is not different from explaining a belief based on judgment.

Rorty's identification of the central problem in empiricism and how it infects the problematic of traditional epistemology ought to be familiar to students of Heidegger, Derrida, and a whole line of poststructuralist writers: the pervasive and constitutive use of ocular metaphors to conceive of the process of knowing, with their implied norms of unmediated and immediately available perceptual knowledge, and the hierarchy of gradually receding mediations and abstractions from that "presence." For Heidegger, as is well known, the "representational" framework that constitutes modern Cartesian and post-Cartesian thought is the essence of Western metaphysics; indeed, this definition provides Heidegger and Derrida with one of the most sensitive tools of antimetaphysical historical inquiry, making possible a radically empirical project that pursues the question of the historically "new" with a tenacious respect for the old. And both the "behaviorists" Rorty draws on (Quine, Sellars, et al.) and the Heideggerians (such as Derrida) would agree on the need to question the foundations that modern philosophy has sought for itself using such metaphors, challenging an entire history of philosophy by interrogating its hidden epistemic norms and values.

Wholes, Things, Theories

The crucial argument against empiricism is based on a reformulation of the relation between things and theories, between, on the one hand, those entities which the empiricist sought to isolate and study to gain knowledge and, on the other, those larger patterns of meaning, those intricate webs of belief and knowledge, which are in some dialectical way related to these entities. Basic to the empiricist program is the idea that the features of the world out of whose analysis we develop our knowledge of the world are themselves available to us as isolatable units. Thus, individual sense data can be scrutinized to understand facts about the world, and individual sensory experiences can be examined to verify whether or not a proposition is meaningful. (The latter idea is at the core of the "verificationist" theory of meaning made popular by the logical positivists in the early years of this century.)[3]

W. V. O. Quine's epistemological holism is a critique of this way of conceiving knowledge. His critique takes the form of a reevaluation of the relation between theories and individual statements (say, about individual units of the world). He attacks the famous verificationist theory of meaning, the notion that the meaning of statements can be confirmed as true (or disconfirmed, as the case may be) by an empiricist process of relating it to "confirmatory experiences."[4] Quine's problem with this conception of meaning is that, like much of the traditional empiricist program, it rests on the idea that "the truth of a statement is somehow analyzable into a linguistic component and a factual component" (p. 41). Quine finds this distinction misleading. Statements cannot be adequately analyzed as isolatable individual units. To put it simply, Quine suggests that one cannot cut up either "language" or

3. The empiricist model of "confirmation" or testing of theories is basic to the positivist accounts of scientific and social explanation. The critique of empiricism Rorty draws on here is central to the realist project as well.

4. W. V. O. Quine, "Two Dogmas of Empiricism," in From a Logical Point of View (Cambridge: Harvard University Press, 1961), p. 41.

"facts" (significant aspects of the *world*) into isolatable units and then proceed to analyze them to gain knowledge about either them or the world. "The idea of defining a symbol in use was . . . an advance over the impossible term-by-term empiricism of Locke and Hume. The statement, rather than the term, came with [Gottlob] Frege to be recognized as the unit accountable to an empiricist critique. But what I am now urging is that even in taking the statement as unit we have drawn our grid too finely. The unit of empirical significance is the whole of science" (p. 42). Then follows that famous passage wherein Quine lays out his holistic view of scientific knowledge:

> The totality of our so-called knowledge or beliefs, from the most casual matters of geography and history to the profoundest laws of atomic physics or even of pure mathematics and logic, is a man-made fabric which impinges on experience only along the edges. Or, to change the figure, total science is like a field of force whose boundary conditions are experience. A conflict with experience at the periphery occasions readjustments in the interior of the field. Truth values have to be redistributed over some of our statements. Reevaluation of some statements entails reevaluation of others, because of their logical interconnections—the logical laws being in turn simply certain further statements of the system, certain further elements of the field. Having reevaluated one statement, we must reevaluate some others, which may be statements logically connected to the first or may be the statements of logical connection themselves. But the total field is so underdetermined by its boundary conditions, experience, that there is much latitude of choice as to what statements to reevaluate in the light of any single contrary experience. No particular experiences are linked with any particular statements in the interior of the field, except indirectly through considerations of equilibrium affecting the field as a whole. (pp. 42–43)

Quine's holism is based on an understanding of "the total field" as "so underdetermined by its boundary conditions, experience, that there is much latitude of choice as to what statements to reevaluate in the light of any single contrary experience." The verificationist procedure of confirming or disconfirming individual statements is, according to Quine, misleading because it assumes that experiential verification bears on all statements *in the same way*, regardless of their position in the totality of knowledge and beliefs.

For Quine, it is not individual statements that have "empirical content" (p. 43), and the distinction between synthetic statements, true by virtue of their empirical content, and analytic statements, true "come what may" (p. 43), is untenable. For if the truth of statements is based on their relation to the whole, "any statement can be held true come what may, if we make drastic enough adjustments elsewhere in the system" (p. 43). Quine suggests the most extreme implication of this conclusion a little later: even physical objects are "posited," "conceptually imported into the situation as convenient intermediaries [for "predicting future experience in the light of past experience"]—not by definition in terms of experience, but simply as irreducible posits comparable, epistemologically, to the gods of Homer" (p. 44). This claim needs to be developed and examined more carefully. At any rate, it points to an important question; if we recall my discussion of Putnam's theory of the reference of natural kind terms, we recognize the need to be clearer about what exactly it means to say that "things" are posited. In fact, the crucial question in the larger debate over the status of the real world concerns the status of such posited *unobservable* entities as germs, electrons, or theories about the microphysical structure of matter. If scientists rely on these just as humans once relied on the idea that the earth is flat or that demons "in fact" possess us when we are seriously ill, then is it enough to say that these are mere posits, beliefs just like any other? If they occupy similar positions in our conceptual schemes, are these posits all "similar"? Should we, then, refuse to judge one set of posits in one conceptual scheme true and the other, by our best lights, false? One science, the other myth?

Rorty comes close to answering yes to these questions. That is because he subscribes to Thomas Kuhn's account of the history of science as a succession of paradigms without any deep theoretical continuity. The issue of relativism hinges on the question of continuity in science and among paradigms in general. But on this crucial point at least, Quine's answer would be different from Rorty's or Kuhn's in one significant respect. Quine's holism is not as "full-blooded" as Rorty's, and it does not lead to Rorty's conclusions in at least one way.

Before we can understand the significance of the differences between Quine's position and Rorty's, it is important to note the general ways in which holism and pragmatism—Rorty's ultimate position is a particular combination of the two—are related. One might be holistic in one's approach to individual propositions or to individual social facts and still believe that truth is not a matter to be left up to convention to define. One could believe, in other words, that even though much of what we think and believe is to be best understood only by reference to a larger web of beliefs and practices which we, as a community, hold, not everything that is true is ultimately reducible to consensus. It would be difficult to see Hegel (from whom we derive our most powerful image of holism in modern social philosophy) compromising the truth of his Absolute Spirit by making it subject to revision. In the same way, a realist could well believe that a web of beliefs and ideas ultimately determines the meaning and truth-value of our individual units of belief, without subscribing to the idea that all facts about the nonhuman universe which science is ever likely to discover are ultimately "made" by humans. It is possible, to put it briefly, to believe that there is a nonhuman universe about which we might find out more and more things (working as we do with imperfect tools and a fallible and infinitely modifiable set of instruments, concepts, and theories), which then change the way we think of our own human world. But to think that we might keep open this empirical possibility does not mean that we are making a sort of rash wager that the nonhuman world out there can be completely described once and for all. A holistic epistemology is perfectly compatible with an open-ended metaphysical position about what there *is* and our relation to "it." There is no reason to accuse such a position of necessarily hankering after metaphysical comprehensiveness, a desire to see it all from a "god's-eye view." Our account of "truth" could, in fact, recognize this partiality of our knowledge and our (human) situation in the world. The full-blooded pragmatism that Rorty advocates is dependent on retaining the holism without this kind of commitment to a respect for the nonhuman universe. His criticism of Quine reveals how he would like to develop a defense of this position. It also reveals the cost of defending this extreme kind of holism. In particular, important problems—the articulation of the "whole," an account of how the whole is sustained and how it changes, and so on—remain unaddressed, and we are left with no way of addressing these questions. The pragmatism that is developed in this account is ultimately unsatisfactory for cultural and social theory, especially a theory interested in questions of historical determination and specific forms of social change.

In the long passage from "Two Dogmas of Empiricism" I quoted, it is clear that Quine's holism is based on the recognition that the "totality" comprising our knowledge and beliefs is *differentiated*, and the implication is that a good account of "reality" is *structured*. The core of this totality is affected in a different way from the periphery, and the "boundary conditions," influenced as they might be by "experience," do not determine the totality enough to change the "interior of the field" directly. What mediates between change in the boundary conditions (say, the disconfirmation on the basis of experience of one of the less central units of belief constituting science) and any change in the whole is a structure of articulated and necessarily hierarchical relations between boundary and interior which defines the whole. Quine devotes a great deal of attention to this very question of how the totality is defined, and it is necessary to examine some of its implications to understand Quinean holism.

In one of Quine's most famous examples, for instance, in the essay "Speaking of Objects," the question of totality is specified through a consideration of translation from a completely foreign language to a known one. Even faced with an obvious instance in which a speaker points to a rabbit and utters a sentence, the linguist from "our" culture is not able to get all that far. Translation of the utterance into an assertion that "this is a rabbit" or "a rabbit is present" or anything seemingly unproblematical of that sort is likely to raise deeper questions about whether or not the foreign language—with a structure all its own—possesses the capacity to identify individual units in our ways or to define the identity of objects in the way our familiar language does. Here is a crucial and delightful moment in Quine's discussion of the issue:

> Given that a native sentence says that a so-and-so is present, and given that the sentence is true when and only when a rabbit is present, it by no means follows that the so-and-so are rabbits. They might be all the various temporal segments of rabbits. They might be all the integral or undetached parts of rabbits. In order to be able to decide among these alternatives we need to be able to ask more than whether a so-and-so is present. We need to be able to ask whether this is the same so-and-so as that, and whether one so-and-so is present or two. We need something like the apparatus of identity and quantification; hence far more than we are in a position to avail ourselves of in a language in which our high point as of even date is rabbit-announcing.
>
> And the case is yet worse: we do not even have evidence for taking the native expression as of the form "A so-and-so is present"; it could as well be construed with an abstract singular term, as meaning that rabbithood is locally manifested. Better just "Rabbiteth," like "Raineth."[5]

Quine's argument is that totalities (languages, conceptual schemes, and so on) are structured in particular ways; they do not just "hang to-

5. W. V. O. Quine, "Speaking of Objects," in *Ontological Relativity and Other Essays* (New York: Columbia University Press, 1969), pp. 2–3.

gether" nonchalantly. We might not be able to define all the details of articulation of this structure, but they can be studied empirically. That there is a hierarchy of articulations is in fact an empirical claim as much as it is a commonsensical idea. This claim Rorty is keen to deny, but that he does so in the spirit of Quinean holism is confusing.

What Rorty questions in Quine's philosophy is its commitment to an image of science as a quest for knowledge of what there is, for an ontology. In *Word and Object*, for instance, Quine argues that science seeks to "limn . . . the true and ultimate structure of reality." Rorty will have none of it, or of the idea that a given theory often in fact depends on a background theory as Quine puts it, "with its own primitively adopted and ultimately inscrutable ontology."[6] In the latter quotation Quine seems to be indicating that theories (particularly those with the largest scope) do not come to us as free-floating choices; often they imply obscurely understood commitments to larger images of reality. The first quotation clarifies Quine's belief that the holistic thesis is compatible with a view of knowledge as hierarchically structured, implying a plausible division of labor in which certain parts of modern science attempt to understand the deepest features of the natural—particularly the non-human—world. For Rorty, by contrast, the question of reality is a red herring. Taking Quine's holism one step further than Quine would, he asks us to consider the idea that the criteria for choosing between different accounts of reality are ultimately "aesthetic" (*PMN*, p. 203). He denies that there might be a hierarchy of the sciences even in relation to the question of reality: "Why do the *Naturwissenschaften* limn reality while the *Geisteswissenschaften* merely enable us to cope with it? What is it that sets them apart, given that we no longer think of any sort of statement having a privileged epistemological status, but of all statements as working together for the good of the race in that process of gradual holistic adjustment made famous by 'Two Dogmas of Empiricism'? Why should not the unit of empirical inquiry be the whole of culture (including both the *Natur-* and the *Geisteswissenschaften*) rather than just the whole of physical science?" (p. 201). But as we have seen in the passage from "Two Dogmas" I quoted, it is not enough to say that Quine argues for "gradual holistic adjustment." Quine's understanding of the totality of science is *specified* by reference to the difference between the "interior" of the field and its boundaries, and this specification has significant implications for his understanding of the

6. The first quotation is from *Word and Object* (Cambridge: MIT Press, 1981) p. 221, the second, from *Ontological Relativity*, p. 51; cited in *PMN*, pp. 199 and 196 respectively.

whole field. No sort of statement has a privileged epistemological status if by privilege we mean that it can establish epistemic truths by itself, but that is not to say that certain statements (and certain domains of inquiry) are not better suited to yield reliable knowledge about the largely impersonal and indeed nonhuman world. And what exactly do we lose in specificity by saying that both physics and cultural criticism help us "cope"? What kinds of questions need to be addressed before we can slide from holism about all of knowledge to this easy-going pragmatism?

Quine's thesis has proved controversial for many reasons that do not concern me directly, but one of the criticisms is worth mentioning, since it raises an issue that always appears in one form or another in various kinds of holism, and a similar problem appears in Rorty's social theory. The criticism is that the thesis does not provide an account of how change takes place or of how the system is kept stable in the first place. The question of stability and change is particularly crucial in the context of holistic theories that attempt to explain social phenomena, and the polemics over continuity and discontinuity which have shaped contemporary cultural theory might be an indication that this issue is charged with all kinds of political meaning. Indeed, as we have seen in several previous chapters, continuity in historiography is identified with an idealist problematic that is ultimately reductive and inattentive to the material complexity of history. The passage from Foucault I quoted in Chapter 5 in fact suggests the links between political respect for the space of the Other and the need to fight such continuist endeavors. Traditional historiography has become so used "to seeking origins," Foucault says, "to pushing back further and further the line of antecedents, to reconstituting traditions, to following evolutive curves, to projecting teleologies," in short, to imposing "rational" patterns and narrative outlines over our pasts and our presents, that we have forgotten how to conceive of "difference." But as I have suggested in various ways throughout this book, the main objection here is to the a priorism inherent in these historiographical choices and decisions. We need to understand both the specific kinds of a priori normative patterns that are imposed in specific contexts and the overdetermined reasons for the success of these patterns. It is misleading to say that we can rule out "continuity" in advance, especially if we understand it as the basic forms of connection and organization which constitute *any* explanation.

Before we choose between a continuist account of a historical phenomenon and an account that posits discontinuity, however, we need to address the empirical and meta-analytical issue of change, how and when we can identify it, when we see something essentially "new" (or "different") emerge, and how our theoretical accounts of the whole (of knowledge, of social structures and historical periods, and so on) enable us to identify and explain such events. An adequate social theory must, it seems, be able to tell us not only how social systems sustain themselves but also how and when the old gives way to the new. Similarly, an adequate historical explanation must go beyond mere descriptions of changing phenomena to help us understand what underlying causes helped bring about the dissolution of the old and the establishment of the new. None of this presupposes, of course, that it is simple to differentiate the old from the new; indeed, I am suggesting—along Quinean lines—that this kind of identification is an eminently theoretical matter, tied to an understanding of how the whole is structured and its components interrelated. I am arguing, in addition, something most modern social theorists would assert—that in the context of social phenomena our analysis of change is essential to any account we might construct of the interrelationships that constitute the whole.

Theory, Bias, and a Naturalized View of Knowledge

Quine's work might not address the question of change directly, but it does give us a clue as to where to look if we are concerned about such issues. I think it is evident in the lesson he wishes to draw for epistemology from the discussions of holism. For Quine the criticism of epistemology as "first philosophy," as the a priori ground on which all further knowledge is to be based, does not lead to what he calls an "epistemological nihilism," which "belittle[s] the role of evidence and . . . accentuate[s] cultural relativism."[7] Rather, he sees the critique of both idealist epistemology and the residual foundationalism of traditional empiricism as bringing into "clear focus" the task of epistemology in our times. Epistemology must be "naturalized"; it must build on the lessons of the empirical sciences, merging in fact with psychology and linguistics. For Quine, the critique of the sharp distinction between theoretical statements and observation statements leads not to a collapsing of the two but to a new way of conceiving the empirical project. Here is a crucial passage with which the pragmatist Rorty would disagree:

7. Quine, "Epistemology Naturalized," in *Ontological Relativity*, p. 87.

The observation sentence is the cornerstone of semantics. For it is . . . fundamental to the learning of meaning. Also, it is where meaning is firmest. Sentences higher up in theories have no empirical consequences they can call their own; they confront the tribunal of sensory evidence only in more or less inclusive aggregates. The observation sentence, situated at the sensory periphery of the body scientific, is the minimal verifiable aggregate; it has an empirical content all its own and wears it on its sleeve.

. . . It is no shock to the preconceptions of old Vienna to say that epistemology now becomes semantics. For epistemology remains centered as always on evidence, and meaning remains centered as always on verification; and evidence is verification. (p. 89)

Holism does not force us to the position that all of "culture" is one undifferentiated whole, or even that there can be no separation—and hierarchy—between the various sciences. In particular, the blurring of the boundaries between the natural and the human sciences which Rorty wants to see does not *follow* from the critique of foundationalism. Put very simply, developing Quine's sketch of a naturalized epistemology will enable us to conceive the hard sciences as providing us with facts about the largely impersonal world we inhabit. Thus even a holist can believe that observation and verification can lead to real knowledge, to knowledge that grows, changes, and revises itself. In this context epistemology serves the valuable function of explaining what we mean by our various observation sentences as well as explaining the revisable process whereby we come to know (propositions about ourselves and about the world in which we live). I don't think this function requires a belief, as Rorty suggests in a slightly different context, that the world can be completely and accurately described. All it requires is that we not deny that the nonhuman world "outside of us" *exists*, and that it can be causally relevant. It can shape our lives in important ways, and we can discover and know (in the sense that we can hold justified beliefs about) it. Indeed, to doubt that would be to doubt that modern science has made any progress at all in developing reliable instruments for predicting features of this natural world.[8]

One way we can place ourselves in a quandary about the reality of the real world is to pitch the discussion too high, to suppose (for no good

8. This argument for realism originates in Richard Boyd's work, and is also used by Hilary Putnam. A good survey of the issues in scientific realism and some of their implications for contemporary literary studies is provided by Paisley Livingston, *Literary Knowledge* (Ithaca: Cornell University Press, 1988), esp. chaps. 3 and 6.

reason I can imagine) that reality is a matter of all or nothing, that it must be conceived as something capable of being described in One True Picture or else that it does not exist outside our minds in any significant way. But the general possibility of a naturalized epistemology, with its open-ended reliance on the empirical sciences, is a more modest and realistic conception of the social organization of human knowledge and human frailties. Without reducing the natural sciences to the human ones, proposing an easygoing pragmatism about all facts about the world, it suggests that scientific inquiry cannot be compartmentalized into different insular domains and that science is a unified process. A student of Quine's who holds a position about the world generally called "metaphysical realism" proposes a diagnosis worth mentioning here as at least a feasible alternative to foundationalist epistemology:

> The thorough-going sceptic sets the standards of knowledge (or rational belief) too high for them ever to be achieved. Our best science shows us this. It shows us, for example, that if knowledge is to be gathered we must eliminate implausible hypotheses without being able, ultimately, to justify that elimination. It shows us that there is always an (empirical) possibility of error with any (normal) knowledge claim. Standards that our best science shows cannot be met short of instantaneous solipsism—a doctrine that is literally incredible— should be ignored. Scepticism is simply uninteresting: it throws the baby out with the bath water. . . .
>
> Having dismissed the quest for certainty, for rock-hard foundations, and for ultimate justification, what then remains for epistemology? It is left with the task of *explaining* our coming to know science (and common sense). There are two parts to this explanation, a descriptive part and a normative part. The descriptive part explains how as a matter of fact we form our opinions. The normative part explains what makes these opinions knowledge. We seek a scientific explanation of our knowing science. The epistemic relation between humans and the world itself becomes the object of scientific study.[9]

Rorty's view is that the world admits of both "extensional" and "intensional" descriptions and that we should not make "invidious comparisons between these modes of description" (*PMN*, pp. 204–5). But nothing in Rorty's arguments convinces me that alternative "descriptions" of disease and what brings them about, provided by science, on

9. Michael Devitt, *Realism and Truth* (Princeton: Princeton University Press, 1984), pp. 63–64.

the one hand, and folk legend, on the other, should not be compared. We can explain how folk legends about disease and its causes developed; we can also explain how the most satisfactory scientific account we have at present came to be accepted. We might appreciate the value of each explanation as helping us "cope" in different ways. But that appreciation does not do away with the question of which is, by our present knowledge of both science and folk legend, in fact causally accurate and thus epistemically reliable. Nor does it do away with the fact that an objective study of the features of the human body and the world can tell us much about what causes a particular disease. As argued in Chapter 2, the fact that in a prescientific time all humans who cared to think about diseases might have held the "folk legend" explanation of them does not invalidate our current belief that we now have a better explanation, and one that matches the way the world is. To believe that we do, we do *not* need to subscribe to the idea that the world-as-it-is can be completely described once and for all in one neutral language, but we do subscribe to the very different idea that the external world exists and might reveal regular processes of functioning which could be identified as "lawlike" by our best scientific procedures of observation and systematization. Some kinds of observation and theorizing reveal factual knowledge of certain aspects of this world, and others, no matter how precise the description, are simply false insofar as underlying causes and laws are concerned.

The view that human knowledge is capable of producing a completely accurate and unmediated picture or representation of the world is in fact one that postpositivist realists would reject on precisely Quinean grounds. No such atheoretical description is possible in principle, and human inquiry is by definition historical and meliorative. In the Quinean antiempiricist perspective, "theory" or "bias" is not only inevitable but also necessary for engendering good accounts of the world. The real question concerns the nature of our actual biases and the epistemic consequences they have.

The view that the world can be exhaustively described (and explained) through only an accumulation of facts betrays a conception of objectivity which the feminist philosopher Louise Antony humorously calls the "Dragnet" theory: "Objectivity, on this view . . . , is the result of complete divestiture—divestiture of theoretical commitments, of personal goals, of moral values, of hunches and intuitions. We'll get to the truth, sure as taxes, provided everyone's willing to be rational and to play by the (epistemically relevant) rules. Got an especially knotty problem to solve? Just the facts, ma'am."[10] A Quinean realist such as Michael Devitt not only has no need for the Dragnet theory of objectivity; he is in fact theoretically committed to the rejection of such a view as epistemologically dangerous and misleading. A naturalized epistemologist is by definition deeply committed to going beneath observable facts and ostensive descriptions to the theories that underlie them. He thinks of such theories, and the epistemic norms they presuppose, as subject to empirical investigation and evaluation. Antony puts this well: "A naturalized approach to knowledge, because it requires us to give up *neutrality* as an epistemic ideal, also requires us to take a different attitude toward bias. We know that human knowledge requires biases; we also know that we have no possibility of getting *a priori* guarantees that our biases incline us in the right direction. What all this means is that the 'biasedness' of biases drops out as a parameter of epistemic evaluation. There's only one thing to do, and it's the course always counseled by a naturalized approach: *We must treat the goodness or badness of particular biases as an empirical question*" (p. 215). Thus an antifoundationalist enterprise that is faithful to Rorty's critique, as well as to that of the various other philosophers he draws on, can produce a social or cultural theory that is not relativistic in the senses identified in the previous chapter. Moreover, it can count on a general and context-specific notion of objectivity which would be essential to analyses of social phenomena. Let us explore these ideas by considering in some detail the issues of continuity and discontinuity, focusing on the question of scientific "progress" as it is formulated by Thomas Kuhn and Rorty.

Kuhn and Rorty both agree that if there is progress in science and human knowledge, it is not a kind of progress that can be charted in theory- or paradigm-independent terms. Neither is an extreme "relativist" (in terms of my discussion in Chapter 5) if by that we mean one who asserts that all paradigms are the same, involving no improvement at all. The main thing they deny is that there is progress toward some objective truth about a world that is "really there." In what sense, then, can we determine whether progress has taken place, particularly if we agree with Kuhn's famous picture of the history of science as a series of total revolutions or breaks with the past? Here at least is one kind of

10. Louise M. Antony, "Quine as Feminist: The Radical Import of Naturalized Epistemology," in *A Mind of One's Own: Feminist Essays on Reason and Objectivity*, ed. Antony and Charlotte Witt (Boulder, Colo.: Westview, 1993), p. 206.

problem: "Revolutions close with a total victory for one of the two opposing camps. Will that group ever say that the result of its victory has been something less than progress? That would be rather like admitting that they had been wrong and their opponents right. . . . When it repudiates a past paradigm, a scientific community simultaneously renounces, as a fit subject for professional scrutiny, most of the books and articles in which that paradigm had been embodied. Scientific education makes use of no equivalent for the library of classics, and the result is a sometimes drastic distortion in the scientist's perception of his discipline's past. More than the practitioners of other fields, he comes to see it as leading in a straight line to the discipline's present vantage. In short, he comes to see it as progress. No alternative is available to him while he remains in the field."[11] From within the field, with the institutional and sociological arrangements and constraints that Kuhn describes in *The Structure of Scientific Revolutions*, progress is seen as inevitable, but Kuhn suggests that this is only the appearance of continuity, of improvement of technique and the emergence of new and better questions. In what sense then do "scientific revolutions" constitute a break with the old?

From a comparative historical perspective, Kuhn sees a more significant discontinuity between the old paradigm and the new. No matter what the victors themselves think about the progress they have made over the paradigm of the vanquished, there really is no way we can identify a set of standards higher than—that is, more general than—the specific terms and categories used by individual scientific communities, for science is the work of a social community, and "in paradigm choice *there is no standard higher than the assent of the relevant community*" (p. 94, emphasis added). Hence what is essential in paradigm choice is not only "the impact of nature and of logic" but, equally significant, "*the techniques of persuasive argumentation* effective within the quite special groups that constitute the community of scientists" (p. 94, emphasis added). Kuhn's emphasis on the rhetorical and ideological underpinnings of scientific activity is an important contribution to our understanding of the politics of science—and claims to scientificity and truth in the natural sciences. But then the question of relativism also becomes a real one, for given such a conception of change in paradigms, we have *no way* of negotiating among these paradigms in terms of their relative claims to truth. Consider Kuhn's more emphatic elaboration in this key passage:

11. Thomas Kuhn, *The Structure of Scientific Revolutions*, 2d ed. (Chicago: University of Chicago Press, 1970), pp. 166–67.

The differences between successive paradigms are both necessary and irreconcilable. Can we then say more explicitly what sorts of differences these are? . . . Successive paradigms tell us different things about the population of the universe and about that population's behavior. They differ, that is, about such questions as the existence of subatomic particles, the materiality of light, and the conservation of heat or of energy. These are the substantive differences between successive paradigms, and they require no further illustration. But paradigms differ in more than substance, for they are directed not only to nature but also back upon the science that produced them. They are the source of the methods, problem-field, and standards of solution accepted by any mature scientific community at any given time. As a result, the reception of a new paradigm often necessitates a redefinition of the corresponding science. Some old problems may be relegated to another science or declared entirely "unscientific." Others that were previously nonexistent or trivial may, with a new paradigm, become the very archetypes of significant scientific achievement. And as the problems change, *so, often, does the standard that distinguishes a real scientific solution from a mere metaphysical speculation, word game, or mathematical play. The normal-scientific tradition that emerges from a scientific revolution is not only incompatible but often actually incommensurable with that which has gone before.* (p. 103, emphasis added)

Paradigms are radically discrete and insulated from one another. The plausible sociological point about differences among particular communities and their criteria of scientificity is here inflated into an epistemological claim. In effect, it is suggested, we cannot distinguish "a real scientific solution" from "a mere metaphysical speculation" if they happen to exist within competing paradigms; that we cannot is what makes these paradigms "incommensurable." Kuhn's qualification "often" is irrelevant, for it is the most extreme case that is of theoretical interest here. What enables us to posit such radical discontinuities? Kuhn does not address this issue too precisely, but there are at least a few related theses one can glean from his account. Kuhn argues against the (positivist) idea that there is a match between the "ontology" of a theory (in Kuhn's definition, the totality of "the entities with which the theory populates nature") and what is "really there." "There is no theory-independent way to reconstruct phrases like 'really there,'" Kuhn argues; "the notion of a match between the ontology of a theory and its 'real' counterpart in nature now seems to me illusive in principle" (p. 206).

The view under attack here is similar to the one Rorty criticizes, for it obviously conceives reality as the world-as-it-is, describable in a complete and accurate way. This reality is a composite of entities, but Kuhn's point is that entities are produced by theory and do not exist outside that framework. A pendulum is, given a theory change, no more than a swinging stone. Pendulums were "brought into existence by something very like a paradigm-induced gestalt switch," Kuhn claims (p. 120); it is fair to conclude that pendulums could disappear from existence given the appropriate kind of paradigm change in the future.

The force of this claim lies to some extent in its vagueness. By implication, "reality" loses all causal force outside specific theoretical contexts: such "posited" entities as gases and germs, electrons and gravitational forces, are real only to the extent that they are underwritten by a theory. All we have to negotiate among theories is the persuasive capacity of scientists situated in social institutions and in history. According to Kuhn, scientific theory can make no theory-independent "ontological" claims because there is no world that it is really about, no nonhuman "nature" that can be partially and incrementally described. Reality, as we saw before in my discussion of Rorty, is an all-or-nothing affair. No possibility is admitted that it might be structured as a causal hierarchy. Recall, for contrast, Quine's view about the different relations that portions of a theory have with observation or experience. The most extreme suggestion in the Kuhnian idea of the "incommensurability" of successive paradigms is that all of reality is up for grabs in moments of paradigm change—not only our local practices of evaluation but all of our observed world.

Why would Kuhn not consider himself a relativist? It is because science does progress, he would say, for it improves its puzzle-solving capacities *across paradigms.* In fact it can improve its capacity for both discovering and solving puzzles. But though these puzzles are, as Kuhn says at one point, "presented by nature" (p. 205), solving them in better ways (say, more easily or more comprehensively) leads us no closer to nature as it really is out there. The reality of the positivist is discarded because it claims too much for scientific inquiry, but a grand claim for theory is surreptitiously made in the process. *It* "makes up" the real world, which in turn is nothing but the "wholes" into which theory constructs it. This view is at the heart of Kuhn's metaphysical position.

Kuhn's contribution to the historiography of science, as I have said, is to make us aware of the complex ways in which scientific inquiry is implicated in social practices and arrangements. For him, theory change in science is a hermeneutical phenomenon (what Rorty would call "conversation"), and the lesson it holds for the historian (of science) is similar to the lesson we saw the sophisticated relativist outline in the previous chapter. The understanding of "out-of-date scientific theories" is akin to the process of translation, and the difficulty is in dealing with "anomalous behavior." Rather than reduce anomalies to the terms of the translator's own logical-illogical grid, the Kuhnian historian must "try to discover what the other would see and say when presented with a stimulus to which his own verbal response would be different" (p. 202). This is close to the Gadamerian injunction to understand social ideas by dialogizing them as a response to an implicit question, and it carries with it the attentiveness to contextual phenomena that most antipositivists advocate. In particular, the gain is ethical—we "refrain from explaining anomalous behavior as the consequence of mere error or madness" (p. 202)—and the hope is that one will have learned to "translate the other's theory and its consequences into his own language and simultaneously to describe in his language the world to which that theory applies" (p. 202).

In rejecting the world, however, Kuhn precludes the possibility that change in the scientific paradigms could be influenced in any way at all by the discovery of "objective" features of this world. The explanation of change in science is provided exclusively in terms of sociological and ideological factors, that is, as we have seen, the capacity of an individual scientific community to persuade another. Kuhn's antirealism draws attention to the question of historical change and, in particular, to the adequacy of his explanation of change. These questions become especially pressing when, as we shall see in the case of Rorty, such an antirealist holistic-hermeneutical approach is the basis on which a social and political theory is elaborated.

Rorty will have nothing to do with Kuhn's metaphysical position. In fact he regrets Kuhn's occasional idealist remarks, such as the one about the "creation" of the pendulum by theory, especially since such remarks distract us from Kuhn's radical hermeneutical suggestions. Rorty wants to argue in effect that as in the history of science, so in the history of philosophy and in human history generally, change is a conversational matter: it involves gestalt switches that are not explainable by any external (objective) factors. This claim, though not advanced explicitly, underlies Rorty's version of pragmatism, which builds on at least two of the ideas I have already discussed in detail: first, a kind of epistemological holism derived from developments in the philosophy of science but without any recognition that (as Quine, for example, emphasizes) the "whole" of scientific knowledge is hierarchically articulated; second, a version of constructivism derived from Kuhn's account of paradigm or theory change in the history of science.

Now the picture of science as a hierarchically organized field, with greater or lesser contact with "observation," is, as we saw earlier, an important epistemic constraint that philosophers such as Quine would like us to acknowledge. For them it provides a cumulatively developed (and revisable) scientific picture of the natural world from which to evaluate and explain theory change. Rorty argues for a thoroughgoing holism that denies this hierarchy, insisting that we collapse the distinction between the natural and the human sciences. Now, Rorty's position is useful inasmuch as the rigid distinction between the two separate spheres of "soft" and "hard" human inquiry itself betrays a positivist prejudice. Rorty's pragmatist move, however, consists not simply in enlarging the problematic of the human sciences to include postpositivist questions raised about natural science but also in making all inquiry into no more than a communal conversation, devoid of transcommunal standards of justification such as truth or objectivity.

Why is this an attractive *political* view? Emphasizing both holism and radical constructivism, Rorty's pragmatist presents a vision of knowledge as social practice and hence ideologically coded and shaped. To deny objectivity is to grant, Rorty insists, that our most sacrosanct norms and principles of justification are revisable, open to historical change. In a key essay that explains the related virtues of the hermeneutical approach in all kinds of human inquiry, scientific and sociocultural, Rorty insists that there is no "objective" realm of truth to serve as a norm for human inquiry.

> From a pragmatist point of view, to say that what is rational for us now to believe may not be *true*, is simply to say that somebody may come up with a better idea. It is to say that there is always room for improved belief, since new evidence, or new hypotheses, or a whole new vocabulary may come along. For pragmatists, the desire for objectivity is not the desire to escape the limitations of one's community, but simply the desire for as much intersubjective agreement as possible, the desire to extend the reference of "us" as far as we can. Insofar as pragmatists make a distinction between knowledge and opinion, it is simply the distinction between topics on which such agreement is relatively easy to get and topics on which agreement is relatively hard to get.[12]

12. Richard Rorty, "Solidarity or Objectivity?" in *Post-analytic Philosophy*, ed. John Rajchman and Cornel West (New York: Columbia University Press, 1985), p. 5.

Rorty argues against what he considers to be the realist position; all there is in this hermeneutical view is "solidarity." Similarly, the gap between "truth" and what we can at present "justify" as knowledge is not to be "bridged by isolating a natural and transcultural sort of rationality" but rather to be seen as "the gap between the actual good and the possible better" (p. 5). The lure of the possible better is what makes Rorty's position so attractive.

But as we saw in my discussion of Quine and a naturalistic account of knowledge, "revisability" is also compatible with a view that leaves open an essential place for a mind-independent real world, gradually and incrementally discovered. Such realists subscribe to the Peircean doctrine of fallibilism, namely, the idea that our fundamental accounts of the world are certainly changeable, but the possibility that they might in principle change in light of new evidence or knowledge in the future is not in itself sufficient grounds for not believing them now. In particular, if by our best standards of reason and evidence we come to see such accounts of the world as true, the Peircean injunction would allow us to commit our beliefs to them.[13] So not only pragmatists can assert that our deepest knowledge claims are essentially revisable and, thus, historical, as becomes particularly clear if we take into consideration versions of realism which are a little more complex—and a little more plausible—than the one Rorty presents. At the heart of any debate between pragmatism and such realist accounts will be the question of explanatory power, in particular the explanation of historical change. The issue then is whether the (Kuhnian) understanding of theory change as a matter of internal persuasion is adequate, and, more important, whether we can extract from it a model of the way *social* change takes place. Considering Rorty's hermeneutical understanding of inquiry as "conversation," I think that with a few qualifications he would assume that the Kuhnian understanding is adequate.

The question of change is central to any respectable social theory in modern times, since we take for granted that social structures are dynamic and internally contested wholes. Rorty has a social and a political vision, but the theory underlying it is developed not in contact with Marx or Max Weber or Emile Durkheim but, a little too quickly, from his antifoundationalist project in philosophy. Thus social change interests him in only the most perfunctory way. The paradimatic form of

13. For a discussion of Peircean fallibilism from a realist perspective, see Nicholas Sturgeon, "What Difference Does It Make Whether Moral Realism Is True?" *Southern Journal of Philosophy* 24 (supplement 1986), 69–78.

change is intellectual-historical or, at best, "cultural," but the change itself is conceived as a kind of gestalt switch, posing no interesting explanatory issue at all. What underlies this approach is an understanding of culture and society—the society in which ideas operate, are accepted and adopted, and are effective—as more or less undifferentiated wholes. Thus one moves briskly from change in one social sphere to another without any consideration of how there might be different levels of causality involved. All Rorty is interested in is the moral lesson to be learned from all this: that we should not hanker after a metatheory that would serve as foundation or transcendental ground:

> When such edifying philosophers as Marx, Freud, and Sartre offer new explanations of our usual patterns of justifying our actions and assertions, and when these explanations are taken up and integrated into our lives, . . . this phenomenon does not require any new understanding of theory-construction or theory confirmation. To say that we have changed ourselves by internalizing a new self-description (using terms like "bourgeois intellectual" or "self-destructive" or "self-deceiving") is true enough. But this is no more startling than the fact that men changed the data of botany by hybridization, which was in turn made possible by botanical theory, or that they changed their own lives by inventing bombs and vaccines. Meditation on the possibility of such changes, like reading science fiction, does help us overcome the self-confidence of "metaphysical realism." But such meditation does not need to be supplemented by a transcendental account of the nature of reflection. All that is necessary is the edifying invocation of the fact or possibility of abnormal discourses, undermining our reliance upon the knowledge we have gained through normal discourses. (*PMN*, p. 386)

But the Kuhnian lesson presented here about not denying the "fact or possibility of abnormal discourses" (Kuhn's "anomalies"), like the claim about the revisability of our theoretical "truths," is not one that *only the pragmatist* can teach us. If that possibility is admitted, the question for Rorty concerns his rather cavalier attitude to social change or, in fact, social processes in general. For a theory (such as Marx's, for instance) that takes causal explanation of social phenomena seriously, such questions as how new "explanations are taken up and integrated into our lives" are important in themselves, to be understood through an analysis of ideologies and institutions; moreover, such an explanation of ideology is dialectically tied to—that is, reciprocally related to—an understanding of larger theses about "theory construction and theory confirmation." An account of cultural change depends on and in turn informs such a larger explanatory account as the one that historical materialism typically provides of class struggle as the motor of historical change. This is a way of connecting "new" social ideas and ideologies to the social interests of various groups, to existing institutions and what interests they express or serve. Now, to the extent that one is a realist in this context, one sees class struggle as an objective element in society, and its status as "theoretical" knowledge does not compromise that objective status. Needless to say, such a realist would remain fallibilistic about historical materialism, open to historical evidence or argument that might change her most basic positions.

Where the realist has an edge over Rorty in this debate is in possessing the resources to provide deeper explanations for social phenomena and, in particular, in taking social change as "caused." Notice, however, that the realist does not thereby commit herself to any understanding of cause as "transcendental" or extrasocial ground. Her explanation nevertheless remains more comprehensive than Rorty's, answerable to new historical data and social analyses. But the analyses provide potentially competing social and historical explanations, pointing to the underlying causal forces that are not purely cultural or intratheoretical.

There is also a political—or at least ethical—vision lurking in the passages I have quoted from Rorty's work. There is the idea that the pragmatist remains more open to the possibility of "abnormal discourses," more tolerant of the "unfamiliar" and the historically new. Here, we recall, is where the rhetorical edge of relativism also lies. In general, the relativist and the antirelativist pragmatist claim to be more open to new historical possibilities and thus to provide a potentially more egalitarian approach. But as we saw in my discussion of cultural relativism, the question of "tolerance" is complex. It would be best to examine what exactly is involved in jettisoning all claims to objectivity and the real world and to consider what a defensible and sophisticated realist position in these matters might be. At issue here for literary studies is the question of causality and in particular the social determination of our practices and our discourses.

How attentive can we be to the new and unfamiliar if we trivialize the question of historical continuity, a question linked to our understanding of the causality inherent in social processes? On this issue, as I shall show in the next section, there is a surprising degree of affinity between contemporary scientific realists and such central poststructuralist figures as Derrida. My reading of the Derridean problematic is unconventional only because of the juxtaposition I am making here;

otherwise, the discussion of the complex relations between continuity and discontinuity in Heidegger's and Derrida's analyses of Western metaphysics is faithful to their own version of the radically "new"—the posthumanist vision that emerges in their critical and genealogical readings.

Deconstruction, Realism, and Historical Explanation

I have shown that Rorty's pragmatism builds on an epistemological holism but is unwilling to grant that human knowledge may be hierarchically organized in such a way that some of the more fundamental theories (or beliefs) might be epistemically prior to others. This denial of the hierarchical structure of knowledge is tied to a rather extreme opposition between (1) causal explanation of knowledge understood as explanation based on transcendent causes and (2) justification as a social practice. Rorty evidently thinks that it is not possible to account for knowledge as *both* socially justified *and* tied, at crucial joints, to our evolving explanation of the causal structure of the natural and social world. This belief is predicated, I have suggested, on the idea that the only existing account of the relation between human knowledge and the world is the positivist one, which sees the world as susceptible to comprehensive description in terms of one true picture. Thus, in Rorty's scheme of things, the "world" exists, but it is of no consequence: that kind of realist thesis is boring, he says. Knowledge as (socially) justified belief has no relation of consequence to the reality of the mind- or discourse-independent world. I have already outlined some of the problems (the nature of historical change and, more generally, the place of causation in the explanation of social phenomena) that Rorty's theory leaves seriously underexamined. Before I suggest what an alternative account of causality and the social justification of knowledge might be, let me turn to one of the ideological implications of this pragmatist definition of truth-minus-the-world.

If all that we can justifiably know is not related in any significant way to the existence of the world that is independent of this knowledge, then the nonhuman world is effectively described as inconsequential, and human history and knowledge are circumscribed within the ambit of who "we" are. The hermeneutical respect Rorty advocates for the "unfamiliar" and the new is then to be understood within this severely "humanized" vision: we might inhabit only the tiniest portion of the universe, but we assume in advance that the nonhuman can in principle have no bearing on who we are and what we know. The ideological nature of such a position becomes clearest when it is contrasted with Derrida's antihumanist problematic.

Wholes, Holes, and the Derridean Critique of Metaphysics

Even at first glance, the incompatibility between Rorty's perspective and that of such poststructuralists as Derrida is clear. For the poststructuralists, the definition of the human is, in fact, what ultimately needs to be located and localized. The goal of the Heideggerian-Derridean antihumanist tradition is to locate the determining infrastructure (for example, the "being" which has always-already been forgotten, the "différance" which is not an "existent" but a tissue that is both continuous and discontinuous with the ontotheology of presence) that shapes our existing definitions of "ourselves" as human. It is this problematic of (over)determination, this set of questions about how our understanding of the human is (perhaps causally) dependent on the nonhuman realm (nonhuman precisely because it escapes the logic of what we happen to call "the human"), which is central to the Derridean project. Even though Derrida has no explicit commitment at all to what scientific realism defines as the natural world, his *methodological* commitment to delimiting the humanist paradigm makes his project less compatible with that of Rorty's pragmatist and much more with that of the postpositivist realist.

From this methodological perspective, the early debates in literary theory over the indeterminacy of textual meaning might not seem terribly relevant or even accurate. The emphasis on the radical play of signifying practices and structures seems to have obscured the genealogical concern in Derrida's work with tracing a fine network of precise determinations or, in other words, a complex causal structure. In the early essay on Georges Bataille, for instance, Derrida is already examining the relation between discourse and nondiscourse: what Bataille calls "sovereignty" exceeds the order of "meaning, truth, and a *grasp-of-the-thing-in-itself*" but is related to it.[14] We should not create a theology of unknowledge but explore this alternative (political) economy in which knowledge and "meaning" are defined.

14. Jacques Derrida, "From Restricted to General Economy," in *Writing and Difference* (Chicago: University of Chicago Press, 1978), p. 270.

> There is no sovereignty itself. . . . Sovereignty is the impossible, there-
> fore it *is not*, it *is*—Bataille writes this word in italics—"this loss."
> The writing of sovereignty places discourse *in relation* to absolute
> non-discourse. Like general economy, it is not the loss of meaning,
> but . . . the "relation to this loss of meaning." It opens the question of
> meaning. It does not describe unknowledge, for this is impossible, but
> only the effect of unknowledge. (p. 270)

We do not approach the realm of "absolute unknowledge" directly; it
is not "a moment of knowledge" (p. 268). As we see, the "writing of
sovereignty" is not opposed to "meaning" as simply the "*loss* of meaning"; it is a determined *relation* to this "loss" and is, in fact, the *effect*
of "unknowledge."

A little earlier in the essay, Derrida gives a formulation of this "relation" between discourse and nondiscourse. Reversing the Hegelian "restricted economy" that situates labor, meaning, and knowledge in the
space of the "negative," Derrida sees Bataille as suggesting an alternative relationship between the "restricted" and the "general" economies:
"Meaning is a *function* of play, is inscribed in a certain place in the
configuration of meaningless play" (p. 260). But then by definition this
"meaninglessness" is not arrived at a priori. We need to proceed cau-
tiously here: it will not be seen as "determined" if by that we mean
"circumscribed by the history of knowledge as a figure taken from (or
leading toward) dialectics" (p. 268). It is not determined—related causally—in the way in which such relations are defined within the "re-
stricted-economic" terms of the ontotheological tradition. Derrida and
Bataille are concerned with the radically new as that other space which
"will be the absolute excess of every *epistemē*, of every philosophy and
every science" (p. 268). But this "excess" (excess to the very extent that
it escapes the order of meaning) is also defined relationally as the constitutive condition of meaning, that which makes meaning possible,
which in fact *produces* it. In "Différance," building on Saussurean semiology, in particular the thesis that relations (of language) are prior to the
individual elements within any given system, Derrida provides some
suggestions about the relation of dependence which exists between a
coherent body of knowledge and that which is *logically* prior to it:
"What is written as *différance*, then, will be the playing movement that
'produces'—by means of something that is not simply an activity—
these differences, these effects of difference. This does not mean that
the *différance* that produces differences is somehow before them, in a

simple and unmodified—and in-different—present. *Différance* is the non-full, non-simple, structured and differentiating origin of differences. Thus the name 'origin' no longer suits it."[15]

The priority of *différance*—or general writing, trace, the general economy—over individual instances of difference is not temporal but logical. It is *implied by* differences, which are *made possible by it.* There is a causal relationship here, if we understand "causation" in a general way: individual differences are brought about by *différance;* without it they would not exist. Causation, however, does not mean here that *différance* exhaustively accounts for individual differences, which "are 'historical' from the outset and in each of their aspects" (p. 11). They are historical because they are "effects," and they "have not fallen from the sky fully formed" (p. 11). They are thus constituted, not given. And their constitution would not be possible without this other set of relationships we call *différance,* but *différance* is not their exclusive "cause"; in historical phenomena, no monocausal relationship is possible.

In classic structuralist fashion (reminiscent of Althusser), Derrida denies such monocausality by emphasizing system over transcendent agent. But there is indeed another conception of causality, in what is an alternative political economy, as it were, and it is defined through a rigorous attentiveness to the determined relation of the known to the unknown. Why is this a determined relationship? Because *"différance maintains our relationships with that which we necessarily misconstrue"* (p. 20; emphasis added). This necessity reveals something about "us," about the specific features of the "human"—the human as it has been historically constituted, defined in and as "metaphysics."

The Derridean critique of ontotheology is antihumanist because it sees *différance,* the logically prior realm, as radically different from what ontotheology defines as human. It posits as a methodological hypothesis an abyss or *Abgrund* underlying the coherent knowledge that traditional ontology constructs; it is in relation to this abyss that the metaphysics of "presence" and plenitude is situated and defined. But this is no more than a methodological hypothesis, because it would be difficult to say what exactly it consists of *in itself.* It would be impossible, in fact, to assign to it the status of an existent because, as we have seen, it is defined only in relational (and hence purely contingent) terms. Its value lies primarily in revealing to us the necessity of our

15. Jacques Derrida, "Différance," in *Margins of Philosophy* (Chicago: University of Chicago Press, 1982), p. 11, hereafter cited in the text as *MP.*

misconstruals, in the process showing us how the ontotheological tradition is historically constituted. (Here the contrast with de Man might be evident.)

The political force of this critique derives from its demonstration that the tradition is a construct, subject to change and revision. It is also, then, historical rather than natural, motivated, not neutral. Developing Heidegger's critique of Leibnizian rationalism, for instance, Derrida introduces the hypothesis of the *Abgrund* to suggest the methodological alternatives available to us. Notice how the hypothesis opens up two "responses" to the rationalist's absolute claim that nothing is without reason and that such reason must be rendered, that existence must be comprehensively explained. The abyss points to the attempt of Leibnizian rationalism to transcend its empirical deficiencies through a circular metaphysical claim:

> To respond to the call of the principle of reason is to "render reason," to explain effects through their causes, rationally; it is also to ground, justify, to account for on the basis of principles or roots. Keeping in mind that Leibnizian moment whose originality should not be underestimated, the response to the call of the principle of reason is thus a response to the Aristotelian requirements, those of metaphysics, of primary philosophy, of the search for "roots," "principles," and "causes." At this point, scientific and technoscientific requirements lead back to a common origin. . . . Not only does that principle constitute the verbal formulation of a requirement present since the dawn of Western science and philosophy, it provides the impetus for a new era of purportedly "modern" reason, metaphysics and technoscience. And one cannot *think* the possibility of the modern university, the one that is restructured in the nineteenth century in all the Western countries, without inquiring into that event, that institution of the principle of reason.
>
> But to answer for the principle of reason (and thus for the university), to answer *for* this call, to raise questions about the origin or ground of this principle of foundation *(Der Satz vom Grund),* is not simply to obey it or to respond *in the face of* this principle. . . . Are we obeying the principle of reason when we ask what grounds this principle which is itself a principle of grounding? We are not—which does not mean that we are disobeying it, either. Are we dealing here with a circle or with an abyss? The circle consists in seeking to account for reason by reason, to render reason to the principle of reason, in appealing to the principle in order to make it speak of itself at the very point where, according to Heidegger, the principle of reason says nothing about reason itself. The abyss, the hole, the Abgrund, the

empty "gorge" would be the impossibility for a principle of grounding to ground itself. This very grounding, then, like the university, would have to hold itself suspended above a most peculiar void. Are we to use reason to account for the principle of reason? Is the reason for reason rational? Not simply; but it would be overhasty to seek to disqualify this concern and to refer those who experience it back to their own irrationalism, their obscurantism, their nihilism. Who is more faithful to reason's call, who hears it with a keener ear, who better sees the difference, the one who offers questions in return and tries to think through the possibility of that summons, or the one who does not want to hear any question about the reason of reason?[16]

The circle consists in trying to account for a narrowly defined reason within its own terms. The hypothesis of the abyss opens up the possibility that "reason" is historically constituted and, hence, is not justified through principles that are self-sufficient; it is rather a social construct. It is thus open to empirical investigation, subject to the kind of sociological analysis that Kuhn suggests we need for scientific theories and their corresponding norms of scientific experiment and validation. In this sense, Leibnizian "reason" is not an absolute principle but rather a paradigm-specific value. It is not valid universally, that is, across competing paradigms of rationality.

What would it mean to claim that "reason" is paradigm-specific? It is clear that in the Heideggerian perspective rationality is seen as a social construction, and reality is understood in a generally constructivist way. But the Derridean thesis that the nonhuman world in some way determines or shapes the human is not simply constructivist, for it makes no such absolute claim about paradigm relativity. Instead, as we have seen, Derrida's central goal is to examine why the nonhuman *cannot* be understood with our conventional and familiar terms. Thus he is interested in the ideological reductionism inherent in "linear" histories of human thought, which he associates with "logocentrism, phonocentrism, semantism, and idealism."[17] Instead, the Derridean project aims to "put philosophy back on stage, on a stage that it does not govern" (p. 50). Philosophy as metaphysics, or more generally the ontotheological tradition as Heidegger and Derrida define it, succeeds in sustaining itself by radically *excluding* the traces of this stage and of the fact that it is not autonomous and self-governing. Deconstruction

16. Jacques Derrida, "The Principle of Reason," *Diacritics* (Fall 1983), 8–9.
17. Jacques Derrida, *Positions* (Chicago: University of Chicago Press, 1972), p. 50; hereafter cited in text as *Pos.*

seeks to open philosophy up to those "external" principles that define the field in which philosophy is located, suggesting in the process not only the fictitiousness of ontotheology's self-definition but also the complex and multiple lines of causal force which connect the inside and the outside. In examining this set of methodological and substantive questions, Derrida reveals one of his persistent concerns, the limits of a certain understanding of holism.

The critique of holism in Derrida's work is evident in two related ways. First, there is the idea that the elements of metaphysics do not exist within a delimitable field called "metaphysics" as such. "I have never believed," Derrida says in the famous interview with Jean-Louis Houdebine and Guy Scarpetta, "that there were *metaphysical* concepts *in and of themselves*," for "no concept is by itself, and consequently in and of itself, metaphysical, outside of all the textual work in which it is inscribed."[18] The claim here is not that concepts always exist in embodied form and that understanding them involves taking into account the forms of their embodiment. Instead, we are told that "concepts" are "metaphysical" to the very extent that they are related to a "textual" force field that gives them their meaning. The "field" determines these concepts as specifically metaphysical, constitutive of the ontotheological tradition. The "textual work in which [the concept] is inscribed" is Derrida's metaphor for the play of determined relationships in which metaphysics is constituted and defined as metaphysics; it is that "outside" which is by implication not just an exterior.

Hence this more specific qualification of holism: "The 'closure of metaphysics' cannot have the form of a *line*, that is, the form in which philosophy recognizes it, in which philosophy recognizes itself. The closure of metaphysics, above all, is not a circle surrounding a homogeneous field, a field homogeneous with itself on its inside, whose outside would then be homogeneous also. The limit has the form of always different faults, of fissures whose mark or scar is borne by all the texts of philosophy" (*Pos.*, pp. 56–57). If holism is the claim that individual elements within a given whole are to be explained by reference to the totality of relationships that constitute the whole, the Derridean perspective opens the field of relationships—and by implication the constitution of the individual elements themselves—to include an other "outside." What marks the division between the outside and the inside is thus the very inability of the interior space—of, say, a given meta-

18. Jacques Derrida, "Positions: Interview with Jean-Louis Houdebine and Guy Scarpetta," *Pos.*, pp. 37–96, 99–114; p. 57.

physical system—to define itself on its own terms, to "govern" the stage on which it appears. Humanist ideology, central to the ontotheological tradition, is unstable and incoherent to the extent that it is dependent on a nonhuman "space." But this nonhuman exterior is not quite a space in any familiar sense of the term, since it is defined as a radically other (nonhomogeneous) structure, different from that which defines the interior. It is in this sense that we understand why for Derrida the Other of ontotheology is to be conceived through metaphors of absolute alterity, through images indicating the limits of what we might consider (humanly) intelligible.

But, we recall, the exterior is not anything that either "is" or can be located; rather it is hinted at, defined only through a purely *methodological* gesture. A new kind of "writing" practice, a new "interpretation of interpretation," it is hoped, will give birth to "the as yet unnamable which is proclaiming itself . . . only under the species of the nonspecies, in the formless, mute, infant, and terrifying form of monstrosity."[19] This monstrosity is different from what Rorty considers the "unfamiliar" since it cannot be located within a (human) conversation. It is not part of the dialectic of historical development, especially a history that is continuous in meaning and conception with the past. Unlike Rorty's vision of the "new," Derrida's image of absolute alterity demands a more thoroughgoing transformation of everything we know about ourselves as a minimum condition for apprehending the "historically" new. Derridean "discontinuity" is an essentially methodological demand. It is related to the critique of holism in its "continuist" versions, especially those like Rorty's, which suggest that the historically new (the unfamiliar, the Other) might be available to us through hermeneutical interchange. The Derridean point would be that this critique "humanizes" the Other, conceiving it in advance as in principle appropriable. There is a radical relativism implied here, but it is not a cultural relativism. Rather, "culture" is implicitly put into question since it is within the field of "the human," within a certain determined notion of the human sanctioned by ontotheology. Hence Derrida's reticence about what exists beyond "writing," beyond purely methodological descriptions and prescriptions. The "text" and the field of textual relations define the complex play of causal determinations which cannot be pinned down to any aspect of "reality"; it is through his unrelentingly nonphilosophical and purely textual practice that Derrida wishes to keep "metaphysics" (the ontotheological tradition) at bay.

19. Jacques Derrida, *Writing and Difference* (Chicago: University of Chicago Press, 1978), p. 293.

The crucial difference between the Rortian pragmatist and the Derridean is then that the Rortian proposes a view close to the constructivist one, emphasizing in the name of holism and the social justification of knowledge that "truth" is ultimately a human, social matter, whereas the Derridean maintains that human knowledge is fundamentally shaped by a network of determined relationships that are not only—and not even centrally—human. In this sense the Derridean is radically antihumanist, suspending our faith in any notion of what it means to be human. But this radical antihumanism is not based on or tied to an alternative view of reality and of human nature, since Derrida has consistently refrained from making any metaphysical commitment whatsoever.

I have been characterizing as "causal" the Derridean description of the relationship of determination which exists between Western metaphysics and its radically nonhuman "outside." Close readers might point out that Derrida does indeed talk about a relationship between metaphysics and its Other in a way that might be called "explanatory," since one realm is said to "produce" the other, but he uses terms such as "produce" in highly qualified ways and casts doubt on the very notion of causation. In "Différance" he in fact specifies that if causation is understood "in the most classical fashion," he would need to add that the "effects" of *différance* have no "causes" (*MP*, p. 12). But what exactly is the "classical fashion" of understanding causation? Derrida explains earlier in the same passage: "Since language . . . has not fallen from the sky, its differences have been produced, are produced effects, but they are effects which do not find their cause in a subject or a substance, in a thing in general, a being that is somewhere present, thereby eluding the play of *différance*" (p. 11).

The notion of cause against which Derrida is cautioning us is built on the idea of self-evidence and "presence"; at its core is the idealist conception of an unanalyzable originary space or power, one that is left up to metaphysical speculation rather than any kind of empirical verification whatsoever. The problem with such notions of causation is that they are profoundly antihistorical, since causal power in this account resides in a transcendental agent or a space that is not subject to scrutiny or analysis on the same plane as the phenomenon being analyzed. (Derrida's critique is similar to Althusser's attack on the essentialism in Hegel's historiography.) Speculative notions of causation residing in Absolute Spirit or racial or national "essences" are examples of illegitimate idealization. They might be seen as the fault lines that reveal ideological rationalization, indicating the ways in which varieties of idealized reason subsume empirical and scientific explanations of social and historical phenomena. In this sense, "causes" short-circuit analysis by trying to "govern" its complex, multiply determined field, establishing reductive continuities and assuming that the "field" is "homogeneous." But causation can be conceived in less speculative ways, and even though Derrida does not say too much about it directly, the deconstructionist program would be quite compatible with a more complex notion of causation and explanation. We can infer that it would from current debates in philosophy of science, particularly from postpostivist realist philosophies that draw on a radically naturalized conception of human inquiry.

The Postpositivist Realist Alternative

The Derridean (and more generally poststructuralist) skepticism toward speculative categories such as transcendental essences and the Absolute Spirit is similar in some respects to empiricism's thoroughgoing methodological suspicion of unverifiable "metaphysical" claims. Empiricists resisted all talk of unobservable entities and forces, equating such talk with metaphysical speculation, that is, bad science. Hume's famous definition of causation is a case in point; it anticipates the Althusserian and Derridean suspicion of invisible agents and idealized substances. Hume argues that causes have nothing to do with necessary connections; they are rather mere conjunctions we observe.

> Upon the whole, there appears not, throughout all nature, any one instance of connexion, which is conceivable by us. All events seem entirely loose and separate. One event follows another; but we can never observe any tie between them. They seem conjoined, but never connected. . . . [I]t is impossible to give any just definition of cause, except what is drawn from something extraneous and foreign to it. Similar objects are always conjoined with similar. Of this we have experience. Suitably to this experience, therefore, we may define a cause to be an object, followed by another, and where all the objects, similar to the first, are followed by objects similar to the second. Or in other words, where, if the first object had not been, the second never had existed. The appearance of a cause always conveys the mind, by a customary transition, to the idea of the effect. Of this also we have experience. We may, therefore, suitably to this experience, form another definition of cause; and call it, an object followed by

another, and whose appearance always conveys the thought to that other.[20]

Thus a cause is defined through a description of observable regularities, with no reference to unobservable causal powers that might reside *in nature*. In this framework, knowledge of causes implies no more than a simple generalization from the observations that provide evidence for it. Such knowledge is thus very closely tied to the contexts of verification and confirmation. Verification is empirical, based on observation and experience; in the empiricist paradigm, verification is confined to observables; and theoretical knowledge in science consists in that which can be confirmed by experiment through direct observation of phenomena. Empiricist method, which rules out that which cannot be confirmed (or disconfirmed) as metaphysical nonsense, thus remains wary of notions of cause which claim any more than what can be verified: "causation" cannot be theoretically investigated. For both the empiricist and the positivist, the notion of explanation is built around this rather truncated notion of cause as perceivable regularity. No reference to causal power or relations as real features of the natural world is possible.[21]

We begin to understand the explanatory cost of the Humean account of causation when we recall the various powerful critiques of empiricist method which have been launched in the twentieth century. Quine's holistic view of knowledge suggested, for instance, that the empiricist view of *confirmation* is itself profoundly mistaken. For Quine, confirmation in science is not really a matter of testing isolated hypotheses against bits of the "real world" but is rather a question of coordinating a large body of interrelated hypotheses, both confirmed and confirmable, in relation to (1) one another, that is, the complex unity they form, and (2) the cumulative results of observation and experience. On this view, held today by most philosophers, scientific practice is necessarily theory laden; there is simply no direct ("atheoretical") access to the observed world. Nelson Goodman has made a similar far-reaching critique of the positivist tradition, pointing out how the empiricist notion of confirmation underlying positivist programs is untenable on its own terms. Goodman's argument is that the generalization from individual

20. David Hume, *An Enquiry concerning Human Understanding*, 2d ed., ed. Eric Steinberg (Indianapolis: Hackett Publishing, 1993), pp. 49–51.

21. Richard Boyd, "Observations, Explanatory Power, Simplicity: Toward a Non-Humean Account," in *Observation, Experiment, and Hypothesis in Modern Physical Science*, ed. Peter Achinstein and Owen Hannaway (Cambridge: MIT Press, 1985), p. 53.

observations and theories to "laws" (so essential to positivist method) cannot be achieved through purely experimental criteria. The positivist generalizes to "lawlike" regularities, Goodman shows, only through specific conceptions about the "projectability" of data and theories, but these conceptions must themselves be nonexperimental—beyond the bounds of what is observed.[22] Scientific methodology is, as Goodman's and Quine's critiques point out, necessarily more "theoretical" than the empiricist believes. Considerations that are not strictly speaking experimental enter into the formulation of scientific knowledge, and theoretical and conventional considerations are in fact constitutive of scientific practice and method.

These far-reaching criticisms of empiricist and the positivist notions of confirmation suggest that the Humean understanding of causation is inadequate, that the model of causal explanation advanced by the positivist tradition is flawed. Confirmation and explanation are linked circularly. The positivist sees confirmation as based on experiments without theoretical commitment to unobservables, which are seen as evidence of metaphysical speculation, since they cannot be empirically confirmed or refuted. Confirmation of theories consists in generalizations from individual instances of confirmation to appropriate "laws," defined as patterns or regularities, which are used to predict the occurrence of phenomena of the kind that have just been confirmed. Explanation, on this positivist view, consists in the *subsumption* of individual cases (in historical inquiry, "events") into such laws.

"To give a causal explanation of an event," writes Karl Popper, "means to deduce a statement that describes it, using as premises of the deduction one or more universal laws, together with certain singular statements, the initial conditions."[23] The "universal laws" are precisely those that have been confirmed by empirical verification. These laws are then seen as being genuinely explanatory because from them, with a few specified "initial conditions" (together they constitute the *explanans*), we can deduce the event being explained (the *explanandum*). Hence the subsumption of a given event into a "law" provides an explanation of the event. This is the famous deductive-nomological model; confirmation and explanation are thus linked methodologically.

22. See Nelson Goodman, *Fact, Fiction, and Forecast*, 3d ed. (Indianapolis: Bobbs-Merrill, 1973).

23. Karl Popper, *The Logic of Scientific Discovery* (London: Hutchinson, 1959), p. 59. For a lucid and informative account of the influence of the positivist model of explanation on the social sciences, see Anthony Giddens, "Positivism and Its Critics," in *A History of Sociological Analysis*, ed. Tom Bottomore and Robert Nisbet (New York: Basic Books, 1978), pp. 237–86.

If the empiricist and positivist understanding of knowledge is flawed in the way Quine indicates, because it ignores the holistic and theory-mediated nature of confirmation, the model of explanation outlined by the positivist tradition must be reexamined as well. In particular, if Quine's holism is accepted, then confirmation involves background theories and auxiliary hypotheses. Explanation must then involve more than deduction of the *explanandum* from laws that predict regularities, and the explanation of an event in the positivist framework can be seen as both too general (too abstract) and too impoverished. It is too general because it sees only lawlike regularities as explanatory and is inattentive to contextual differences. (This has been one of the main charges leveled against positivist methods in the social sciences.) It is too impoverished because it considers the perception of regularities to be an adequate explanation. It does not, for instance, attempt to explain why the event came about, under what conditions it would not have come about, and so on. These "deeper" causal explanations are not possible, given the positivist definition of explanation as "deductive-nomological"; and it is defined in this way because it is based on the Humean empiricist understanding of causation as no more than constant conjunction.

Developing these critiques of positivism, contemporary realist philosophers in particular have pointed out that the Humean notion of causation is inadequate to explain actual scientific practice. Realists such as Richard Boyd accept Goodman's point about the "nonexperimental" criteria that the empiricist confirmation procedures must presuppose. But Boyd insists that these criteria cannot be just "pragmatic": they must possess *epistemic* value as well.[24] It is in this claim about the epistemic value of auxiliary or background theories and nonexperimental criteria that we notice one of the crucial differences between the realist and the pragmatist. (Both the pragmatist and the empiricist can however, agree that such theories and criteria are purely conventional.)

Boyd maintains that the empiricist cannot deny the real status of theoretical entities—the thesis, that is, that theories are true (or approximately true)—if he is to subscribe to the ideal of the "unity of science," which is of fundamental importance to the history of empiricism as a philosophical tradition. The empiricist gets into trouble, for instance, when he acknowledges that his confirmation procedures depend on background theories. His empiricist ontology implies a commitment to the idea that such theories cannot refer to anything real; all we can say,

24. Boyd, "Observations," pp. 75–76.

the empiricist is committed to saying, is that they are "instrumentally reliable." This limitation is embarrassing for the empiricist, Boyd points out, because it implies the confirmation (as instrumentally reliable) of theories that could not yet have been tested:

> Since no knowledge of theoretical entities is supposed to be possible, it would be initially natural for the empiricist to hold that when a theory is confirmed all that is confirmed is the approximate instrumental reliability of the theory itself. Recognition of the crucial role of auxiliary hypotheses in the testing of theories suggests replacing this instrumentalist conception with a broader one according to which the experimental confirmation of a theory amounts to the confirmation of the conjoint reliability of the theory together with the other theories that have been employed as auxiliary hypotheses in testing it. The "unity of science" principle requires a much broader conception. Experimental confirmation of a theory is supposed to constitute evidence for its instrumental reliability even when it is applied conjointly with other well-confirmed theories not even discovered at the time the evidence for the first theory was assessed! (p. 72)

Theoretical embarrassments of this kind are avoided, the realist would argue, if we do not fight shy of the realist proposal that, when a scientific theory is confirmed through experiment, the theory, together with its background theories and auxiliary hypotheses, might be *true*, might refer accurately to *real features of the world*. Their truth or approximate truth consists in a "fit" between the structure of these theories and the way the world is. If we are not to get into the same awkward situation as the empiricist, claiming that theories that have not in fact been tested are instrumentally reliable, we need to acknowledge the more modest and reasonable realist claim that the reliability of theories (main and auxiliary) is due to the fact that they are true or approximately true of the way the world is. Not only the observational claims but also the theoretical ones are, then, true in this sense.

Such realist critiques of the empiricist view of the status of theories imply a need to reorient my earlier discussion of causation, for claims about "causal" forces and powers are fairly typical *theoretical* claims. That they can be true, in the sense that they can describe actual properties of the world, follows from the holistic view of scientific knowledge and practice I have already discussed. Holism does not lead to a thoroughgoing pragmatism (with no commitment to the truth of theories beyond their "instrumental reliability"). When we consider the nonpositivist implications of actual scientific practice, we recognize that it is congruent with a realist view of causation. This understanding of causation, Boyd points out, is radically non-Humean:

> The ["unity of science"] principle is tenable only on the assumption that knowledge of theoretical entities is possible, and it presupposes that the univocality judgments for theoretical terms that scientists actually make are reliable judgments about reference relations between theoretical terms and theoretical entities. This, in turn, requires that scientists have reliable knowledge of causal relations between unobservable causal factors and their own use of language. The "unity of science" principle thus presupposes just the sort of knowledge that the Humean conceptions are designed to "rationally reconstruct" away, and the Humean conceptions are thus philosophically untenable. (p. 73)

The antimetaphysical thrust of the Humean definition of causation is thus unwarranted by the very principle (the unity of science) on which modern science is founded. "Causes," like all theories that are used reliably in scientific practice, are more than mere observable empirical regularities. They can refer to true or approximately true features of the world as it is. The Humean definition of cause is too impoverished to account for the achievements of modern scientific practice. On the realist view, we need to distinguish between speculative metaphysics and the (revisable) metaphysical posits of scientific inquiry. Skeptical antimetaphysical positions can themselves be dogmatic if they dismiss all "theoretical" knowledge of the world as speculative. The realist metaphysical conclusion that many theoretical entities are "true" is the least unreasonable one.

The postpositivist realist view of causation is part of a more general naturalist view of knowledge. Given the holistic nature of confirmation and the reliability of good scientific practice, causation should itself be seen as a natural phenomenon, subject to empirical investigation. It is not one uniform phenomenon or process to be found in every area of human inquiry; rather, the nature of causation is tied up with the variety of contexts human inquirers study. Thus contemporary realist philosophers typically criticize the positivist assumption that causation is an a priori matter, related to universally applicable laws. The positivist, says the realist, does not see that since causation is a "natural" process, it needs to be conceptualized in a flexible and context-sensitive way. Let me explain in some more detail what causation might look like on this view.

Repudiation of the Humean conception of cause enables the realist to accept that causal powers and relations are features of nature; she is not frightened in advance, as is her empiricist colleague, that talk of real causal power necessarily leads to illegitimate speculation. The realist thus finds it unnecessary to reduce all causal phenomena to noncausal terms in order to avoid the dangers of such speculation. Indeed, from the realist perspective causation is not an analytic concept but fundamentally a project of theoretical inquiry based on empirical research. Boyd maintains, for instance, that "what causation is and what causal interaction amounts to are theoretical questions about natural phenomena . . . , so it is hardly surprising that answers to them should depend more upon the empirically confirmed theoretical findings of the various sciences than should answers to more abstract (and more typically philosophical) questions about the nature of knowledge, reference, or explanation" (pp. 79–80). Notions of "cause" are like notions of various natural kinds (see Chapter 2); they do not possess "analytic definitions" (p. 80).

If causation is not an inflexibly general concept given in advance but a context-sensitive notion defined in relation to the variety of natural phenomena (including social and cultural ones) we encounter, then in what way is it to be conceptualized? Richard Miller, an antipositivist philosopher working within a perspective generally sympathetic to Boyd's, says that "causation" is to be understood as a "core concept," in much the same way as "work of art" or "number." Miller suggests that "cause" is like these two concepts in that it resists description "by a positivist rule."[25] They are "based on a diverse core of elementary varieties, extended to further cases by rational but unpredictable processes of discovery and criticism" (p. 74). The concept is elaborated by extension in contact with empirical phenomena, especially new cases that resist explanation in terms of the previous core concept. The process of inquiry is naturalistic; causes, as Boyd would say, are features of the real world. Here is Miller's definition of this "rational" process of theoretical inquiry:

In grasping the concept [of causation], we understand that the elementary instances are supposed to serve certain purposes through certain activities. If we encounter new contexts in which the old purposes, or very similar ones, are served in similar ways by new varieties, the

25. Richard Miller, *Fact and Method* (Princeton: Princeton University Press, 1987), p. 74.

latter are included as instances of the concept. (Or perhaps one should say that it is then reasonable to include them, and that if most experts take advantage of this permission they are included.) Thus the old purposes of measuring and calculation motivated the further inclusion of the square root of 2. At a certain point in the calculations of area and perimeter, the old numbers proved insufficient. Roger Fry and others showed that Cézanne was doing many of the things that Rembrandt was doing, despite superficial differences. Once new varieties are included and become established, they can be part of a core, in the sense that new candidates are vindicated by relevant resemblance to them, even if there is insufficient resemblance to the elementary varieties. (p. 75)

Causation understood in this way is a theoretical concept developed in contact with empirical research; it remains sensitive to historical change and to differences in the contexts of inquiry. The question whether a "new" cause is really a cause is settled by reference to empirical data, together with suitable respect for the evolving protocols of discipline-specific methodology. In adopting such a "naturalist" view of causation, the realist respects what Rorty calls the "unfamiliar," but does so by approaching it in the context of explanation. The general point is similar to the hermeneutical arguments of Donald Davidson and Charles Taylor (discussed in Chapter 5). The new (the Other) is apprehended not only through comparison but also as part of an explanatory project. To determine some phenomenon as "new," we need to explain (at least partially) its relationship with the old and the familiar. The determination of this relationship is best achieved through *causal* comparison, not simply through a description of "differences." We cannot, in other words, talk about the "new" without an adequate causal account of social and historical change.

On the realist view, causation and explanation are deeply linked. In approaching the natural world as well as social phenomena, to explain adequately is to determine the causal relations that exist between phenomena and events and the world. Causal explanations provide accounts of what brings something about, attempting to understand under what conditions, given certain features of the world, the "new" phenomenon might *not* have come about as well. If the notion of causation is sketched in a naturalist and context-sensitive way, no methodological gulf necessarily separates the "natural" from the "human" sciences. The traditional humanist suspicion of "scientific" method was due to the inflexibility of positivist (universally applicable) norms of rationality, explanation, and confirmation. It was axiomatic for those who stressed the hermeneutical nature of the human sciences to claim that these were different from the "hard" sciences because they were "historical" and thus not susceptible to scientific confirmation. Classic writers in the hermeneutical tradition, such as Dilthey and Gadamer, sometimes take the division between the two kinds of inquiry for granted, emphasizing the need for different "modes" of inquiry— scientific confirmation for one, empathy and tact for the other. Even when the division is not seen in quite such extreme terms, the dominant assumption has been that "scientific method" is too demanding and reductionistic in its understanding of confirmation and explanation to be suitable for the areas of inquiry defined by the humanities and the social sciences.[26] But the picture of scientific practice which emerges in this chapter—from Quine through the contemporary realists—is far from the positivist picture scholars in the human sciences have resisted. What, then, does explanation look like in the postpositivist realist perspective, and what claims to "scientificity" can it make? How do we go from "history"—with its irreducible emphasis on change, novelty, and difference—to scientific knowledge?

The postpositivist realist position is that the positivist understanding of scientific inquiry needs to be "softened" to accord with everything we know about how scientists actually pursue their work. In this, the realist agrees with Quine and Kuhn, accepting the claim about the holistic nature of objective knowledge in science. The realist differs from the (Rortian) pragmatist in considering such phenomena as causation to be central aspects of the natural world; the realist asserts, in fact, that the real world is causally relevant to our justificatory practices. Her perspective on human knowledge is, moreover, unlike that of the pragmatist and more like that of the Derridean philosopher because the realist stresses the radically determined nature of "the human," shaped as it is by the nonhuman universe in which the human takes shape. While the Derridean remains metaphysically shy, however, faithful to his methodological rigor and skeptical of any claims about the "real" world which have not been textually demonstrated, the realist—given the further commitment to the naturalist conception of inquiry based on the "unity of science"—is open to acknowledging the scientific "division of labor" in which "cultural" studies must be responsive to the most current "reasonable" conclusions about the nature of the world we inhabit. Objectivity might be context specific, but the realist notion of

26. See Hans-Georg Gadamer, *Truth and Method*, 2d ed. (New York: Crossroad, 1989), pp. 6–8.

scientificity includes an account of the social organization of our current practices of inquiry. The general approach is based on a rejection of a prioristic notions of knowledge; the focus, as Philip Kitcher puts it, is on "the cognitive enterprise (including the ventures of science), on its history and on the capacities of those who participate in it, to achieve *corrigible* formulations of the goals of the enterprise and *corrigible* accounts of promising strategies for achieving those goals."[27]

The realist's postpositivist notion of scientific methodology as epistemically reliable is thus itself open to the claims of history, that is, to change and revision. "The epistemic reliability of scientific methods is logically contingent," Boyd writes. "It depends upon the historical emergence of relevantly approximately true theoretical traditions . . . and also upon logically contingent features of our individual and collective capacities for theoretical imagination. Thus, principles of scientific methodology are not defensible a priori but have empirical presuppositions" (p. 92). The conception of objectivity implied by the realist view is radically antifoundationalist. It is based on a conception of human inquiry as profoundly historical and socially mediated; no a priori incorrigible epistemological principles are possible. Human knowledge is a socially constructed knowledge of the real world; the world exists as an analyzable causal structure, and it shapes our knowledge of it. The world exists independently of our knowledge of it; it is not paradigm specific. But significant portions of it, namely, the social and cultural aspects of it, including much of the natural world, are also causally affected by our actions, our theories, and our knowledge-gathering procedures: we do not only "discover" reality; we "make" it as well. This dialectical view of knowledge and the social organization of inquiry is radically antifoundationalist and antiidealist without being shy of justified metaphysical claims.

In the second part of this book I have been considering the general view in contemporary cultural theory and philosophy that the challenge of history is the challenge of difference and novelty, that to do justice to history a theoretical perspective must provide us with a capacity for greater tolerance for the new and the unfamiliar. Whether in the Kuhnian-Rortian version or in the poststructuralist one, claims about discontinuity are meant to alert us to the reductive rationalism inherent in most idealist philosophies of history. If "history" is to be explained

27. Philip Kitcher, "The Naturalists Return," *Philosophical Review* 101 (January 1992), 58.

by a preformulated reason that is supposed to underlie it, then these alternative theoretical positions show us how such a conception of reason is fundamentally antihistorical. I have suggested that at least since the Herderian attack on Enlightenment universalism, such general critiques of rationality have opened up a valuable area of theoretical inquiry, although they have been articulated in terms of a number of quite different arguments. It is clear that not everyone who shares Herder's anti-Enlightenment stance in historiography would want to subscribe to the relativist position, especially in its more extreme formulations. Similarly, although Rorty and Derrida might share a suspicion of positivist epistemologies and an implicit preference for holism of Quine's kind, they would disagree in their definitions of radical alterity, the position from which to criticize one's current cultural perspective. What I have been arguing, in effect, in these chapters is that the claims of history are real and quite important, but they cannot be adjudicated by a debate between a too hastily construed universalism, on the one hand, and some form of constructivism or relativism, on the other. In particular, I have tried to show that debates in recent philosophy of science have much to teach us about cultural and historical inquiry. The postpositivist realist position gives us a way of evaluating an alternative to traditional notions of rationality, scientificity, and objective method; at the same time it brings to the center of our attention the cross-disciplinary issues surrounding causation and explanation, evidence and confirmation. If my critique of relativism in the previous chapter is convincing, these methodological issues might then have a direct bearing on the cross-cultural preoccupations of contemporary criticism and theory.

Objection 1: But History Is Not Like That!

As I suggested earlier, one popular argument against the positivist model of explanation in the historical sciences is that science may work in that way but history does not. Historical phenomena cannot be subsumed into laws, it might be claimed, because each event in history is "unique." It can also be suggested that historical method demands "empathy"; scientific explanation is irrelevant in the human sciences, where we need to "understand" and "interpret" rather than "explain." In all these instances, the crucial point would be not that empathy and imagination are necessary for interpreting historical phenomena but that they are sufficient. History, it might be claimed, has nothing to do with science as the positivists understand it.

Now what happens when we entertain the postpositivist realist thesis that science is not quite like the positivist model of it? In particular, recall that scientific confirmation is not an atomistic enterprise, a question of matching individual theoretical statements with an unmediated reality. If, as we have seen, such a confirmation procedure is not in fact what goes on in scientific practice, we are led to appreciate the crucial significance of background theories in determining whether a given test of a theory is successful. We recognize the possibility that the "deductive-nomological" model of explanation is flawed even in the context of natural science, since it is (among other things) built on a narrowly empiricist notion of causation.

Scientific epistemology, the realist argument goes, cannot be resistant to acknowledging the real status of "unobservables" if such "theoretical" posits (for example, germs, electrons, causal powers) have proved essential in explaining natural phenomena in a series of interlocking explanatory theories. Such resistance, the realist argues, is unreasonable or even dogmatic, deriving from a residual empiricist suspicion of metaphysical speculation. But the realist's account of modern scientific practice, and the history of science, is precisely that a wide variety of such unobservables, including a number of inadequately tested theories, in fact form the "background" necessary for any kind of scientific inquiry to be possible at all. The presence of such background or auxiliary theories (some of which may in fact include the unconfirmed "lore" scientists draw on) implies that the positivist epistemology is deeply flawed and that we need to understand scientific confirmation and explanation in the light of these flaws. We need, realists such as Boyd maintain in effect, to appreciate the "dialectical" nature of all inquiry. Scientific knowledge is a result of a "reflective equilibrium" rather than the accumulation of individually tested theoretical statements, and central to its ongoing dialectic of testing, confirming, and "applying" theories is the recognition that theories that work are at least approximately true of the world as it is. "Truth" is the property not only of those statements that can be empirically verified in terms of observables but also of statements about unobservable processes and powers, "things" and also, in an ineliminable way, "theories." Thus from this postpositivist perspective the gap between natural science and social inquiry cannot be absolute, since it cannot be based on the false positivist opposition between (observable) scientific data and the unobservable world of, say, meanings and values. And this point anticipates the second objection.

Objection 2: But You Can't "Explain" Everything!

It can be argued that it is wrong to seek explanations for many human phenomena because they do not involve "knowledge" in the sense that science does. In crucial areas of our cultural lives, for instance, we might claim to be doing significant things without basing them on any kind of cognitive ground. An example of this kind of reasoning arises in ethics; the most famous kinds of demystification of dominant traditions of morality—from Nietzsche and Marx to many contemporary writers—reveal the ideological basis of moral systems. Surely here, if anywhere, some form of social constructivist thesis is the most adequate explanation? (And hence the importance of constructivism for literary and cultural studies.)

This position might offer us useful analyses of the way morality works in actual societies, but it is important to see in what ways it can be misleading. The main reason it is an inadequate general account of moral processes is that it assumes once again a too easy dichotomy between scientific knowledge and moral knowledge. On this view, scientific knowledge is possible because it is based on facts about the natural world, facts that can be tested through observation. Moral knowledge, however, can draw on no such "facts," for there are none in the area of morality. In morality, at least, we need to accept the pertinence of some sort of relativism. In fact it is only in this way that we can demystify dominant moralities, showing their connection with social power. Morality, it might be claimed, is primarily attitudinal; our debates about various competing moral positions cannot appeal to anything like a moral *knowledge* that can be reasonably evaluated. At best we claim allegiance to general "principles" and "beliefs" about moral issues and supplement them with nonmoral facts about social reality. Morality is not a cognitive activity; its disputes cannot be settled by any moral "facts of the matter."

Now this is a very basic and simple sketch of a wide range of positions—from nihilism to skepticism to some forms of ideology critique—but it is useful to clarify that the central argument relies on some form of noncognitivism, and it is this that sanctions positions in contemporary theory which assume that questions of truth, objectivity, and scientific method are irrelevant in many areas of "cultural" inquiry.[28]

28. For a particularly forceful statement of the ethical possibilities of this position, see Barbara Herrnstein Smith, *Contingencies of Value* (Cambridge: Harvard University Press, 1988), esp. chap. 7. My difference is not with Smith's ethical position but rather with her metaethical stance.

"Explanations" are thus by definition reductionist in these contexts. But the lesson to be drawn from the critiques of positivism and empiricist epistemology in science is this: if "science" is not a hard enterprise that seeks—and can provide—pretheoretical observation and confirmation but is profoundly theory dependent, then "ethics" does not have to be that fundamentally different from science.[29]

Rational, "scientific," inquiry in ethical matters need not involve confirmation of the positivist kind; instead, such inquiry is rational to the extent that it relies on reasonably accurate interlocking theories and assumptions about right and wrong, about the dignity of the individual and the nature of the good society, about the just distribution of goods and resources, and so on. On this view, moral inquiry typically relies on various "objective" moral claims, which themselves involve theses about social and political arrangements, about human nature and conceptions of moral "personhood," and so on. Judgments about the rightness or wrongness of particular actions typically involve such other judgments, whether or not they are consciously drawn on at any given time. The repertoire of "facts" and theories on which moral judgments draw is large, and moral and social inquiry are based on our evolving knowledge of human history, on human cognitive powers and adaptive capacities. Morality is thus not a precognitive enterprise in a world of hard scientific inquiry about "external" reality.

In fact, as I suggested in the previous chapter in discussing why cultural relativism might be an inadequate position, cross-cultural inquiry cannot avoid questions about human agency, rationality, and "personhood." Answers to these questions often involve moral evaluations tied to large explanatory visions and projects; rational debate between competing positions on these issues is possible to the extent that we do not retreat to a noncognitivist position. That such debates are "rational" does not entail that they will lead to one true answer; since these inquiries are open to historical change and contingency and to the fallibilism inherent in our knowledge-gathering procedures, we must reasonably expect a plurality of outcomes. But this plurality is not predicated on our considering moral and historical inquiry to be either noncognitive or irrational. In the next chapter, I develop such general arguments by grounding them in a realist account of cultural identity and personal experience, and a pluralist—specifically multiculturalist—vision of ethical and political practice.

29. For a discussion of these issues, the reader may wish to consult the debate between Gilbert Harman and Nicholas Sturgeon in their contributions to the collection *Essays on Moral Realism*, ed. Geoffrey Sayre-McCord (Ithaca: Cornell University Press, 1988).

7

IDENTITY, MULTICULTURALISM, JUSTICE

What would a realist account of social and cultural diversity look like? I have been claiming in a general way that a (realist) metatheoretical understanding of objectivity as a social achievement is necessary for a genuinely progressive social and cultural theory. In this chapter, I intend to substantiate that claim by showing how belief in objectivity can enable realists to develop a rich notion of cultural diversity as a social good and how it can help them ground their conception of ethics in a cogent theory of culture and society. It is in fact my account of the interdependence of moral and cultural processes that makes my realist version of multiculturalism stronger than the relativist or liberal versions I have examined. I understand multiculturalism as an aspect of a theory of social justice. This understanding draws upon specifically realist definitions of human agency, cultural identity, and moral knowledge—definitions that in principle leave room for objectivity as well as for error and mystification.

The thesis about agency and personhood I introduced in Chapter 5 was that in cross-cultural inquiry we should recognize one crucial limit to relativist arguments. No matter how different cultural Others are, they are never so different that they are—as typical members of their culture—incapable of acting purposefully, of evaluating their actions in light of their ideas and previous experiences, and of being "rational" in this minimal way. Without the capacity for such rational agency, I suggested, they would not be capable of social existence, since they could not develop the kind of adaptive mechanism that enables them to learn and survive, to possess a "history."

My basic point builds on the widely shared Kantian position in moral
and political theory that the capacity for rational agency is universal,
and it provides the grounds for claims about the "dignity" or "intrinsic
worth" of every human individual.[1] Such a capacity thus defines human
personhood, which is in this context a moral notion that carries a great
deal of *political* force, for the most powerful philosophical ally of all
modern struggles for equality and social justice is this universalist view
that individual human worth is absolute: it cannot be traded away, and
it does not exist in degrees. "Human worth" in this sense has nothing
whatsoever to do with "merit," since these claims about an individual's
intrinsic value (and the rights accruing from it) do not depend on the
individual's achievements or even on the extent to which she has exercised and developed her capacity for rational agency. It is the necessarily
abstract (that is, acontextual) universalist moral claim that makes such
radical demands for equality and democracy possible. So I am not convinced by some recent (vague) claims that universalism needs to be par-
ticularized before it can "acknowledge difference."[2] I think this sort of
argument confuses the levels on which the claims about universality
(versus particularity) work. The Kantian statement about human worth
or dignity as a universal phenomenon does not, and should not, depend
on the knowledge of any particularity, since it defends a radical principle that needs no contextual qualification or substantiation. That abstraction from (social and historical) context is in fact necessary,
because it is the source of the principle's power to claim the widest
applicability: any contextual qualification would compromise its radical scope. The universalist claim concerns a basic capacity shared by all
humans, rather than a comprehensive account of human nature. Hence
it is perfectly compatible with different ways of particularizing and

1. "Now I say that man, and in general every rational being, exists as an end in himself
and not merely as a means to be arbitrarily used by this or that will. He must in all his
actions, whether directed to himself or to other rational beings, always be regarded at the
same time as an end. . . . Whatever has a price can be replaced by something else as its
equivalent; on the other hand, whatever is above all price, and therefore admits of no
equivalent, has a dignity. Whatever has reference to general human inclinations and needs
has a market price; whatever, without presupposing any need, accords with a certain taste,
i.e., a delight in the mere unpurposive play of our mental powers, has an affective price;
but that which constitutes the condition under which alone something can be an end in
itself has not merely a relative worth, i.e., a price, but has an intrinsic worth, i.e., dignity."
Immanuel Kant, *Grounding for the Metaphysics of Morals* in *Ethical Philosophy*, 2d ed.,
trans. James W. Ellington (Indianapolis: Hackett, 1994), pp. 35–40 (Ak: 428, 434–35).
2. For example, see Chantal Mouffe, "Radical Democracy: Modern or Postmodern?"
in *Universal Abandon? The Politics of Postmodernism*, ed. Andrew Ross (Minneapolis:
University of Minnesota Press, 1988), p. 36.

specifying given situations and the kinds of additional rights and entitlements they call for. Indeed, this kind of contextual specification is precisely what is demanded by the universalist principle. It invites specification, but it does not depend on specification for support of the basic claim.[3]

Social analysis across cultures needs to be based on a philosophical anthropology that reveals the constructed and conventional nature of cultural meanings but does not reduce human nature to the purely conventional. The general Kantian argument I am developing is that without the capacity for second-order thoughts (the definition of the minimal rationality required for agency) humans cannot be capable of social existence. Thus the claim about agency is an aspect of social theory, not of speculative ethics. Such claims (about agency, and the model of rational capacity it implies) are no less "objective" for being culturally and "theoretically" mediated. There is no reason to assume that philosophical analysis of agency is necessarily discontinuous with the analyses of the empirical sciences; indeed a naturalistic epistemology of the kind I described in Chapter 6 suggests that there is a necessary continuity of substance and method between the "empirical-scientific" and the "philosophical." The rationality of human agents is one such area, the province of psychology and the social sciences rather than of speculation and polemic, involving a set of questions for various kinds of research to specify and develop. What resources of self-understanding do human agents typically possess, and in what ways do physiological constraints define them? How do humans come to believe what they do, in fact, believe? What relation is there between the way they come to hold certain beliefs and the question of how they ought ideally to justify them? How is rationality not just a matter of ideal justification but also related to our biological and social adaptive functions? These are genuine questions for research, and they ought not to be obscured by a holistic cultural relativism. If these researches do yield convincing answers about human cognition and action, about commonalities across cultures which cannot be explained away as culturally determined local phenomena, then questions about agency and practical rationality can yield reasonably objective answers.

But it may bear repeating that the objective knowledge we can expect

3. My discussion of (Kantian) universalism in this chapter is indebted to Gregory Vlastos, "Justice and Equality," in *Social Justice,* ed. Richard Brandt (Englewood Cliffs, N.J.: Prentice-Hall, 1962), pp. 31–72; Onora O'Neill, *Constructions of Reason* (Cambridge: Cambridge University Press, 1989); and Barbara Herman, *The Practice of Moral Judgment* (Cambridge: Harvard University Press, 1993), esp. pp. 184–207.

to gain here is not to be understood as free of (theoretical and indeed evaluative) presuppositions. As may be clear from my discussion in Chapter 6, that essentially positivist notion of objectivity—the Dragnet theory—is not only unattainable in social inquiry but an undesirable goal as well, for presuppositionless inquiry would lack those very background assumptions that guide the trajectory of our questions and even (as constructivists such as Kuhn show) determine our "observations." More crucial, as various hermeneutical thinkers from Hans-Georg Gadamer to Sandra Harding have argued, our presuppositions are themselves often repositories of knowledge, indexes of our individual or collective "standpoints" in relation to the world. Inquiry that is interested in examining its own social embeddedness will thus wish both to explain and to evaluate its own (subjective) moorings, its half-disguised values and interests, its visions of history and social change. In the postpositivist realist framework, there is a need to examine these presuppositions critically, for although they are all considered significant, there is no claim that they are all equally valid. Presuppositions and biases are epistemically essential, but they don't all illuminate equally well.

Cultural identities are good everyday instances of our deepest social biases; even when they are openly espoused, they are often based on submerged feelings and values, reflecting areas of both sensibility and judgment. They are neither to be dismissed as mere social constructions, and hence spurious, nor celebrated as our real unchanging essences in a heartless and changing world. We have the capacity to examine our social identities, considering them in light of our best understanding of other social facts and our other social relationships. Indeed this is what we do whenever we seek to transform ourselves in times of social and cultural change. On the realist view I have been advocating in this book, when we strive for objectivity in inquiry (whether in the academic disciplines or in everyday life), we seek to produce an account of the socially based distortions as well as the socially based insights that constitute our presuppositions, including our more sophisticated "theories." An examination of these distortions and insights will help us develop more general naturalistic accounts of "truth" as well as "error," accounts on the basis of which we formulate our understanding of "objectivity" as an ideal of knowledge. To develop these points, let me turn to what is clearly an urgent issue in contemporary cultural politics—the question of identity, especially of what is called identity politics. My intent is ultimately to specify the political implications of our debates over objectivity, especially the objectivity of our deepest evaluative and subjective claims. I do so in part through an interpretation of Toni Morrison's *Beloved*—a novel that is centrally about the status of social identity—explaining the theoretical connections among the projects of radical writers and critics, social activists and progressive theorists.

On the Epistemic Status of Cultural Identity

Several closely related practical and theoretical questions concerning identity emerge from current debates about cultural diversity. If multiculturalism is to be a goal of educational and political institutions, we need a workable notion of how a social group is unified by a common culture, as well as the ability to identify genuine cultural differences (and similarities) across groups. Whether cultures are inherited or consciously and deliberately created, basic problems of definition—who belongs where or with whom, who belongs and who doesn't—are unavoidable the moment we translate our dreams of diversity into social visions and agendas. Debates about minority literatures, for instance, often get bogged down in tedious disputes over genuineness or authenticity, but it is difficult to eliminate these disputes entirely. That is because they point to what is in many cases a practical problem: who can be trusted to represent the real interests of the group without fear of betrayal or misrepresentation? Every "obvious" answer (such as "it'll have to be one of us, of course!") begs the question, indicating why our views about cultural identity always involve theoretical presuppositions. The most basic questions about identity call for a more general reexamination of the relation between personal experience and public meanings—subjective choices and evaluations, on the one hand, and objective social location, on the other.

So it is not surprising that recent theoretical writings on cultural identity have focused on the status of personal experience, examining the claims to representativeness we might make on their behalf. The two dominant alternative views on cultural identity—the view associated with identity politics and characterized as essentialism and the position of postmodernism—are in fact seen as providing conflicting definitions of identity because they understand the relation between the experiences of social actors and the theoretical construct we call "their identity" very differently. Simply put, the essentialist view would be that the identity common to members of a social group is stable and more or less unchanging, since it is based on the experiences they share. Opponents of essentialism often find this view seriously misleading, since it ignores historical changes and glosses over internal differences within a group by privileging only the experiences that are common to everyone. Postmodernists in particular insist that identities are fabricated and constructed rather than self-evidently deduced from experience, since—they claim—experience cannot be a source of objective knowledge.[4] My central task here is to show, first, that the relation between experience and identity is a genuine philosophical or theoretical issue, and, second, that there is a better way to think about identity than might be suggested by the alternatives provided by the essentialists and the postmodernists. I develop this view by examining what I shall call the epistemic status of cultural identity. After outlining some of the key theoretical issues implied in discussions of identity, I explore these questions further through an analysis of Toni Morrison's remarkable novel, *Beloved*, which is directly concerned with the relations among personal experience, social meanings, and cultural identities.

One of the main components of the postmodernist case against identity politics is the charge that "experience" is not a self-evident or reliable source of knowledge and cannot be seen as grounding a social identity. Postmodernists typically warn against the desire to consider experience a foundation of other social meanings; they point out that personal experiences are basically rather unstable or slippery, and since they can only be interpreted in terms of linguistic or other signs, they must be heir to all the exegetical and interpretive problems that accompany social signification. This specifically poststructuralist view contains an epistemological thesis. Jonathan Culler's formulation of the thesis in his 1982 discussion of experience and "reading" is one of the most frequently cited: " 'Experience' always has [a] divided, duplicitous character: it has always already occurred and yet is still to be produced—an indispensable point of reference, yet never simply there."[5] This claim, with its Derridean allusions (Derrida usually couches it as a critique of specifically idealist or phenomenological notions of experience), leads to the following conclusion about the relation between ex-

4. Diana Fuss, in *Essentially Speaking: Feminism, Nature, and Difference* (New York: Routledge, 1989), provides an intelligent discussion of various kinds of essentialism and identity politics. Since my focus in the first half of this chapter is primarily on postmodernism, I have found it expedient to accept the simple definition of identity politics in terms of an ahistorical essentialism. I attempt, however, to answer some of the fundamental questions raised by proponents of identity politics (e.g., the status of experience, the epistemological privilege that the oppressed might have, and so forth) in terms that are not available through the postmodernist-essentialist debate as it is currently understood, even in resourceful reinterpretations such as the one Fuss provides.

5. Jonathan Culler, *On Deconstruction* (Ithaca: Cornell University Press, 1982), p. 63.

perience and identity: "For a woman *to read as a woman* is not to repeat an identity or an experience that is given but to play a *role* she *constructs* with reference to *her identity* as a woman, which is *also a construct*, so that the series can continue: a woman reading as a woman reading as a woman. The noncoincidence reveals an interval, a division within woman or within any reading subject and the 'experience' of that subject" (p. 64, emphasis added).[6]

I think, however, that this argument about the relation between experience and cultural identity can be best appreciated as part of the more general suspicion of foundationalism in contemporary thought, for there is nothing peculiar to experience as such which warrants its rejection on epistemological grounds. The critique of epistemological foundationalism, as we have seen, contains the suggestion that we naturalize epistemology, that is, examine the production, justification, and regulation of belief as social processes. We have seen why many antifoundationalists contend that the growth of empirical knowledge about the practices and protocols of justification in the various sciences ought to shape our understanding of epistemological questions. In this sense neither a "method" of justification nor some privileged class of foundational beliefs can be seen as existing outside the social contexts of inquiry.[7]

6. For a selective survey of the various critiques of experience in modern European philosophy, see Alice A. Jardine, *Gynesis* (Ithaca: Cornell University Press, 1985), pp. 145–55. Jardine, however, is not too helpful when it comes to basic distinctions such as that between Hegel's *Erfahrung* and the ordinary idea of everyday experience Culler and other poststructuralist critics wish to question. For a useful account of some of the responses to Culler's position, see Fuss, *Essentially Speaking*, pp. 23–37. For a postmodernist position on identity which draws on a variety of sources and identifies itself as "postcolonial," see Homi Bhabha, "Interrogating Identity: The Postcolonial Prerogative," in *Anatomy of Racism*, ed. David Theo Goldberg (Minneapolis: University of Minnesota Press, 1990), pp. 183–209; the relevant epistemological claims (as I understand them) are presented on pp. 191–94.

The current skepticism about the claims of experience can be traced back to Nietzsche, especially his critique of idealist notions of consciousness and subjectivity as self-sufficient and self-authorizing. See, e.g., *The Will to Power*, trans. Walter Kaufmann and R. J. Hollingdale, ed. Kaufmann (New York: Vintage, 1968), pp. 263–67, secs. 477–80. Nietzsche's central argument is an antipositivist one about the theory dependence of experience and facts. Whether recognition of theory dependence should lead to a denial of objectivity is one of the main questions I am addressing here. Postmodernists say that it does; Nietzsche was at least ambiguous on the subject. For Nietzsche's conception of objectivity (through the mediation of theories and perspectives), see *On the Genealogy of Morals*, trans. and ed. Walter Kaufmann (New York: Modern Library, 1968), p. 555, 3d essay, sec. 12. His conception is compatible with the antirelativist theory I am outlining here.

7. For a brief statement of the naturalistic view of philosophy as "continuous with science," rather than an "a priori propaedeutic or groundwork for science," see W. V. O. Quine,

I suggest that we consider the postmodernist critique of identity politics in analogous terms, as a critique of experiential foundationalism. If we were not to specify the critique in this way, the general postmodernist skepticism toward experience could lead to the strange conclusion that the experiences of social actors are irrelevant to explain, say, their moral or political growth. Alternatively, we could be led to conclude that moral or political change (growth or decline) is never real because it is tied to experience and can thus never be justified. The antifoundationalist thesis I have tried to retrieve from postmodernism brings into focus the accurate and damaging critique that postmodernists can make of identity politics, but by itself, it does not entail either of the two extreme conclusions to which their skepticism can lead us. The naturalist-realist account of experience I defend here is neither foundationalist nor skeptical; it maintains that experience, properly interpreted, can yield reliable and genuine knowledge, just as it can point up instances and sources of real mystification. Central to this account is the claim that the experience of social subjects has a cognitive component. Experiences can be "true" or "false," can be evaluated as justified or illegitimate in relation to the subject and his world, for "experience" refers very simply to the variety of ways humans process information. (This conception carries none of the normative baggage that comes with Hegelian *Erfahrung*, which is always tied to a particular model of ethical development. Neither does it presuppose, as Dilthey's conception of *Erlebnis* does, a necessary opposition between "lived experience" and scientific thinking.) It is on the basis of this revised understanding of experience that we can construct a realist theory of social or cultural identity in which experiences would not serve as foundations because of their self-evident authenticity but would provide some of the raw material with which we construct identities. As we shall see, to say that experiences and identities are constructed is not to prejudge the question of their epistemic status.[8] Radical skepticism about the cogni-

---

Ontological Relativity and Other Essays (New York: Columbia University Press, 1969), pp. 126–28.

8. I think it is a belief in the cognitive component of experience (and the knowledge it can give us about our social location) that is behind Houston Baker's impatience with Anthony Appiah's "debunking" account of the reality of race (both in *"Race," Writing, and Difference*, ed. Henry L. Gates Jr. [Chicago: University of Chicago Press, 1986]). Appiah's critique of racial essentialism is not based on postmodernist premises, but his response to Baker on the question of experience is evasive and might point to a vagueness in his conception of identity. See "The Conservation of 'Race,'" *Black American Literature Forum* 23 (Spring 1989), 37–60.

One way of evaluating my theory of experience and identity is to see how it responds to

tive implications of cultural identity is not the only alternative to an ahistorical essentialism.

A Realist Approach to Culture and Politics

The first claim I wish to advance is that "personal experience" is socially and "theoretically" constructed, and it is precisely in this mediated way that it yields knowledge. Let me develop this idea by drawing in part on work done by feminist theorists in the last decade and a half, beginning with an insightful essay by the philosopher Naomi Scheman.[9] Writing from an explicitly antiindividualist perspective on such things as emotions and feelings, Scheman explains how the notion of our emotions as our own "inner" possessions is fundamentally misleading. She focuses on the anger that women who have been members of feminist consciousness-raising groups often come to feel. This anger, Scheman says, should not be seen as a fully formed emotion that was waiting to be released or expressed in the context of the group. Rather, the emotion becomes what it is through the mediation of the social and emotional environment that the consciousness-raising group provides. Part of what constitutes this environment is an alternative narrative or account of the individual's relationship with the world, and these alternative accounts are unavoidably theoretical. They involve notions of what a woman is supposed to be angry about, what she should not tolerate, what is worth valuing—notions that are not merely moral but also so-

---

the challenge the historian Joan Scott has formulated quite well: "Experience is not a word we can do without, although it is tempting, given its usage to essentialize identity and reify the subject, to abandon it altogether. But experience . . . serves as a way of talking about what happened, of establishing difference and similarity, of claiming knowledge. . . . Given the ubiquity of the term, it seems to me more useful to work with it, to analyze its operations and to redefine its meaning. . . . The study of experience . . . must call into question its originary status in historical explanation." Scott, " 'Experience,' " in *Feminists Theorize the Political*, ed. Judith Butler and Joan Scott (London: Routledge, 1992), p. 37. Scott points out that postmodernist attacks on experience are a critique of a certain kind of epistemological view. I am not sure, however, that I agree with her assumption that a "genuinely nonfoundational[ist] history" is possible only "when historians take as their project *not* the reproduction and transmission of knowledge said to be arrived at through experience, but the analysis of the production of that knowledge itself" (p. 37). I suggest that once we acknowledge the cognitive status of experience, as well as its necessary theory dependence, we can conceive legitimate ways of reproducing and transmitting "knowledge said to be arrived at through experience." As I shall show, this is in fact the best way to understand the "epistemic privilege" of, say, the oppressed, as well as how it demands hermeneutical respect from the historian.

9. Naomi Scheman, "Anger and the Politics of Naming," in *Women and Language in Literature and Society*, ed. Sally McConnell-Ginet, Ruth Borker, and Nelly Furman (New York: Praeger, 1980), pp. 174–87.

cial-theoretical in nature. They imply social visions and critiques of what exists; at the very least they suggest that it is perfectly okay to feel dissatisfied about certain relationships and social arrangements. Scheman's point is that in many important instances such alternative accounts and notions help organize inchoate or confused feelings to produce an emotion that is experienced more directly and fully. It follows then that this new emotion, say anger, and the ways it is experienced are not purely personal or individual. A necessary part of its form and shape is determined by the nonindividual social meanings that the theories and accounts supply. It would be false to say that this emotion is the individual's own "inner" possession, and that she alone has "privileged access" to its meaning or significance (p. 179). Rather, our emotions provide evidence of the extent to which even our deepest personal experiences are socially constructed, mediated by visions and values that are "political" in nature, that refer outward to the world beyond the individual.

> The structure that consciousness-raising groups provide for the interpretation of feelings and behavior is overtly political; it should be immediately obvious that one is presented with a particular way of making sense of one's experience, a way intimately linked with certain controversial political views. Consciousness-raising groups are not, however, unique in this respect. What they are is unusually honest: the political framework is explicit (though often vague) and openly argued for. The alternative is not "a clear space in which to get your head together" but a hidden political framework that pretends not to be one. (p. 186)

There are different ways of making sense of an experience, and the way we make sense of it can in fact create a new experience.

Consider Scheman's example, Alice, who joins a consciousness-raising group and in the safe and supportive environment provided by other women like her learns to recognize that her depression and guilt, though sincerely felt, may not be legitimate. In fact, they hide from her her real needs and feelings, as well as the real nature of her situation. "The guilt and depression," the group might argue and Alice might come to acknowledge, "are a response to and a cover for those other feelings, notably feelings of anger. Alice is urged to recognize her anger as legitimate and justifiable in this situation" (p. 177). Here is where the "political" nature of the views Alice is now asked to ponder comes in: she is not seen as merely bringing to the surface something she, as a lone individual, knew and felt all along. Rather, her emotion (the anger) is constituted in part by the "views" about the world, about herself in it, and the details of what is acceptable and unacceptable in this new theoretical picture. She comes to experience anger by reinterpreting her old feelings of depression, guilt, and so on, but she does so unavoidably with the aid of theory, an alternative, socially produced construction of herself and the world. Now, "we may describe [Alice] as having discovered that she had been angry, though she hadn't previously recognized it. She would, in fact, have denied it if she were asked: 'Why *should* I be angry?' It is significant," Scheman goes on, "that a denial that one is angry often takes the form of a denial that one would be justified in being angry. Thus one's discovery of anger can often occur not from focusing on one's feelings but from a political redescription of one's situation" (p. 177). The reason we say that Alice "discovers" she has been angry is that the anger underlay her vague or confused feelings of depression or guilt; now it organizes these feelings, giving them coherence and clarity. And our judgment that the anger is deeper than the depression or guilt is derived from (and corroborated by) our understanding of Alice's changing personal and social situation, an understanding that is based in part on a "theory."[10]

Here we discern what might be the strongest argument against the essentialist picture of cultural identity. The constructed nature of experience shows why there is no guarantee that my experiences will lead me to some common core of values or beliefs that link me with every other member of my cultural group. Our experiences do not have self-evident meanings, for they are in part theoretical affairs, and our access to our remotest personal feelings is dependent on social narratives, paradigms, and even ideologies. In fact, drawing on a Nietzschean theme, the postmodernist might declare that we need to go further, that the kind of theory dependence I have just identified leads to a radical perspectivism or relativism. When we choose among these alternative ways of organizing and interpreting experience, we make a purely arbitrary choice, determined by our social locations or our prerational ideological commitments. "Experience" remains unstable and unreliable. Why, then, speak of the cognitive component of personal experience, as though we might be able to glean objective knowledge from it?[11]

10. This theory-mediated process of coming to acknowledge one's genuine feelings is central to any form of political consciousness raising. The antiracist work done by the "freedom schools" in the South also drew on normative theories of personhood and racial justice in order to enable victims of racism to interpret their experiences and their needs accurately. Such "interpretations" are, I suggest, never purely intellectual.

11. I am thinking here of the kind of extreme thesis about "drives" and "needs" which

Oddly enough, this postmodernist response turns out to reveal a disguised form of foundationalism, for it remains within a specifically positivist conception of objectivity and knowledge. It assumes that the only kind of objective knowledge we can have is independent of (socially produced and revisable) theoretical presuppositions and concludes that the theory dependence of experience is evidence that it is always epistemically suspect. But what if we reject as overly abstract and limiting this conception of objectivity as presupposition-free knowledge? What if we give up both radical perspectivism and the dream of a "view from nowhere" in order to grant that all the knowledge we can ever have is necessarily dependent on theories and perspectives? We might then be able to see that there are different kinds and degrees of theory dependence and understand how theory-laden and socially constructed experiences can lead to a knowledge that is accurate and reliable.

Consider Scheman's example again. Alice's emotion, "anger," is the result of a political redescription of herself and her world, but if that new description happens to explain adequately and cogently—as social, psychological, and moral theory—the constituent features of Alice's situation, then Alice's experience of the emotion leads us to conclude that she has just come to know something, something not merely about her repressed feelings but also about her self, her personhood, and the range of its moral and political claims and needs. She comes to this knowledge by discovering or understanding features of the social and cultural arrangements of her world which define her sense of self, the choices she is taught to have, the range of personal capacities she is expected to exploit and exercise. And she does so in the process of learning to trust her judgments about herself, recognizing how others like her have done so as well. If this is the case, Alice's anger is not merely a personal or private thing inside, as it were, her own "innermost" self; rather, her anger is the theoretical prism through which she views her world and herself in it correctly. Hers is then an objective assessment of her situation, and in this strong sense, her anger is rational and justified.[12]

Nietzsche sometimes combined with his valid antipositivist insights: "Against positivism, which halts at phenomena—'There are only *facts*'—I would say: No, facts is [sic] precisely what there is not, only interpretations. We cannot establish any fact 'in itself': perhaps it is folly to want to do such a thing. . . . It is our needs that interpret the world; our drives and their For and Against. Every drive is a kind of lust to rule; each one has its perspective that it would like to compel all the other drives to accept as a norm" (*Will*, p. 267, sec. 481).

12. In emphasizing that Alice comes to know something about her world through her emotion, I wish to show how Scheman's account of emotion is a realist one. Scheman does

The example also suggests why emotions do not have to be seen as fully explicit beliefs or clear processes of reasoning for us to appreciate their cognitive role. We misunderstand the way Alice's anger gives coherence and shape to her previously confused feelings if we do not also appreciate the extent to which her experience of anger is a process whereby she weighs one vaguely felt hunch against another, reinterprets and reevaluates the information she considered relevant to her feelings and her situation, and thus redefines the contours of "her world." This sifting and reinterpretation of information sometimes happens quite suddenly; at other times, it becomes clearer and more lucid slowly and only in retrospect. The emotion is this not-entirely-explicit way Alice learns to reanalyze or even discern crucial features of her situation.

Emotions fall somewhere between conscious reasoning and reflexlike instinctual responses to stimuli. They are, as Ronald de Sousa has proposed, ways of paying attention to the world. They fill the "gaps" between our instinctually driven desires, on the one hand, and our fully developed reasoning faculties, on the other, especially when we need to decide what to do or believe. Emotions are "determinate patterns of salience"; like Kuhn's scientific paradigms, says de Sousa, they provide our half-articulated "questions" about the world. Emotions are "what we see the world 'in terms of,' " and therefore, like the scientific paradigm, they "cannot be articulated propositions."[13] It is significant that the focus her anger provides allows Alice to discover some of the constitutive features of her world. Emotions enable and encourage specific interpretations or evaluations of the world, and our judgment that Alice's anger is rational, justified, or "appropriate" (de Sousa's term) is a judgment about the accuracy of the interpretation and the objectivity of the evaluation. In Aristotelian terms, an essential component of Alice's moral development would be the increased capacity of her analytical and affective faculties to work together for cognitive purposes. Emotional

---

not identify her position as realist, perhaps because she thinks (wrongly, to my mind) that realism about emotions can only lead to a sort of physicalism: e.g., "types of psychological states (like being angry or in pain) actually are types of physical states (like certain patterns of neurons firing)." Naomi Scheman, "Individualism and the Objects of Psychology," in *Discovering Reality*, ed. Sandra Harding and Merrill B. Hintikka (Dordrecht: Riedel, 1983), p. 225. My interpretation of emotions in this chapter should suggest a better conception of the realist view. For a cognitivist-realist understanding of emotions compatible with mine, see the many valuable suggestions in Audre Lorde, *Sister Outsider* (Trumansburg, N.Y.: Crossing Press, 1984), esp. pp. 54–58.

13. Ronald de Sousa, "The Rationality of Emotions," in *Explaining Emotions*, ed. Amélie Oksenberg Rorty (Berkeley: University of California Press, 1980), pp. 136–38.

growth would be central to moral growth, and both presuppose the post-positivist notion of theory-mediated objectivity I am defending.[14]

There is no commitment here to the silly idea that all emotions are equally justified or rational. Questions about the legitimacy of emotions are answered by looking at the features of the subject in her world, and it is possible to glean an accurate picture of these features not only through the right theory (or narrative or description) but also through the relevant information that we can examine and share. "The difference between someone who is irrationally angry and someone who is not," Scheman explains, "may not be a difference in what they *feel* so much as a difference in what sorts of feelings, under what sorts of circumstances they are ready to take as anger. When we judge that people are right to deny the name of anger to their irrational reactions, we are often judging that their situation, unlike Alice's, does not really call for anger" (pp. 178–79). If Alice's father or husband were to become angry at Alice for supposedly betraying their trust by going to the consciousness-raising group meetings and by becoming dissatisfied with her personal relationships, we would evaluate these emotions as we do Alice's. The anger may be sincerely felt, but whether or not we consider it justified or legitimate would depend on what we think of the underlying political and moral views of these men about the role of women in society, as well as the information (about themselves, about their society, and so on) they draw on—or ignore—to support these views. This kind of assessment is naturally both complex and difficult. But the difficulty is not due to anything peculiar to emotions. All experience—and emotions offer the paradigm case here—is socially constructed, but the constructedness does not make it arbitrary or unstable in advance. Experiences are crucial indexes of our relationships with our world (including our relationships with ourselves), and to stress their cognitive nature is to argue that they can be susceptible to varying degrees of socially constructed truth or error and can serve as sources of objective knowledge or socially produced mystification.

14. "A person of practical insight," writes Martha Nussbaum, imaginatively and resourcefully elaborating Aristotle's view of moral development, "will cultivate emotional openness and responsiveness in approaching a new situation. Frequently, it will be her passional response, rather than detached thinking, that will guide her to the appropriate recognitions. 'Here is a case where a friend needs my help': this will often be 'seen' first by the feelings that are constituent parts of friendship, rather than by pure intellect. Intellect will often want to consult these feelings to get information about the true nature of the situation. Without them, its approach to a new situation would be blind and obtuse. . . . Without feeling, a part of the correct perception is missing." Martha Nussbaum, *Love's Knowledge* (Oxford: Oxford University Press, 1990), pp. 78–79.

This kind of argument about the cognitive component of experience helps strengthen the claim made by feminist standpoint theorists that in a gender-stratified society women's experiences are often significant repositories of oppositional knowledge, but this does not mean that experience serves to ground feminist knowledge. "It is rather," Sandra Harding maintains, "the subsequently articulated observations of and theory about the rest of nature and social relations" which help us make sense of "women's lives" in our sexist social structure.[15] "Women's lives" constitute an "objective location" (p. 123) from which feminist research should examine the world, because without it we would not be able to explain a significant feature of our society. "Women's lives" is a theoretical notion or construct, but it involves the kind of social theory without which we could not make sense of—explain—a central feature of our world. The theoretical notion "women's lives" refers not just to the experiences of women but also to a particular social arrangement of gender relations and hierarchies which can be analyzed and evaluated. The standpoint of women in this society is not self-evidently deduced from the "lived experience" of individual women or groups of women. Rather, the standpoint is based in "women's lives" to the extent that it articulates their material and epistemological interests. Such interests are discovered by an explanatory empirical account of the nature of gender stratification, how it is reproduced and regulated, and the particular social groups and values it legitimates. Our definition of social location is thus closely tied to our understanding of social interests.[16]

15. Sandra Harding, *Whose Science? Whose Knowledge?* (Ithaca: Cornell University Press, 1991), p. 124.

16. This explanatory notion of "objective interests" implies comparison with other competing explanations of the same phenomena. When marxists talk about the objective interests of the working class, they are trying to explain the location of the class in terms, on the one hand, of the relations of production and, on the other, of their theories about human freedom and social justice. Ernesto Laclau and Chantal Mouffe's criticism of the notion of objective interests thus seems to be either hasty or disingenuous: "In our view," they write, ". . . it is necessary to . . . discard the idea of a perfectly unified and homogeneous agent, such as the 'working class' of classical discourse. . . . [F]undamental interests in socialism cannot be *logically* deduced from determinate positions in the economic process." Laclau and Mouffe, *Hegemony and Socialist Strategy: Towards a Radical Democratic Politics*, trans. Winston Moore and Paul Cammack (London: Verso, 1985), p. 84. The theoretical assumption here is that "fundamental interests in socialism" can either be "logically deduced" on the basis of "determinate positions in the economic process" or else not discovered at all. The view that "interests" might be inferred (or deduced, in their stronger language) solely on the basis of "determinate positions" without the mediation of any theory is clearly based on a positivist understanding of explanation. Having rejected this view, Laclau and Mouffe leap to the postmodernist conclusion that a social group's inter-

An important metatheoretical consequence follows from this. Objectivity is inextricably tied to social and historical conditions, and objective knowledge is the product not of disinterested theoretical inquiry so much as of particular kinds of social practice. In the case of social phenomena such as sexism and racism, whose distorted representation benefits the powerful and established groups and institutions, an attempt at an objective explanation is necessarily continuous with oppositional political struggles. Objective knowledge of such social phenomena is in fact often dependent on the theoretical knowledge that activism creates, for without these alternative constructions and accounts, Harding notes, our capacity to interpret and understand the dominant ideologies and institutions is limited to those created or sanctioned by these very ideologies and institutions (p. 127). Moreover, as Richard Boyd shows in an important essay, even moral knowledge (for example, knowledge of "fundamental human goods") is to a great extent "experimental knowledge," dependent on social and political experiments. "We would not have been able to explore the dimensions of our needs for artistic expression and appreciation," Boyd points out, "had not social and technological developments made possible cultures in which, for some classes at least, there was the leisure to produce and consume art. We would not have understood the role of political democracy in [shaping our conception of the human] good had the conditions not arisen in which the first limited democracies developed. Only after the moral insights gained from the first democratic experiments were in hand, were we equipped to see the depth of the moral peculiarity of slavery. Only since the establishment of the first socialist societies are we even beginning to obtain the data necessary to assess the role of egalitarian social practices in fostering the good."[17]

The claim that political activity is in various ways continuous with attempts to seek scientific, objective explanations of social reality un-

---

ests cannot be identified through an objective explanation: There is no "constitutive principle for social agents [interests or anything else] which can be fixed in an ultimate class core" (p. 85). This leads to the more general assertion that "[u]nfixity [is] the condition of every social identity" (p. 85). The glib antiobjectivism of many postmodernist positions is based on such positivist presuppositions about the nature of inquiry. For a useful point of contrast, see the accounts of Marx's conception of scientific and moral objectivity in Peter Railton, "Marx and the Objectivity of Science," in *The Philosophy of Science*, ed. Richard Boyd, Philip Gasper, and J. D. Trout (Cambridge: MIT Press, 1991), pp. 763–73, and Alan Gilbert, "Marx's Moral Realism," in *After Marx*, ed. Terence Ball and James Farr (Cambridge: Cambridge University Press, 1984), pp. 154–83.

17. Richard Boyd, "How to Be a Moral Realist," in *Essays on Moral Realism*, ed. Geoffrey Sayre-McCord (Ithaca: Cornell University Press, 1988), p. 205.

derscores that objective knowledge should not be sought by meta-theoretically sundering the realm of "hard facts" from the realm of values. In the postpositivist picture of knowledge I am outlining here, some evaluations—from vaguely felt ethical judgments to more developed normative theories of right and wrong—can in crucial instances enable and facilitate greater accuracy in representing social reality, providing better ways of organizing the relevant or salient facts, urging us to look in newer and more productive ways. We have seen in the case of Alice how this epistemic reorientation takes place on a very personal level, where an individual's recognition and conscious acceptance of her feelings makes possible the search and discovery through which she comes to discern crucial features of her situation. For such emotional growth is a form of epistemic training as well. When we speak of collective political struggles and oppositional social movements, we can see how the political is continuous with the epistemological. In fact, one may interpret Marx's famous eleventh thesis on Feuerbach as making just such an epistemological argument. It does not urge us to give up the job of interpreting the world (in the interest of changing it) but instead points out how the possibility of accurately interpreting our world fundamentally depends on our coming to know what it would take to change it, on our identifying the central relations of power and privilege which sustain it and make the world what it is. And we learn to identify these relations through our various attempts to change the world, not merely by contemplating it as it is.[18]

We can thus see how the unavoidability of theory, one of the key ideas of postpositivist intellectual culture, leads to an important nonrelativist insight about the political moorings of knowledge: there are better or worse social and political theories, and we can seek less distorted and more objective knowledge of social phenomena by creating the conditions for the production of better knowledge. Given the pervasiveness of both sexism and individualism in Alice's culture, it is more likely that she will come to discover the reality about herself and her situation in a feminist consciousness-raising group than by herself at home. Research institutions that employ scientists from a wide variety of social backgrounds (and do not confine decision making about research topics or the allocation of funds to a handful of individuals from the socially advantaged groups) will be less likely than other institutions to betray unconscious racial or gender bias in their research agendas. Objectivity is something we struggle for, in a number of direct and not so obvious

18. See Railton, "Marx and the Objectivity of Science," pp. 770–71.

ways, and this struggle puts into perspective the epistemological privilege "experience" might give us. Feminist standpoint theorists such as Harding both develop and clarify Marx's argument about the political bases of knowledge production. A standpoint, says Harding, "is not something that anyone can have simply by claiming it" (p. 127). Since "experience" is only the raw material for the kind of political and social knowledge that constitutes a feminist standpoint, it cannot guarantee or ground it. A standpoint is thus "an achievement" (p. 127), both theoretical and political. The objectivity we achieve is profoundly theory dependent and thus postpositivist. It is based on our developing understanding of the various causes of distortion and mystification. I believe a naturalistic conception of human inquiry best suits the various examples I have been discussing. An essential part of this conception of inquiry would be an understanding of fallibility which is developed and specified through explanations of how different kinds and degrees of error arise. Precision and depth in understanding the sources and causes of error or mystification help us define the nature of objectivity, and central to this definition would be the possibility of its revision and improvement on the basis of new information. This conception of fallibility is thus based on a dialectical opposition between objectivity and error. Since error in this view is opposed not to certainty but rather to objectivity as a theory-dependent, socially realizable goal, the possibility of error does not sanction skepticism about the possibility of knowledge. Such skepticism (postmodernist or otherwise) is usually the flip side of the quest for certainty.[19]

19. One way to evaluate different versions of postmodernism is to examine the conception of objectivity they define themselves against; another is to look carefully at precisely how they develop their notion of fallibility. Donna Haraway has suggested in a well-known essay that we need to go beyond "realism" (by which I think she means positivism) to conceive the world (i.e., the object of knowledge) as a "coding trickster with whom we must learn to converse." See Haraway, "Situated Knowledges: The Science Question in Feminism and the Privilege of Partial Perspective," in Simians, Cyborgs, and Women (New York: Routledge, 1991), esp. pp. 198–99, 201. "The Coyote or Trickster," she argues, "embodied in American Southwest Indian accounts, suggests our situation when we give up mastery but keep searching for fidelity, knowing all the while we will be hoodwinked" (p. 199). The image suggests the epistemological injunction to acknowledge "the agency of the world" by "mak[ing] room for some unsettling possibilities, including a sense of the world's independent sense of humour" (p. 199). This view is for the most part compatible with the postpositivist epistemology I am developing here, but Haraway's conception of fallibility is not precise enough to be very helpful. It is important to know more than that "we will be hoodwinked," formulated here as a generalized possibility. We do not begin to understand the hoodwinking until we appreciate why and where we were wrong in our expectations (or theories). In many situations—many more than Haraway's image suggests—it is barely useful to know that we were wrong unless we are also led to a more

My proposal is that we reorient our theorizing of cultural identity in the following way: instead of conceiving identities as self-evidently based on the authentic experiences of members of a cultural or social group (the conception that underlies identity politics) or as all equally unreal to the extent that they lay any claim to the real experiences of real people because experience is a radically mystifying term (this is the postmodernist alternative), we need to explore the possibility of a theoretical understanding of social and cultural identity in terms of objective social location. To do so, we need a cognitivist conception of experience, as I have been suggesting, a conception that will allow for both legitimate and illegitimate experience, enabling us to see experience as source of both real knowledge and social mystification. Both the knowledge and the mystification are, however, open to analysis on the basis of empirical information about our social situation and a theoretical account of our current social and political arrangements. Whether we inherit an identity—masculinity, being black—or we actively choose one on the basis of our radical political predilections—radical lesbianism, black nationalism, socialism—our identities are ways of making sense of our experiences. Identities are theoretical constructions that enable us read the world in specific ways. It is in this sense that they are valuable, and their epistemic status should be taken very seriously. In them, and through them, we learn to define and reshape our values and commitments, we give texture and form to our collective futures. Both the essentialism of identity politics and the skepticism of the postmodernist position seriously underread the real epistemic and political complexities of our social and cultural identities.

Postcolonial Identity and Moral Epistemology in "Beloved"

These complexities are at the heart of Toni Morrison's postcolonial cultural project in her remarkable novel *Beloved*.[20] Central to the novel

---

precise understanding of the sources of our error. I agree with Haraway that we should give up (foundationalist) "mastery" in favor of (postpositivist) "fidelity," but our conception of that fidelity will be richer to the extent that we can specify and deepen our understanding of the conditions that lead to our "hoodwinking." Objectivity and error are the products of social practice, and we should attempt to understand as much as we legitimately can about them (in naturalistic terms) before we generalize about our condition of original epistemic sinfulness.

20. Toni Morrison, *Beloved* (New York: Knopf, 1987), hereafter cited parenthetically in the text.

is a vision of the continuity between experience and identity, a vision only partly articulated in the juxtaposition of the dedication ("Sixty Million and more"), with its claim to establish kinship with the unnamed and unremembered who perished in the infamous Middle Passage, together with the epigraph's audacious appropriation of God's voice from Hosea, quoted by Paul in Romans, chapter 9: "I will call them my people, / which were not my people; / and her beloved, / which was not beloved."

Laying claim to a past often serves simply to create an ancestry for oneself. What makes this juxtaposition of allusions in *Beloved* especially significant is that it suggests how the claim is going to be spelled out later in the novel, the terms in which one's relationship with the past is going to be conceived. The community sought in *Beloved* involves as its essence a moral and imaginative expansion of oneself, in particular one's capacity to experience. Only in the context of this expanded capacity can we understand the trajectory of the moral debate that informs and organizes the narrative: the debate between Paul D and Sethe about the nature and limits of Sethe's "mother-love." Is Sethe's killing of her "crawling already?" child to prevent her from being captured and enslaved an instance of a love that's too "thick," as Paul seems to think, an emotional attachment that makes Sethe forget that she is transgressing the limits of what is morally permissible for humans? "You got two feet, Sethe, not four," Paul says incomprehendingly when he hears what she has done (p. 165). How we evaluate Sethe and this incipient moral debate depends on how we interpret Paul D's growth in the second half of the novel and how we define the relationship between his ability to understand and his emotional capacity to respond to the dead and absent members of the community of the oppressed.

Sethe's defiant maternal cry that she has "milk enough for all"—repeated insistently over the course of the novel—is as much a response to Paul D's specific moral accusation as it is a reminder of her powerful will to survive. For she claims to have had will enough to survive the indignity of the rape in which her owners steal her milk from her, and also the determined love to nourish the generations of children—alive and dead—who will together create the community she seeks. Sethe's argument would be, I suppose, that there is no way to respond to Paul D's question on its own terms. The moral injunction—you are human after all, Sethe, and there are things you simply cannot do!—is too abstract. The political vision of a community of the oppressed, which the novel seeks primarily through the agency of its women characters, provides the context in which Paul's challenge can be specified, given historical resonance and meaning. We should begin, then, by acknowledging the need for this community, a need that is from Sethe's perspective not only affective but also epistemic.

To create this community, the survivor of slavery must begin by facing the immediate past more directly, and neither Sethe nor Paul D is able to do so alone. Only when they are together, and together in a very specific way that I shall describe in a moment, are they able to face the horror of Sweet Home. The act of remembering, Morrison's text insists, is not simply an attempt to know the past by recapitulating its events. The cognitive task of "rememory" is dependent on an emotional achievement, on the labor of trusting—oneself, one's judgments, one's companions. Paul D's arrival at 124 Bluestone Road opens up the possibility of Sethe's renegotiation with her own past, for that past is unavoidably collective. Like Alice's in Naomi Scheman's example, Sethe's capacity to know herself is tied up with her capacity to feel with others: "The morning she woke up next to Paul D . . . she . . . thought . . . of the temptation to trust and remember that gripped her as she stood before the cooking stove in his arms. Would it be all right? Would it be all right to go ahead and feel? Go ahead and *count on something?*" (p. 38). Trusting enables remembering because it organizes and interprets crucial new information about one's life: it might be safe, now, to acknowledge one's feelings; one might be justified in counting on the relative safety of this environment. This safe environment is based on cooperation, on the most basic form of social activity, and it restores to Sethe some of her most intimate and personal experience of herself: "To push busyness into the corners of the room and just stand there a minute or two, naked from shoulder blade to waist, relieved of the weight of her breasts, smelling the stolen milk again and the pleasure of baking bread[.] Maybe this one time she could stop dead still in the middle of a cooking meal—not even leave the stove—and feel the hurt her back ought to. Trust things and remember things because the last of the Sweet Home men was there to catch her if she sank?" (p. 18). Trusting involves emotional labor because Sethe has to reorganize her feelings toward others and herself; she has to come to acknowledge what is appropriate to feel. So trusting depends in part on her ability to judge whether something is appropriate, that is, to appraise relevant information about her changing situation and about her needs and desires. The assurance that Paul would be "there to catch her if she sank" changes her world profoundly, makes possible a cognitive reorientation. Paul is important because he can raise the possibility of trust, because he can help create the emotional conditions in which a new kind of knowing is possible.

Indeed, the main argument for seeing Paul D as a central participant in the moral debate the novel stages is that from the very beginning he reveals a capacity for an extraordinary kind of sympathy. That is in fact why we take his later charge ("You got two feet, Sethe, not four") seriously, acknowledging the potential force of his judgment. Although male and an outsider in Sethe's world of dead and living kinfolk, Paul D has a moral and imaginative life that can take him far beyond what traditional individualist notions of feeling and emotion might lead us to expect.

Notice in the following extraordinary passage how a kind of braiding of consciousnesses is achieved, a weaving together of emotional perspectives, through which a memory is relived and a new meaning created. Sethe and Paul have just finished having sex, and it has been disappointingly short, abrupt, and meaningless. As they lie together in discomfort and embarrassment, a fused memory wells up without having been verbalized. Sethe remembers both her wedding night and the first time she had sex with her husband, Halle, in the cornfields in Sweet Home; Paul's related memory of that not-so-private event adds counterpoint and resonance. The perspectives shift back and forth, occasionally without warning, and "fusion" is achieved gradually. The text points to new knowledge as well as a way of knowing, both registered in the word "free" and its gentle but deliberate modulation:

> Halle wanted privacy for [Sethe] and got public display. Who could miss a ripple in a cornfield on a quiet cloudless day? He, Sixo and both of the Pauls sat under Brother [the tree] pouring water from a gourd over their heads, and through eyes streaming with well water, they watched the confusion of tassels in the field below. . . .
>
> Paul D sighed and turned over. Sethe took the opportunity afforded by his movement to shift as well. Looking at Paul D's back, she remembered that some of the corn stalks broke, folded down over Halle's back, and among the things her fingers clutched were husk and cornsilk hair.
>
> How loose the silk. How jailed down the juice.
>
> The jealous admiration of the watching men melted with the feast of new corn they allowed themselves that night. Plucked from the broken stalks that Mr. Garner could not doubt was the fault of the raccoon. . . . [N]ow Paul D couldn't remember how finally they'd cooked those ears too young to eat. What he did remember was parting the hair to get to the tip, the edge of his fingernail just under, so as not to graze a single kernel.

The pulling down of the tight sheath, the ripping sound always convinced her it hurt.

As soon as one strip of husk was down, the rest obeyed and the ear yielded up to him its shy rows, exposed at last. How loose the silk. How quick the jailed-up flavor ran free.

No matter what all your teeth and wet fingers anticipated, there was no accounting for the way that simple joy could shake you.

How loose the silk. How fine and loose and free. (p. 27)

Paul's and Sethe's memories fuse in the repeated image of the cornsilk and the juice, and the resonance of the word "free" the second time it appears is much greater than the reference to the loose cornsilk or the jailed-up juice might suggest. The fusion of perspectives suggests something new, something that Sethe and Paul in fact have in common—a concern with the moral implications of being enslaved and being free. After she has arrived in Cincinnati, Sethe realizes that freedom for the slave involves more than a flight from the legal condition of bondage: the colonial condition continues unless it is faced as a fundamental ethical challenge. "Freeing yourself was one thing," she thinks, articulating the constitutive cultural challenge of the postcolonial condition, "claiming ownership of that freed self was another" (p. 95).

In fact the disagreement between her and Paul D is defined by a question about the real implications of political freedom. Can you really be free, Paul seems to ask, if your love is so "thick" that it binds you to the level of the subrational, that it demeans your essential human self by distorting your capacity to determine which actions are simply not morally permissible for humans? Part of Sethe's response to this charge is evident in the passage I have just analyzed. Sethe is not simply reliving the first time she had sex with Halle; she thinks also about her wedding night and her relationship with her husband. Mrs. Garner is surprised that Sethe insists on a ceremony to make her union with Halle a formal event. She sews her own dress, refusing to be lowered to the level of the breeder that slavery insisted she be. For Sethe, freedom—even under slavery—appears as the ineliminable human need for self-determination, with the capacity for moral agency at its core. So it is not enough to be free from legally imposed bondage; one must also claim ownership of one's freed self. And this ownership, Sethe might have argued with Paul, cannot be a purely individual affair. To understand this ownership adequately, we need access to the buried memories and experiences of others who might have shared our experience. We need to reconstruct what our relevant community might have been, appreciate the social and historical dimensions of our innermost selves. Paul's moral accusation is unfair and simplistic to the very extent that it seems like the application of a general law to an isolated individual act; Sethe suggests that Paul's judgment itself needs to be reevaluated in the context of the knowledge of their common historical experience, a knowledge that remains unavailable to the individual by herself.

For both Sethe and Paul, reclaiming community involves personal growth in their rational and affective capacities to deal with their traumatic pasts. In psychoanalytic terms, the novel traces their developing ability to "work through" the implications of their complex cathectic relations with Sweet Home and everything that followed. In the early chapters both characters reveal a deep resistance to confronting their pasts on any level, which is manifested in their inability to narrate their own personal stories by themselves. If for Sethe surviving was predicated on "keeping the past at bay" (p. 42), keeping it from forming a coherent narrative with the present and the future, the attempt to construct and narrate the story together with Paul can succeed only if the past ceases to be a form of uncontrolled repetition, "acted out" by the subject rather than integrated cognitively and affectively into her life. Even when it is successful, the narrating is at best fitful and uneasy; "working through" the traumatizing past involves dealing with the way it effectively arrests one's agency: "[Sethe] was spinning. Round and round the room. Past the jelly cupboard, past the window, past the front door, another window, the sideboard, the keeping-room door, the dry sink, the stove—back to the jelly cupboard. Paul D sat at the table watching her drift into view then disappear behind his back, turning like a slow but steady wheel. . . . [T]he wheel never stopped" (p. 159). To go beyond this image of motion and energy without real movement, Sethe has to integrate more fully into her emotional life the theoretical knowledge she both has and resists: if her past is not just hers alone, she can regain its meaning only through collective effort—with Paul, with Denver and Beloved. Her anxieties about trusting, herself as well as others, cannot be resolved at a purely intellectual level.[21]

21. Mae Henderson has provided an insightful analysis of the historiographical project of *Beloved*, focusing on Morrison's views about memory and narrative. See Henderson, "Toni Morrison's *Beloved*: Remembering the Body as Historical Text," in *Comparative American Identities*, ed. Hortense Spillers (New York: Routledge, 1991), pp. 62–86. For an application of psychoanalytical concepts such as "acting out" and "working through" to the historian's relationship with his or her object, see Dominick LaCapra, "Representing the Holocaust: Reflections on the Historians' Debate," in *Probing the Limits of Representation: Nazism and the "Final Solution,"* ed. Saul Friedlander (Cambridge: Harvard University Press, 1992), pp. 108-27, 356–60. This theme is developed in what is easily one of

Morrison indicates in several ways why historical memory might be available to human subjects only if we expand our notion of personal experience to refer to ways of both feeling and knowing, and to include collectives as well as individual selves. The braiding and fusing of voices and emotions makes possible the new knowledge we seek about our postcolonial condition. That it does is evident even more clearly in the searching, exploratory quality of the chant of the black women who at the end help Sethe exorcise the ghost, searching for something that is, once again, both the stuff of history and a new knowledge: "When the women assembled outside 124, Sethe was breaking a lump of ice into chunks. . . . When the music entered the window, she was wringing a cool cloth to put on Beloved's forehead. . . . Sethe opened the door and reached for Beloved's hand. Together they stood in the doorway. For Sethe it was as though the Clearing had come to her with all its heat and shimmering leaves, where the voices of women searched for the right combination, the key, the code, the sound that broke the back of words. Building voice upon voice until they found it, and when they did it was a wave of sound wide enough to sound deep water and knock the pods off chestnut trees. It broke over Sethe and she trembled like the baptized in its wash" (p. 261). The dense allusions in the images bring to mind the varieties of ways people join to transcend their present condition, to recreate past and future through an act of collective imagination and will. And this act is something one learns; one searches for the knowledge to be able to do it right. Images of water evoke both the unremembered dead of the Middle Passage and the power of giving birth; the Clearing brings to mind the collective healing ritual presided over by Sethe's dead mother in law, the ritual that makes possible the communal life of the survivors of slavery. In every instance the collective effort produces something new, the fusion of voices (the call and response, the braiding of sounds that breaks the back of words) leads to possibilities that could not have been created by the effort of an individual by herself.

The image of braiding I have been using suggests that in the very way it is written Morrison's novel advocates a specific moral epistemology. If the narrative is organized around a moral debate between Sethe and Paul, we see in crucial passages such as the ones I have been analyzing

the most honest and illuminating articles on the de Man controversy: LaCapra, "The Personal, the Political, and the Textual: Paul de Man as Object of Transference," *History and Memory* 4 (Spring/Summer 1992), 5–38, where the focus is less on de Man's World War II journalistic writings and their moral implications and more on the responses of some of his more illustrious defenders.

why the debate cannot be adequately understood in its stark or abstract form as a disagreement in judgment. Rather, Sethe's response to Paul is elaborated by precisely such moments of narrative braiding of perspectives, suggesting how much more Paul will need to know about his communal past, as well as the way he might go about seeking this knowledge. The almost insular world of Sethe, Denver, and Beloved represents the most complex instance of the kind of intersubjective knowing that Paul and the reader must learn to appreciate. For in their search for reconciliation, mother and daughters, victims all, reclaim one another by deepening our understanding of what it means to call something or someone one's own. Again, the narrator often deliberately makes it difficult to separate the voices, but notice in the first passage from Beloved's monologue how the community of the dead from the Middle Passage is invoked in a way that frames and lends meaning to the later passage in which Sethe, Denver, and Beloved acknowledge one another's needs and demands.

> We are not crouching now we are standing but my legs are like my dead man's eyes I cannot fall because there is no room to the men without skin are making loud noises . . . the woman is there with the face I want the face that is mine they fall into the sea which is the color of the bread she has nothing in her ears if I had the teeth of the man who died on my face I would bite the circle around her neck bite it away I know she does not like it now there is room to crouch and to watch the crouching others it is the crouching that is now always now inside the woman with my face is in the sea a hot thing (p. 211)

> Beloved
> You are my sister
> You are my daughter
> You are my face; you are me
> I have found you again; you have come back to me
> You are my Beloved
> You are mine
> You are mine
> You are mine
>
> I have your milk
> I have your smile
> I will take care of you
> You are my face; I am you. Why did you leave me who am you?
> I will never leave you again
> Don't ever leave me again
> You will never leave me again

You went in the water
I drank your blood
I brought your milk

You forgot to smile
I loved you
You hurt me
You came back to me
You left me

I waited for you
You are mine
You are mine
You are mine (pp. 216–17)

Beloved reconnects us with the dead and unremembered of the Middle
Passage but also specifically with Sethe's mother who had come from
Africa. The "face" that Beloved claims is not just her grandmother's,
however, for the images of claiming kinship reverberate outward. "The
face I want" becomes "the face that is mine," suggesting the appropriation of another to oneself. But in the very next lines the distance in-
creases, to register an other who might need help: she has an iron ring
around her neck that she "does not like" or—more emphatic still—"the
woman with my face is in the sea a hot thing."

Loving, forgiving, acknowledging, helping, even making demands or
accusations—all these are woven together through the different voices
in the second passage, suggesting the complexity of coming to know
oneself and one's family or community through sustained emotional
labor. But the allusion to Sethe's mother in Beloved's monologue opens
out from one's immediate purview to include those from the past whose
lives frame one's own. If Sethe's mother survived the Middle Passage,
she did so only to be hanged later. Sethe remembers her primarily
through her absence, and through her struggle to communicate to her
daughter a lineage that Sethe would barely register: "She must of nursed
me two or three weeks—that's the way the others did. Then she went
back in rice and I sucked from another woman whose job it was. She
never fixed my hair nor nothing. . . . One thing she did do. She picked
me up and carried me behind the smokehouse. Back there she opened
up her dress and lifted her breast and pointed under it. Right on her rib
was a circle and a cross burnt right in the skin. She said, 'This is your
ma'am. This,' and she pointed" (pp. 60–61). Sethe is too young and ignorant of history to know what the sign meant, and why her mother is
hanged later with, as she says incomprehendingly, "a lot of them" (p.

61). The surrogate mother Nan, whose job it was to nurse babies and who spoke the same African language Sethe's mother spoke, fills in a portion of the lost narrative with a moral insistence that Sethe can appreciate only in retrospect.

> Nighttime. Nan holding her with her good arm, waving the stump of the other in the air. "Telling you. I am telling you, small girl Sethe," and she did that. She told Sethe that her mother and Nan were together from the sea. Both were taken up many times by the crew. "She threw them all way but you. The one from the crew she threw away on the island. The others from more whites she also threw away. Without names, she threw them. You she gave the name of the black man. She put her arms around him. The others she did not put her arms around. Never. Never. Telling you. I am telling you, small girl Sethe." (p. 62)

What Sethe's perspective—mediated through Denver, Beloved, and the dead women characters—offers Paul is a new understanding of the historical achievement of motherhood. It had the function not just of giving birth and nurturing, but—when fatherhood was denied the slave family—the most basic historical role of positing meaning and continuity as well. Mothering becomes a central trope in the novel because it is defined as a key feature of the moral and historical imagination. The slave mother persevered to create identity, both personal and familial; in her image—and on her body—were inscribed the twin imperatives to survive and to create new meaning. The recurring images of water, milk, and blood combine in the novel to suggest some of the material conditions in which one creates the conscience of the race, for the race needs to survive, both physically and in our imaginations, before we can examine its moral choices. Sethe insists that the community of the colonized includes not just the living survivors of the slave plantations but also, beyond it, the absent, those who need to be reclaimed, who need in fact to be asked to make their claims on us. The novel's central thesis about black motherhood subtends the moral issues Paul raises; it deepens, qualifies, and historicizes it. It suggests in effect that Paul's question—can a human do that?—is indeed too abstract, bereft of historical and contextual depth. In order to pose the question appropriately, we need the cognitive context that only the community of the colonized—dead and living, slave and nonslave—can provide. It is this that Paul D begins to realize when he finally returns to 124 Bluestone Road.

Paul achieves this realization by coming to terms with Beloved, the ghost, and the powerful spell she cast on him. By coming to understand that he both needed Beloved and was afraid of her, he learns the historical lesson for which the narrative has prepared us. Before his reconciliation with Sethe, Paul D must acknowledge that his dependency on Beloved is a sign of his connection with the past he has up till now misunderstood, the past of water and death and ocean-deep emotion which threatens to engulf him and to liberate him. Through this reliving of his relationship with the exorcised ghost-child, Paul comes to have faith in the intergenerational lineage of black women whose primordial presence frames his moral questioning because it makes possible his historical and cultural present:

> There is the pallet spread with old newspapers gnawed at the edges by mice. The lard can. The potato sacks too, but empty now, they lie on the dirt floor in heaps. In daylight he can't imagine it in darkness with moonlight seeping through the cracks. Nor the desire that drowned him there and forced him to struggle up, up into that girl like she was the clear air at the top of the sea. Coupling with her wasn't even fun. It was more like a brainless urge to stay alive. Each time she came, pulled up her skirts, a life hunger overwhelmed him and he had no more control over it than over his lungs. And afterward, beached and gobbling air, in the midst of repulsion and personal shame, he was thankful too for having been escorted to some ocean-deep place he once belonged to. (pp. 263–64)

If coupling with Beloved is something to which Paul was blindly and "brainless[ly]" driven, it is paradoxically because it evoked a "life hunger" in him which he only now begins to understand. His need for her was like the need for air, the "clear air at the top of the sea," but the life he unwittingly seeks is his own unclaimed history, the "ocean-deep place" of the dead female ancestors to whom he once "belonged." This belonging is what brings Paul to his final moment of reconciliation with Sethe, and this reconciliation is as much an intellectual growth as it is an emotional acknowledgment of his historical indebtedness. It is a moment that emblematizes the general cultural phenomenon Hortense Spillers indicates, the essential moral education through which the African-American male comes to "regain the heritage of the mother" as "an aspect of his own personhood—the power of 'yes' to the female within."[22]

22. Hortense Spillers, "Mama's Baby, Papa's Maybe: An American Grammar Book," *Diacritics* 17 (Summer 1987), 80.

Note how in the scene of reconciliation the earlier image about the morality of infanticide gets revised, the stark demand of the abstract moral law—"be human"—is softened and humanized in its turn, for it is located in culture, in history, in life. Sethe is ill and exhausted when Paul returns, and she is lying in Baby Suggs's bed:

"Don't you die on me! This is Baby Suggs' bed! Is that what you planning?" He is so angry he could kill her. He checks himself, remembering Denver's warning, and whispers, "What you planning, Sethe?"
"Oh, I don't have no plans. No plans at all."
"Look," he says, "Denver be here in the day. I be here in the night. I'm a take care of you, you hear? Starting now. First off, you don't smell right. Stay there. Don't move. Let me heat up some water." He stops. "Is it all right, Sethe, if I heat up some water?"
"And count my feet?" she asks him.
He steps closer. "Rub your feet." (pp. 271–72)

This transformation from law to human understanding, from abstract humanity to real feeling, is predicated on the enlargement of Paul's personal capacity to experience, but if my reading of the novel is convincing it suggests how much historical knowledge, indeed how much theoretical knowledge, is involved in Paul's growth. His new relationship to Sethe and to Beloved is based on a new understanding of his history, of a history constructed and sustained by generations of black mothers. Morrison's novel is one of the most challenging of postcolonial texts because it indicates the extent to which the search for a genuinely noncolonial moral and cultural identity depends on a revisionary historiography.[23] We cannot really claim ourselves morally or politically until we have reconstructed our collective identity, reexamined our dead and our disremembered. This is not simply a project of adding to one's ancestral line, for as we have seen, it often involves fundamental discoveries about what ancestry is, what continuity consists in, how cultural meanings do not just sustain themselves through history but are in fact materially embodied and fought for.

Sethe's act of infanticide resonates differently after we have reconsidered the role of motherhood under slavery. We think, for instance, of

23. It is of course not only the colonized who need to worry about the way their search for a noncolonial identity depends on an adequate historiography. For an account of the colonizer's identity, and how it might survive in postcolonial contexts precisely to the extent that its genealogy is not traced, see my "Drawing the Color Line: Kipling and the Culture of Colonial Rule," in *The Bounds of Race*, ed. Dominick LaCapra (Ithaca: Cornell University Press, 1991), esp. the concluding section.

Sethe's unnamed mother, who throws all her children except Sethe away as an act of resistance to rape and racial humiliation. It is something of this order that Sethe decides to do in slitting her child's throat. If Paul speaks in terms of the abstraction we call "the human," Sethe's situation and that of other slave mothers reminds us that humanity is itself measured in terms of a moral personhood, a capacity for self-determination, which the institution of slavery denied the slave. "Anybody white could take your whole self for anything that came to mind. Not just work, kill, or maim you, but dirty you. Dirty you so bad you couldn't like yourself any more. Dirty you so bad you forgot who you were and couldn't think it up. And though she and others lived through and got over it, she could never let it happen to her own. The best thing she was, was her children" (p. 251). We may or may not agree with Sethe's argument, but we need to come to terms with the historical community she claims as her own, and reexamine the moral theory we bring with us. That is what Paul does at the end, as he seeks reconciliation with Sethe.

> "Sethe," he says, "me and you, we got more yesterday than anybody. We need some kind of tomorrow."
> He leans over and takes her hand. With the other he touches her face. "You your best thing, Sethe. You are." His holding fingers are holding hers.
> "Me? Me?" (p. 273)

He claims her community as his own and, through her, reclaims an aspect of his own personhood, but his words of acceptance and reconciliation suggest a new challenge, a new way of conceiving the postcolonial tomorrow. Sethe's argument had been that she could not let her children be enslaved because they were "her best thing"; Paul does not condemn her action now as he had done in the past, but he suggests a different emphasis: "You your best thing, Sethe. You are." This is not quite a disagreement so much as an indication that the distinctly postcolonial challenge lies in leaving part of the past behind, in working through it to imagine agency and selfhood in positive terms, inventing new dimensions of cultural possibility.

Morrison's novel suggests that the community that defines our cultural identity is constructed through a complex and ongoing process involving both emotional and cognitive effort. Central to this effort is the work of the moral imagination that learns to "remember" with honesty and integrity. Morrison's vision of the writer's historical task, as she described it in a 1987 lecture, is what we would call realist or cognitivist:

> The act of imagination is bound up with memory. You know, they straightened out the Mississippi River in places, to make room for houses and livable acreage. Occasionally the river floods these places. "Floods" is the word they use, but in fact it is not flooding; it is remembering. Remembering where it used to be. All water has a perfect memory and is forever trying to get back to where it was. Writers are like that: remembering where we were, what valley we ran through, what the banks were like, the light that was there and the route back to our original place. It is emotional memory—what the nerves and skin remember as well as how it appeared.[24]

Needless to say, such remembering is never easy, nor is the moral growth that is closely tied with it irreversible, for fallibility, or at least the danger of forgetting what is essential, is always a historical possibility. What we need to recognize is that such forgetting would not be simply a personal failure but rather a loss of community, of necessary social meaning—hence the tone of loss and mourning that frames the scene of Paul and Sethe's reconciliation. There are images of "dead ivy," "shriveled blossoms," and a "bleak and minus nothing" (p. 270). As the novel ends, it is not just Beloved who is forgotten "but the water too and what it is down there" (p. 275). Integral to the postpositivist realist view of experience and identity is thus the necessary caution that our cultural identities (or the moral and political knowledge we might seek through them) are defined in a way that is historically open-ended, never frozen or settled once and for all: "Down by the stream in back of 124 [Beloved's] footprints come and go, come and go. They are so familiar. Should a child, an adult, place his feet in them, they will fit. Take them out and they disappear again as though nobody walked there" (p. 275).

Cultural Difference and Social Power

Let me summarize part of my central argument in outlining some of the advantages of the realist view of experience and identity. First, this account of cultural identity explains an important way in which identities can be both constructed (socially, linguistically, theoretically, and

24. Toni Morrison, "The Site of Memory," in *Inventing the Truth: The Art and Craft of Memoir*, ed. William Zinsser (Boston: Houghton Mifflin, 1995), pp. 98–99.

so on) and "real" at the same time. Their "reality" consists in their referring outward, to causally significant features of the social world. Alice's gendered identity is theoretically constructed, to be sure, insofar as she elaborates and consolidates it in the context of the conscious-ness-raising group and the alternative descriptions of the world she en-counters and debates there. But if this description happens to be accurate as an explanation of the key causal factors that make this world what it is, that is, make this world this world, then Alice's new feminist cultural and political identity is "real" in the following sense: it refers accurately to her social location and interests. Alice discovers that what defines her life in her society is that she belongs to a group defined by gender. Gender is a social fact that is causally relevant for the experiences she has and the choices and possibilities that are avail-able to her. Her world is what it is because in it social power is sustained through the hierarchical organization of gendered groups, including the cultural meanings they share. The collective identity Alice consciously forges through reexamination of the accepted cultural meanings and values, the given definition of her personal and political interests, is then as much her discovery as it is a construction. For good social and political theories do not only organize pregiven facts about the world; they also make it possible for us to detect new ones. They do so by guiding us to new patterns of salience and relevance, teaching us what to take seriously and what to reinterpret. To say that theories and iden-tities "refer" is thus to understand the complex way they provide us knowledge about the world. Beyond the elementary descriptive rela-tionship that individual signs might have with unique and static ob-jects, "reference," postpositivist realists say, should be understood dialectically and socially as providing us degrees of "epistemic access" to reality. On this view, there can be both partial and successful refer-ence. In some cases, theories (like signs) can fail to refer accurately, but reference should not be conceived as an all-or-nothing affair. Thus, when I say that cultural identities refer, I am suggesting that they can be evaluated using the same complex epistemic criteria we use to evaluate "theories."[25]

So the second advantage a realist theory of identity offers is this: it helps explain how we can distinguish legitimate identities from spuri-ous ones. In fact, it gives us the way to appreciate different degrees of

25. This way of understanding reference builds on the "causal" account discussed in Chapter 2. See esp. Boyd, "Metaphor and Theory Change: What Is 'Metaphor' a Metaphor For?" in *Metaphor and Thought,* 2d ed., ed. Andrew Ortony (Cambridge: Cambridge University Press, 1993), pp. 481–532; see also, below, pp. 243–45.

legitimacy and spuriousness. It does so by urging us to take the epistemic status of personal experience very seriously, seriously enough in
fact to consider why Alice's anger and her father's are not equally justified, and how Paul D's initial moral judgment of Sethe's action can become subtler and deeper, more adequate to the reality they share.
Alice's evolving personal experience plays an epistemic role since it reveals to her some of the determining features of her social location and
her world and where, objectively speaking, her personal interests might
lie. To say that Alice (like Paul or Sethe) learns from her experience is
to emphasize that under certain conditions personal experience yields
reliable knowledge about oneself and one's situation.[26] And since different experiences and identities refer to different aspects of one world,
one complex causal structure that we call "social reality," the realist
theory of identity implies that we can evaluate them comparatively by
considering how adequately they explain this structure. This comparison is often a complex and difficult negotiation (since it can involve
competing interpretations and only partially overlapping bodies of information), but it is facilitated by making buried explanations explicit,
by examining the social and political views involved in what seem like
purely personal choices and predilections. Experiences and identities—
and theories about them—are bits of social and political theory themselves and are to be evaluated as such.

The cultural radicalism of the postmodernist position I identified earlier is based on the argument that all identities are constructed and are
thus contingent and changeable. But it cannot adequately explain what
difference different kinds of construction make. Since it refuses to take
the epistemic dimension of experience seriously, it cannot explain how
(as, say, in the case of Alice or Paul D) changes in our cultural identity
reflect moral and political growth, an increase both in our personal capacities and in knowledge. Once we consider the theoretical option to
postmodernism provided by the realist account of identity I have proposed here, it might also be clearer why we should not frame our questions about cultural identity in terms of a rigid opposition between
essentialism, claiming unchanging "reality," and (social) construction-

26. For two realist accounts that define political identity by reference to social location,
common interests, and shared contexts of struggle, see A. Sivanandan on "black" people
in Britain, in *Communities of Resistance: Writing on Black Struggles for Socialism* (London: Verso, 1990), and Chandra Talpade Mohanty on third-world women in "Cartographies
of Struggle: Third World Women and the Politics of Feminism," in *Third World Women
and the Politics of Feminism*, ed. Mohanty, Ann Russo, and Lourdes Torres (Bloomington:
Indiana University Press, 1991), pp. 1–47.

ism, emphasizing social and historical ideology. Both this unhelpful opposition and efforts to transcend it through such weak theoretical compromises as are suggested by such terms as "strategic essentialism"[27] are based on an evasion of the difficult but unavoidable epistemological questions that the postmodernist confronts. If the identities of social actors cannot be deduced from experiences whose meanings are self-evident, is there anything objective we can say about these identities? How do we determine that one social identity is more legitimate than another? How do we justify one "strategy" over another? Is such justification purely a matter of pragmatic calculation, or does it obey some epistemic constraints as well? Does what we know about the world (independently of specific questions about identity) have any bearing on our understanding of this justification? I have suggested some answers to these questions by emphasizing the continuity of accounts of cultural identity with accounts of the social justification of knowledge, especially the knowledge involved in our ethical and political claims and commitments.

The third, more specific, advantage of the realist approach to experience and identity is that it explains how the oppressed may have epistemic privilege, but it does so without espousing a self-defeating or dubious kind of relativism with separatist implications. To have a cognitivist view of experience is to claim that its truth content can be evaluated, and thus potentially shared with others. As we saw in my discussion of a theory of emotions, the individualist "privileged access" theory is wrong because it denies that personal experience is fundamentally theory-mediated. A realist theory of the kind I have outlined would both acknowledge the constitutive role played by theory and respect the ways specific theories—and social situations, conditions of research, and so on—provide better or worse ways of detecting new and relevant information about our world. I have said (drawing on Harding, Boyd, and Marx) that certain social arrangements and conditions—social struggles of dominated groups, for instance—can help produce more objective knowledge about a world that is constitutively defined by relations of domination. That would help explain why granting the possibility of epistemic privilege to the oppressed might be more than a sentimental gesture; in many cases in fact it is the only way to push us

27. See Gayatri Chakravorty Spivak, *In Other Worlds* (New York: Methuen, 1987), pp. 202–11; and for a position that is both more complex and more lucidly discussed, Fuss, *Essentially Speaking*, esp. pp. 118–19. I think Fuss's overall project would be better served by a fully developed realist theory of experience than by the Althusserian one she invokes in her concluding discussion.

toward greater social objectivity. For granting that the oppressed have this privilege opens up the possibility that our own epistemic perspective is partial, shaped by our social location, and needs to be understood and revised hermeneutically. One way to read my account of Paul D's growth over the course of the novel is that he grows because Sethe challenges him to become aware of his partiality. His recognition of the nature of his dependence on Beloved—the particular needs she fulfilled, the ocean-deep place to which he had lost access which she restored—is a historical lesson that is learned by becoming less forgetful and more fully human, more aware of the cultural sources of his own personhood.

This is a general lesson whose implications every historian confronts, as theorists have lately been pointing out. Reviewing the cultural debate among German historians about the centrality of the Holocaust in the writing of objective national history, Dominick LaCapra shows why the historian of the period must overcome the kind of false objectivity that is derived from a denial of one's "subject position." What is needed, instead, is an understanding of the variety of affective responses to the past, responses shaped by one's location. For the historian's interpretation to be more objective than might otherwise be possible, she must attend to the ethical implications of her discursive stances:

> The Holocaust presents the historian with transference in the most traumatic form conceivable—but in a form that will vary with the difference in subject position of the analyst. Whether the historian or analyst is a survivor, a relative of survivors, a former Nazi, a former collaborator, a relative of former Nazis or collaborators, a younger Jew or German distanced from more immediate contact with survival, participation, or collaboration, or a relative "outsider" to these problems will make a difference even in the meaning of statements that may be formally identical. Certain statements or even entire orientations may seem appropriate for someone in a given subject position but not in others. (It would, for example, be ridiculous if I tried to assume the voice of Elie Wiesel or Saul Friedlander. There is a sense in which I have no right to these voices. There is also a sense in which, experiencing a lack of a viable voice, I am constrained to resort to quotation and commentary more often that I otherwise might be.) Thus although any historian must be "invested" in a distinctive way in the events of the Holocaust, not all investments (or cathexes) are the same and not all statements, rhetorics, or orientations are equally available to different historians.[28]

28. LaCapra, "Representing the Holocaust," p. 110.

LaCapra goes on to characterize "statements, rhetorics, or orientations" as specific choices about "how language is used" (p. 110), but in the context of my present discussion it is possible to see that they point to epistemic choices and stances as well. They "orient" inquiry by suggesting where we might be reflexive or critical, where attention to seemingly irrelevant subjective information can lead to greater objectivity. When we acknowledge that the experiences of victims might be repositories of valuable knowledge, and thus allow that they have epistemic privilege, we are not thereby reduced to sentimental silence. Entailed in our acknowledgment is the need to pay attention to the way our social locations facilitate or inhibit knowledge by predisposing us to register and interpret information in certain ways. Our relation to social power produces forms of blindness just as it enables degrees of lucidity. The notion of epistemic privilege is thus inseparable from the cognitivist account of experience and cultural identity I have sketched, and it explains how objectivity in historical and moral inquiry can be found not by denying our perspectives or locations but rather by interrogating their epistemic consequences.

My arguments should indicate that these consequences are not so severe that we need to retreat into skepticism. Even when we are discussing such slippery things as personal experiences and cultural meanings, it is not clear that postmodernist skepticism is warranted. Either to base definitions of identity on an idealized conception of experience (as essentialists do) or to deny experience any cognitive value whatsoever (as postmodernists might) is to cut with too blunt a theoretical knife. The realist-cognitivist account of identity I have proposed here, a definition implicit in Toni Morrison's novel, might suggest to some a viable alternative to these dominant theoretical positions.

Universalism, Particularism, and Multicultural Politics

One implication of the realist account of identity I have provided may surprise some readers. This theory reconciles the claims of certain forms of identity politics with moral universalism. Indeed, it enables us to respect social difference while deepening the radical potential of universalist moral and political claims. The notion of epistemic privilege I outlined, a notion central to the realist understanding of identity, shows us why this should be the case. If our views about our identities are partly explanations of the world in which we live and these explanations are based on the knowledge we gather from our social activities, then the claim that oppressed social groups have a special kind of knowledge about the world as it affects them is hardly a mysterious one requiring idealist assumptions about cultural essences or inaccessible particularities. Rather it is an empirical claim, tied to a wider (empirical and theoretical) account of the society in which these groups live. And therefore any claim about the epistemic privilege of a particular social group will be only as convincing as the social theory and description that accompany it. On the view I am defending, claims about the epistemic privilege of a particular group are necessarily embedded in wider explanatory theories of history and of the society in which the group lives. Both the claim of epistemic privilege and the identity politics based on it need to be evaluated as any social and historical explanation should be; they are prone, like all explanatory accounts of the world, to error—both empirical and theoretical.

But when such a claim about a particular social group is true, its implications are general, not merely limited to the subjective experiences of the group in question. The knowledge we gain is "objective." This conclusion shows why we need to be wary of those overly abstract universalist visions of morality or social justice which focus on only the most general features that the various social groups (or individuals) have in common and exclude consideration of relevant particularities, relevant contextual information. Part of Sethe's response to Paul D's moral indignation is that he has inadequate understanding of the social context in which he, as a (black) man, has developed his moral views about infanticide. Paul's understanding is deepened by his recognition of his partiality, his—historically and socially produced—ignorance about the role of motherhood in the slave family. Sethe does not defend infanticide; she widens the scope of the moral debate to include the relevant contexts of her action, and thus makes it more complex.

Paul's growth is predicated on his coming to know Sethe's perspective, on learning to acknowledge both the partiality of his knowledge and the reason Sethe knows something that he does not about the world in which they both live. Sethe's epistemic privilege is not an accident; it derives from her experience of being a slave mother, that is, her resistance to being a reproducer of slaves. Paul comes to recognize that both motherhood and the gendered division of labor on which slavery was built are objective historical and social facts that shape what he knows and what he does not, that—consequently—influence the moral judgment he makes. But Paul's response—in fact the genuineness of his emotional and moral growth—is predicated on his acceptance of Sethe's claim about motherhood as an empirical fact about slave society. I have not maintained that Paul *has* to accept this claim, and Morrison's novel gives the reader the same option. If the historical claim is seen as cogent, however, it is incumbent upon us to pay attention to the special knowledge that slave mothers have. But in that case such attention would not derive from sentimental respect for motherhood but would rather be sound epistemic practice. Such subjective perspectives often contain deep sources of information and knowledge, or even alternative theoretical pictures and accounts of the world we all share. An adequate appreciation of such "particular" perspectives and viewpoints makes possible a richer general picture, a deeper and more nuanced universalist view of human needs and vulnerabilities, as well as—by implication—human flourishing. In such cases, the (cultural or historical) particular and the (moral) universal complement and substantiate each other.

Thus, with all their flaws and obvious limitations, identity-based political struggles can be built on genuine political insights. Once we acknowledge, as the realist theory requires, that such struggles cannot be based on a priori claims to political or moral knowledge, we can understand how they can legitimately draw on personal experiences and histories to deepen our knowledge of society. A feminist political consciousness often develops, for instance, through a recognition of the overwhelming significance of the personal, of the way gender relations and inequalities are played out in our most intimate relationships (including our relationships with ourselves). As we saw in Alice's case, an adequate appreciation of the political effects of gender often depends on a personal reorientation or growth, involving both the affective and the deliberative faculties. And the relation between the personal and the political is complex and indeed dialectical. The recovery of an individual's sense of personal worth and the development of her capacity for the right kind of anger or indignation partly depend on finding the right social and political theory. In Alice's case, such a theory or such deeply theoretical hypotheses are what the consciousness-raising group provides. The group also gives Alice the appropriate epistemic and emotional context in which to examine such hypotheses, and thus Alice's political growth, the growth in her knowledge about herself, her capacities, and her world, is predicated on her acknowledgment of her inherited social identity and its effects.

What cultural and social conditions make identitarian politics a necessary (though certainly not sufficient) form of social struggle, even of social inquiry? Alice's situation is by no means uncommon. What makes Alice's "identity" so central to her moral and political growth is a crucial feature of the world in which we all live: hierarchical and un-equal gender relations are produced and reproduced by a process through which Alice is taught in effect to devalue her personal experiences as a source of knowledge about her world and even about herself as a person—that is, as someone with genuine needs and capacities, rights and entitlements. Alice learns to value these experiences again and to glean from them—as well as from the fact that she has been taught to ignore them—crucial information about both herself and her world. "Learning" to value and imagine in such new ways is relevant not only for the disadvantaged but also for the historically privileged, for both privilege and privation can produce (different kinds of) moral and political blindness. Cultural decolonization often involves an inter-rogation of the epistemic and affective consequences of our social loca-tion, of historically learned habits of thinking and feeling. For both Alice and Paul D the developing recognition of aspects of their inherited identities amounts to a form of decolonization, a necessary political education. Through his extended dialogue with Sethe, Paul comes to acknowledge both his indebtedness to his community and his own par-tial knowledge—a partiality fostered at least as much by his gendered identity as by any purely personal trait or idiosyncracy.

For Paul and Alice, as for so many others in the modern world, an identity-based politics becomes a necessary first step in coming to know what an oppressive social and cultural system obscures. Such "obscuring" is often a highly mediated and almost invisible process, implicit in traditional forms of schooling as well as in less formal prac-tices of education and socialization. The institutions of social reproduc-tion and cultural transmission—schools, libraries, newspapers, and museums, for instance—are oriented to the dominant cultural and so-cial perspectives. Much of their bias is often invisible because of the relatively benign form the transmission of cultural information takes: it seems utterly natural, part of the scheme of things. In such instances, cultural assimilation amounts to a repression of alternative sources of experience and value. That repression would explain why the feelings of minority groups about their "racial" or cultural identities are so tena-cious, for instance, or why claims about the significance of gender or sexual identity represent more than the simple "politics of recogni-tion."[29] Quite often, such claims and feelings embody alternative and

29. Charles Taylor sees contemporary demands for multiculturalism as primarily the demand for "recognition." See "The Politics of Recognition," in *Multiculturalism and the Politics of Recognition: An Essay by Charles Taylor*, ed. Amy Gutmann (Princeton: Princeton University Press, 1992), pp. 25–73. It should be evident by now why I think he underestimates the multiculturalist claim.

antihegemonic accounts of what is significant and in fact necessary for a more accurate understanding of the world we all share.

Thus, in analyzing identity-based politics, claims about the general social significance of a particular identity should be evaluated together with its accompanying assumptions or arguments about how the current social or cultural system makes some experiences intelligible and others obscure or irrelevant, how it treats some as legitimate sources of knowledge about the world while relegating others to the level of the narrowly personal. Both the claims and the underlying assumptions refer to the social world; they amount to explanatory theses with both empirical and theoretical content. They need to be engaged as such and evaluated as we evaluate other such descriptions and theories about society. This realist attitude does not guarantee that a particular version of identity politics is justified; that justification will depend on the details of what is being claimed. We need to ask if these details mesh with the world as we know it, and to see how the accompanying theories compare with our best moral and political accounts. Thus, for instance, parallel claims and assumptions can be made by both the kind of feminist identity politics that Alice practices and a retrograde form of religious fundamentalism, and we have no way of choosing between them in advance. It would be hasty to dismiss both Alice's feminist identity and the fundamentalist religious identity *in the same way*, simply because both appeal to personal experience and make some claim to epistemic privilege. As I have been emphasizing, realism about identity requires that we see identities as complex theories about (and explanations of) the social world, and the only way to evaluate such theories is to look at how well they work as explanations. "Good" social and cultural identities are quite simply (based on) good explanations of the social world. Such explanations are not purely empirical, and what makes them "good" is in part the cogency of the background theories they draw on, which often necessarily have deep moral and evaluative content. But such necessary interdependence of the empirical and the theoretical, the factual and the evaluative, is, the postpositivist realist will point out, not evidence of the unique epistemic status of cultural identities; as we have seen in various ways this interdependence is a feature of all inquiry, scientific and moral, and adjudicating between different identity claims is not fundamentally all that different from adjudicating between two fairly complex accounts of the natural or social world. There simply is no easy way out, for a lot depends on the details. What we lose by looking for an easy way out—for example, by denying all identities validity because they are always tied to personal experience and subjective judgments—is the capacity to make useful and important distinctions between different kinds of identity, different kinds of value and judgment.

At its best, an identity-based politics is a kind of education, for members of the group as well as for outsiders, about the historically produced *vulnerabilities* of social agents; as such it plays a necessary compensatory role in political education. The growth of moral and political maturity depends not only on learning the appropriate rules and general principles (for instance, infanticide is always wrong; socialist internationalism is superior to cultural nationalism) but also on the deepened knowledge and sensibility it takes to ground such principles in real social and historical contexts. Such knowledge and sensibility do not come automatically with the general rules and principles, because they also involve the capacity to judge well, and judgment is by definition not an abstract matter but is rather grounded in particulars, developed through subjective (including even emotional) experience.[30] The kind of identitarian politics I am defending here as, in some cases, a necessary step in moral and political education thus involves training that is simultaneously affective and epistemic.

Since cultural identities are not mysterious inner essences of groups of people but are fundamentally about social relations, especially relations among groups, the realist view gives us a way to envision multiculturalism as an inevitable part of a theory of justice in societies defined by deep and pervasive cultural inequalities. To the extent that our societies are constitutively unequal, and "cultures" bear the mark of our colonial pasts by encoding within them false hierarchies and evaluations, respect for marginalized cultures is merely sound epistemic practice, especially given the kinds of prejudice and ignorance we have inherited. In societies where cultural inequality is pervasive, the identity-based struggles of subordinate cultural groups is often a necessary component of multicultural politics. One of the assumptions behind this view of multiculturalism is that our cultural environments provide us with necessary affective sustenance and training, and thus when such environments are healthy they enable individuals to grow and flourish in many important ways. As we have seen in the examples of Alice and Paul, such affective sustenance can make it possible for people to be sound rational agents as well, since it often teaches us how to ask the right sorts of questions about our world. Perhaps this view of

30. This is a fundamentally Aristotelian idea. See esp. bks. 2, 3, and 6 of the *Nicomachean Ethics*.

the importance of culture is what Emma Goldman had in mind when she suggested that for her dancing was a necessary part of the revolution: we should dance not only to celebrate victories but to dream revolutionary dreams, to deepen our vision of reality by widening our sense of the possible.

Multiculturalism as Epistemic Cooperation

An adequate appreciation of the epistemic role of "culture" will make it possible to see why multiculturalism and diversity are necessary social ideals even when cultural inequalities are no longer pervasive. I have shown why, in democratic societies that are attempting to ameliorate the effects of cultural inequality (inherited, in some cases, from their colonial pasts), some kinds of identity-based political struggles will be inevitable components of general multicultural agendas. When cultural equality has been more or less achieved, however, the essential value of pluralism and diversity becomes clearer. Multiculturalist policies will no longer be seen as compensatory; instead, they will be seen as enabling the kind of cross-cultural cooperation that always existed as a radical potential within culturally diverse societies. This view has been implicit in my critiques of relativism and of postmodernist skeptical stances toward cultural others, but let me now develop it explicitly and in some detail. Here are the two theses that make my general view clearer: (1) "Cultures" need to seen as fields of moral inquiry; and (2) Multiculturalism should be defined as a form of epistemic cooperation. Both theses grow out of the realist theories of knowledge and society I have been outlining, and they explain how a nonrelativist understanding (and defense) of diversity and pluralism can be developed.

Cultural relativism, I have said, cannot give us an adequate understanding of the force that others' choices and values have for us because it makes such choices and values purely conventional and context specific. In contrast, the realist maintains that just as we can be wrong, so can the other. Central to this view are the notion of error and the implicit idea that cultural practices are forms of inquiry like any other. There is no absolute distinction, in this perspective, between the scientific and the cultural, the epistemic and the affective. In fact, cultural practices—ways of living, of creating, of choosing to value one thing over another in our daily lives—are an essential form of experimental inquiry. Cultures are more like laboratories than anything else; they do not only embody values and beliefs, they also test and modify these values and beliefs in practical ways. Values, which involve more than our conscious beliefs, are the very substance of such experiments. New forms of living—forms of cooperation in the household or the workplace, ways of dividing up work and play, production and reproduction—help us interrogate old ideas and deepen new hunches. Hunches develop both into programs for action and into theories. Notions of the just society and of the moral status of individuals are developed out of intuitions that arise in the practices of everyday social life. Our everyday social practices, Heidegger reminds us, rest on deep assumptions that we might even call "theoretical." It would follow, then, that social life has significant epistemic content, and what we call culture is a field of (moral) inquiry.[31] And for this reason—and not because of any relativist or romantic understanding of cultural uniqueness—we need to begin with the presumption that individual cultures have something of value to teach all of us.

Cultural practices embody and interrogate rich patterns of value, which in turn represent deep bodies of knowledge of humankind and of human flourishing. Given this view, it would seem perfectly natural that a realist theory of knowledge and society would demand cultural diversity, because such diversity is essential for innovation and progress in moral inquiry. If we see moral inquiry, following Hume and Boyd, as based on observation and experimentation (in this—Boyd argues—it is no different from scientific inquiry), and we define cultures the way I have, as laboratories of moral practice and experimentation, then it would follow that without a healthy diversity of cultures, a robust multiculturalism, inquiry into the human good will be limited and parochial. Cultural diversity ensures that more of the relevant information will be available and that our questions themselves will be shaped and honed by a reasonable array of competing theoretical perspectives.[32]

31. My view of culture here thus owes a great deal to the hermeneutical tradition that derives from Heidegger—to thinkers as different as Gadamer and Charles Taylor. But I am also indebted in a more general way to the socialist and anarchist traditions. In particular, Mikhail Bakunin's and Rudolf Rocker's point that workers' cooperative organizations contain the germs of the future has deepened my appreciation of the central role of culture in political struggles. See, e.g., Bakunin, "Geneva's Double Strike," in The Basic Bakunin: Writings 1869–1871, trans. and ed. Robert M. Cutler (Buffalo, N.Y.: Prometheus Books, 1992), pp. 148–49; Rocker, Anarcho-Syndicalism (London: Pluto, 1989), esp. pp. 118-19. Noam Chomsky provides an excellent introduction to anarchism in "Notes on Anarchism," in For Reasons of State (New York: Vintage, 1973), pp. 370–86.

32. See Hume, "Of the Standard of Taste," in Essays, Moral, Political, and Literary, rev. ed., ed. Eugene F. Miller (Indianapolis: Liberty Fund, 1987), pp. 226–49, for a discussion of the role of relevant comparison in sound aesthetic judgment. My general understanding of culture as moral experimentation is based in part on a Humean view of the social basis of moral and aesthetic practice.

Thus a realist (moral) epistemology requires that we promote cultural diversity for epistemic, not sentimental, reasons. Cultural diversity, says the realist, will tend to draw attention to those of our own cultural assumptions which are morally dogmatic, because it will widen the field of historical inquiry. The realist approach I am advocating here rewrites the relativist critique of the Enlightenment as a critique of false universalism, rather than of universalism per se. On this view, social diversity both extends and specifies the critique of false universalism and deepens our understanding of the kind of moral universalism on which so many progressive political movements have been based.

But this kind of moral universalism is itself grounded in our growing understanding of those features of human nature which are not purely cultural or conventional but are shared by all humans across cultures. On this understanding is based a view of those minimal requirements for human welfare—those spelled out in the various declarations of human rights are an example—which no culture or society may deny its members. But beyond that, of course, there is a great deal of room for cultural difference and disagreement even over some core values. Indeed, given the realist view that culture is a laboratory of moral practice and inquiry, it would make sense that differences will arise among cultures about how to apportion and distribute the range of human goods we all recognize. Metatheoretical commitment to the objectivity of values ensures that the realist will seek in cultural disagreement precisely such instances of meaningful conflict of value. Such conflict over how to understand particular values or what priority to give different values (Is the ability to understand abstract principles of justice more important than the ability to form deep intimate relationships? Do the dictates of friendship trump the need for impartiality and fairness? and so on) suggests deep theoretical commitments. But it also often reveals questions that cannot be adequately addressed without a great deal—and variety—of empirical knowledge that only social and cultural practice can provide.

It would be part of the realist's goal, then, to try to specify differences as much as possible, to distinguish differences where there is no common reference from ones where there is what Charles Taylor calls "incommensurability." "Incommensurable" values and activities are defined by entirely different theoretical views, even when they occupy the same general space. Then part of the challenge is to see how the theories differ in their practical implications: "how their range of possible activities," as Taylor puts it, is different from ours.[33] In many cases, a culture's range of possible activities reveals the substructure of its system of explicit values, the genuine choices and exclusions that define them. Belief in the possibility of seeking objective knowledge about morality and cultural values will thus make the realist more eager to attend to difference, to those areas of disagreement that—however mediated by theories and presuppositions—might point to relevant information and new knowledge. It is in the interest of objectivity that the realist will be wary of monist positions on a whole range of values and practices. Recognizing the complexity of human nature and the deeply theoretical nature of moral and cultural practice, the realist will favor cultural diversity as *the best social condition* in which objective knowledge about human flourishing might be sought.

One of the assumptions behind my epistemological defense of diversity and multiculturalism is that our deepest evaluative terms are often necessarily imprecise because they refer not only to what we mean by them now but also to a fuller range of human possibilities than we, given our social and cultural history, know. This inadequacy is not a defect of our language or our analytical skills, to be eliminated through finer conceptual analysis and linguistic rigor. It is a referential incompleteness that reveals the limits of what we know, and the way precision might depend on greater empirical and theoretical knowledge than we possess at present. In such instances, the imprecision reveals an underlying cognitive bias shaped by our social and historical conditions— and such bias can be understood, specified, and (in some instances) corrected only through cooperative inquiry across cultures.

Evaluative concepts such as "individuality," for instance, based as they are in the modern Western sense on the notions of rational agency, autonomy, and a certain kind of uniqueness of the individual agent, may be further refined when they come into conflict with other definitions tied to the patterns and value hierarchies of other cultures. How much is individual *uniqueness* a constitutive feature of genuine individuality? one might ask through such a cross-cultural examination.[34]

33. Charles Taylor, "Rationality," in *Philosophy and the Human Sciences*, vol. 2 of *Philosophical Papers* (Cambridge: Cambridge University Press, 1983), pp. 145–146.

34. For a discussion of how "uniqueness" as a value is central to the modern Western notion of individuality, see Gregory Vlastos, "Justice and Equality," in *Social Justice*, pp. 48–53. A Buddhist may challenge the value of the pursuit of uniqueness without denying that healthy individuality is a desirable goal of human beings. She would simply refuse to define individuality in terms of "uniqueness." Contemplation and meditation, she may claim, enhance genuine individuality through a kind of "unselfing," an ability to transcend

Once we take such a question seriously as a legitimate form of inquiry into the nature of "individuality" as a desirable good for human beings, we see how the term "individuality" as the modern West defines it might refer only partially and inadequately to the good toward which it points. The Western use of the term may pick out some but not all key features of the term. But on the realist view, this partiality is not evidence that the Western use of the term is *merely* conventional and arbitrary or, in other words, completely culture specific. The point is that an adequate explanation of individuality as a moral good for humans may well depend on a much greater specification of *both* the cluster of desirable personal qualities *and* the social arrangements that produce and enhance such qualities. And if, say, our knowledge of such social arrangements is itself quite limited, then the social experiments of other cultures may be quite directly relevant to us, since their practices extend our own and deepen, by comparison or contrast, our knowledge of what is possible for humans.[35] On this view, individuality as a moral good is not a trait of isolated individuals—there are no such beings!— but rather the quality of individuals in one or another social arrangement or system. If we agree, for the sake of argument, that our modern notion of individuality is inadequate and imprecise, since we simply do not know enough, then it is through an understanding of a greater array of cultural and social experiments that we can learn how to refine our knowledge of the term. We refine it by specifying the reference of the term "individuality" in ways that go beyond what we can conceive now.

Deeply evaluative terms refer "outward," beyond the local meanings associated with them by a particular culture, both to what we now know about human nature (our needs and capacities, for instance) and to genuine human (social and political) possibilities. These social and political "possibilities" involve alternative "causal" relations between social organization and human flourishing than the ones with which we are familiar at present. Here is an example of what I mean: A society

one's narrow egocentric notions of who one is and should be. This view is similar to the kind of Platonic position Iris Murdoch articulates in her various books. I am clearer on this point about uniqueness and individuality because of correspondence with Jennifer Whiting.

35. This notion of the reference of moral terms, which extends the ideas discussed in Chapter 2, draws on Richard Boyd's elaboration of the causal theory. See Boyd's definition of reference as a theory of "epistemic access" in "Metaphor and Theory Change" and "How to Be a Moral Realist." See also Hartry Field's important work on "denotational refinement" in the history of science, esp. "Theory Change and the Indeterminacy of Reference," *Journal of Philosophy* 70 (August 16, 1973), 462–81.

at an early stage of its development, for which warfare is a dominant fact of everyday life, will probably identify "courage" almost exclusively with the physical bravery that warriors display on the battlefield. For another society, which has succeeded (for whatever historical reasons) in developing more peaceful social practices and institutions, courage may well come to refer (also) to inner qualities that are closer to patience, emotional fortitude, and the capacity for rational deliberation, qualities and virtues that help an individual deal with, say, a prolonged illness. These two societies could also represent two different historical stages of the same one, in which case we can see how the development of more rational and humane social institutions and practices can lead to a deepening or widening of the reference of the evaluative concept, "courage." The development of peaceful social forms allows members of the society to see how and why such "inner" qualities are valuable or, even more basically, that humans are indeed capable of developing such qualities. New forms of social organization can thus enable us to discover aspects of human nature (our capacities in particular) and of human welfare (say, the relative importance of our different needs), aspects we could not even imagine before. Such "causal" links between social organization and the moral and theoretical imagination of human agents, the realist will suggest, point to hypotheses that can be empirically tested and developed. And since values often refer to such causal connections, they cannot be seen as purely private mental states, even though they are realized in the behavior and beliefs of individual subjects. They involve—fundamentally and essentially—social relations among individuals and groups. In many crucial instances, then, imprecision (or incompleteness) of reference of evaluative terms and concepts is instructive and necessary. Moral inquiry, like other forms of human inquiry, is a social matter, dependent on the highly contingent state of our social and political knowledge and on the coordination of our epistemic and political efforts.

My emphasis on the epistemic role of culture, on culture as moral inquiry, is an implicit critique of that strand of the Enlightenment—in particular the radical materialist tradition—which subordinated the role of culture to "rational" social progress. The views of thinkers like Condorcet, Holbach, Bentham, Helvetius, and others were based on faith in the capacity of human reason to overcome superstition and religion, but they were also often limited by their espousal of a reductive "materialist" approach to human nature and welfare.[36] In *Système de la*

36. For one of the most even-handed critical discussions of this strand of the Enlightenment, see Charles Taylor, *Sources of the Self* (Cambridge: Harvard University Press, 1989), chap. 19.

nature, Holbach captures the essence of such an approach, seeing in Newton's explanation of the physical world the key to human nature:

> Self preservation is thus the common goal toward which all energies, forces, and human faculties seem continuously directed. Scientists have named this tendency or direction gravitation to a centre. Newton calls it force of inertia, moralists have called it in man self-love, which is but the tendency to preserve oneself, the desire for happiness, the love of well-being and pleasure.[37]

The "desire for happiness" is equated with "the love of well-being and pleasure"; for Bentham and the utilitarian tradition, "pleasure" becomes the single yardstick by which human welfare is to be measured. All social customs and traditions get in the way of the kind of disengaged and purely neutral "reason" that can lead us to welfare thus construed. A reductive moral ontology underwrites this near-absolute opposition between reason and social custom, between historical progress and the cultural past. It is this ontology and this view of culture which counter-Enlightenment thinkers such as Hamann and Herder opposed so vociferously, arguing instead for the unique value of individual cultures. My defense of cultural pluralism is not based on religious grounds like Hamann's, and it is an attempt to rewrite Herder's vision of cultural diversity in the form of a cogent and modern social theory, eliminating his exaggerated and confusing use of organic metaphors and his vague notions of the *Volk.*[38] Notice that in the realist theoretical account I have sketched here, cultural self-determination and autonomy are defended not for romantic or relativist reasons, in abstraction from moral considerations, but precisely because cultural diversity is likely to promote the best kind of moral experimentation and knowledge even in a world where cultural inequality has been eliminated. In such a world, diversity ensures that moral and political speculation will be grounded in a sufficient number of different contexts, and a rich variety of theoretical programs and perspectives will flourish.

On the realist view, prolonged disagreement or cross-cultural conflict

37. Holbach, quoted in ibid., p. 325.

38. For Herder's use of organic metaphors, see esp. "National Genius and the Environment," a collection of extracts from his *Reflections on the Philosophy of the History of Mankind,* abridged and with an introduction by Frank E. Manuel (Chicago: University of Chicago Press, 1968), pp. 3–78. For an excellent introduction to Herder's critique of the Enlightenment and the general context in which such a critique was made, see Isaiah Berlin, "The Counter-Enlightenment," in *Against the Current: Essays in the History of Ideas* (New York: Viking Press, 1980).

will in many instances point to genuinely open-ended questions, for which we may indeed possess no answers at the moment—that is, given the state of our knowledge and the extent to which our capacities for formulating the questions themselves have evolved. This situation is not all that different, however, from what happens in any mature science. In my view, we need to fight against arbitrary imposition of homogeneous perspectives in cultural practice for the very reason that we do so in scientific practice in modern societies. The history of science shows why political decentralization and autonomy of inquiry are not luxuries, to be wished for only after all other social problems have been solved; they are the very minimal conditions for the maturing of any science. If my definition of culture as a form of moral and political inquiry is at all convincing, then it should be clear why cultures are like all forms of inquiry—part empirical, part conjectural, always necessarily presupposing deep bodies of theoretical knowledge and insight which cannot be fully articulated. If this is the case, however, it would be easy to see exactly why, at their best, multicultural societies would embody the advanced and complex cooperative structure of an ideal epistemic community. Difference and individuality are not opposed to a deeper commonality, a community of purpose. Even in a world that is not fundamentally structured by (cultural) inequality, healthy pluralism is more likely than cultural homogeneity to lead to the fruitful coordination of our epistemic efforts. That is, I believe, the strongest argument that can be made for multiculturalism, and it is based not on moral or cultural relativism but rather on a realist account of the cognitive component of cultural practice and the objectivity of value.

On Realism and Reason

But it should be clear why this view of cultures as naturally occurring moral experiments cannot by itself support the demand for multicultural diversity, for if such experiments represented inquiries into entirely different bodies of moral information and knowledge—in other words, if human welfare were a purely conventional or culture-specific affair—there would be no need for the kind of diversity I am defending here. There would be no compelling argument in favor of promoting diversity, especially if it did not already exist, for cultural variety as such would offer no epistemic advantage, and tolerance of the variety that *already* exists would be needed only to prevent conflict and to ensure peaceful coexistence. It might be clear now why I said (in Chapter 5) that the relativist or liberal conceptions of multiculturalism provide weak and anemic visions of cultural pluralism. What I oppose to this view is a richer picture of diversity as a form of social cooperation, based on a (universalist) belief that humans, across cultures and societies, are creatures capable of rational agency and hence of cultural and political self-determination. This (Kantian) kind of universalism is also a strand of the Enlightenment, and it does *not* imply a monolithic view of human welfare or a comprehensive account of human nature. If we combine this view of human nature as grounded in (at least) a universal capacity for practical rationality, together with the social-theoretical claim I am making about the centrality of culture to moral and political experimentation and inquiry, it would be difficult to maintain that the growth of objective moral knowledge will lead to cultural homogeneity or the flattening of difference. Indeed, my way of developing (and qualifying) the Enlightenment's moral and political universalist project enables us to envision a social theory and a political practice that *demand* respect for cultural others.

Decentralized political systems and structures, a realist will say, tend to promote the welfare of creatures like us, whose welfare consists in part—but quite fundamentally—in the development of our ability to determine our lives through our own choices and decisions, mistakes and all. This is the key Enlightenment idea that Kant refined and radicalized: ordinary people have the ability to govern themselves, and political freedom is thus not the reward given to mature individuals but rather the precondition for such (moral and political) maturity. It is from such radical claims that all anticolonial movements of our times have drawn their best arguments, and it is these universalist moral and political positions that have been behind the demands for socialism, for the equality of women or the abolition of slavery—in short, behind so many of the struggles to extend and deepen democracy which constitute our modernity. Multiculturalism, as I have defined it here, is such a democratic project. It is based on a realist moral epistemology and a naturalistic view of cultural practice as experimentation and inquiry.

It might be evident that behind the realist-naturalist position I am outlining lies a positive and substantive conception of reason as not only a practical capacity but also an evolving epistemic norm. I began this book by citing the influential critique made by the marxist philosophers Adorno and Horkheimer of the Enlightenment conception of reason. That critique was based on the claim that Enlightenment reason had ossified into a schematic formula, a set of algorithmic guidelines for achieving our (predetermined moral or political) ends. Part of this charge against the Enlightenment certainly sticks; as we saw, the reductive moral ontology of such thinkers as Holbach and Bentham did leave

room for a conception of reason as pure instrument, as in itself noneval-
uative, only the means to predetermined ends.[39] In our contemporary
polemics against the status of reason, it is this purely instrumental conception that is often invoked. In modern technocratic societies and intellectual cultures, such a notion of reason, based as it is on an absolute
(and quite convenient) separation of the "real" world from the world of
value, is understandably pervasive, for it tethers reason to the dominant
social values and interests, clipping its political wings. But for other
politically radical Enlightenment thinkers, such as Rousseau and Kant,
reason represents the human moral and political capacity to be free, to
submit the dictates of arbitrary authority—whether externally imposed
or deriving from one's own "self-incurred immaturity" *(Unmündig-
keit)*—to critical scrutiny. Kant's thorough deconstruction of the excesses of speculative reason (in the first *Critique*) leads him to ground
reason in a public space that can in principle be shared by all. Enlightenment or maturity, the development of the capacity for moral autonomy,
is a process, not a finished product possessed by a few. And reason is the
value embodied in and articulated by this inherently social and political
process through which humans grow and mature.

This account of the social basis of reason both supports and is built
upon the claim that the growth of the individual is impossible to imagine without the appropriate political context. "Maturity" requires not
only autonomy (an abstract capacity) but also, as the *Critique of Judgment* makes clear, the maxim of "enlarged thought" in which the socially situated thinker "reflects upon" his own judgment "from a
universal standpoint."[40] The universal standpoint that reason represents is not of any existing community of humans, but that of the *possible* community of beings capable of reflection and rational agency, the
community that Kant calls the "kingdom of ends."[41] When we adopt

39. Compare Hume's famous remark that " 'Tis not contrary to reason to prefer the
destruction of the whole world to the scratching of my finger." Hume, *A Treatise of
Human Nature*, ed. L. A. Selby-Bigge (Oxford: Clarendon Press, 1975), p. 416. In the *Treatise*, Hume defines reason as "perfectly inert" (p. 458) in relation to the setting of goals and
ends: that is the job of the "passions." For an account of how Hume's conception of reason
changes, becoming, especially in his essays, more social and evaluative, more than the
means to predetermined ends, see chapters 4 and 5 of Annette Baier, *Moral Prejudices:
Essays on Ethics* (Cambridge: Harvard University Press, 1994), pp. 51–94. For one of the
best short accounts of the reductionist modern view of reason and nature, as well as an
explanation of what an alternative, more "dialectical" view of science and the world would
look like, see the discussion of "Cartesian reductionism" in Richard Levins and Richard
Lewontin, *The Dialectical Biologist* (Cambridge: Harvard University Press, 1985), esp. pp.
267–88.

40. Immanuel Kant, *Critique of Judgment* (New York: Hafner Press, 1951), p. 137.

41. "All rational beings stand under the law that each of them should treat himself and

the standpoint of such a community, we accept the moral imperative to conduct our political reflection and behavior in such principled ways that we respect the (actual or potential) claims of other rational creatures to be "ends in themselves." Indeed, as Kant argues, accepting such an imperative enables us to be fully participating "members" of the kingdom of ends, that is, rational agents who can "legislate . . . universal laws while also being [themselves] subject to these laws."

> A rational being belongs to the kingdom of ends as a member when he legislates in it universal laws while also being himself subject to these laws. . . .
> [Morality] consists in the relation of all action to that legislation whereby alone a kingdom of ends is possible. This legislation must be found in every rational being and must be able to arise from his will, whose principle then is *never to act on any maxim except such as can also be a universal law and hence such as the will can thereby regard itself as at the same time the legislator of universal law.*[42]

The respect that we accord (in principle) to other humans is thus the respect for the "humanity" in all of us, which is the rational capacity to be free and self-legislating members of a radically democratic polity. Thus the universalist moral and political ideal is opposed in principle to ethnocentrism, and it is such a vision, simultaneously moral and political, that is embodied in the Kantian conception of reason.

The necessarily abstract universalism explains why the basic principle should not be violated or superseded for historical expediency or convenience. But even the staunchest defenders of this core universalist principle will acknowledge that it will not yield an adequately comprehensive moral or social vision, and that such a radical principle demands specification and elaboration through its grounding in particular social and cultural contexts. It is in these contexts that we develop a fuller knowledge of human nature and its possibilities, as well as of the vulnerabilities and the resources of socially situated human agents. In defending both a certain kind of moral universalism and a form of cultural pluralism, I am drawing on a conception of reason that is in part abstract while being necessarily dependent for its elaboration on histor-

---

all others never merely as means but always at the same time as an end in himself. Hereby arises a systematic union of rational beings through common objective laws, i.e., a kingdom that may be called a kingdom of ends *(certainly only an ideal)*, inasmuch as these laws have in view the very relation of such beings to one another as ends and means." Immanuel Kant, *Grounding*, pp. 39–40 (Ak: 433); emphasis added.

42. Ibid., p. 40 (Ak: 433–34); emphasis added.

ical contexts, cultures, identities—that is, on the local and the particular.

This is thus not an instrumental but a fundamentally evaluative conception of reason. Indeed, it implicitly rejects the metatheoretical sundering of fact and value, for reason, as our deepest epistemic and social ideal, is itself grounded in "nature"—in evolving human nature, and what we discover about it through our social experiments. Part of what we "discover" are new cooperative and democratic possibilities, including the genuine human capacities on which these possibilities are based; such discoveries, in turn, extend our understanding of the positive claims of reason. It was the achievement of the Enlightenment to have given us a conception of reason which could be naturalized in this way and elaborated in social and political activities. It would be difficult to justify or substantiate our best theories about justice and morality, our programs of political struggle and our notions of genuine and meaningful democracy, without such an evolving epistemic norm. In arguing that the demands of universalism are not necessarily opposed to those of cultural difference, I have been relying on such a conception of reason as both evaluative and empirically grounded; it is universal in scope but necessarily context sensitive. And in reformulating the claims of cultural autonomy in terms that are neither romantic and essentialist nor in principle separatist, I hope to have suggested how a moral universalism demands to be rationally examined—and elaborated—in a diverse, multicultural social and political space.

Objectivity and Literary Theory: A Concluding Note

The association of "literary theory" with various kinds of claims about the conventional and constructed nature of the world in which we live has, as I suggested in the introductory chapters, been both liberating and limiting. Marxist critics and deconstructionists, feminists of various persuasions, and Deweyan pragmatists have all been attracted to the antimetaphysical stance and sometimes even to the extreme skepticism that defines the postmodernist position. I would like to end with the proposal that we go beyond the bounds of a purely text-based literary theory to engage more directly the substantive findings of the various scientific disciplines. Our discussion of important questions regarding subjectivity, for instance, will be confined to purely negative and critical gestures unless we make serious contact with the growing knowledge about the natural and social world and come to terms with the empirical implications of our claims (or unstated positions). We cannot expect to discuss such questions seriously until we consider alternative perspectives available in contemporary philosophy and the social sciences. Similarly, our claims about language cannot be validated by a narrow circular reference back to the literary. To the extent that these claims are embedded—as I showed in Chapters 1 and 2—in views about the relation between knowledge and the world, or texts and society, we need to consider theoretical positions from fields other than literary and cultural studies, bringing to center stage such methodological issues as "explanation" and "confirmation" and examining alternative definitions of theory and knowledge.

Beyond that, it seems to me, we need to be ready to countenance the possibility of legitimate "metaphysical" inquiry in many areas. In the postpositivist realist perspective, for instance, plausible and empirically grounded theories about human nature or aesthetic and moral value are indeed attempts to trace the contours of our world, but they are not idealist speculations about the essence of nature. Instead, they are sober and reasonable attempts to explain the variety of causal relations and dependencies that define human reality. Thus they can provide suggestive hypotheses for social inquiry and textual interpretation. Literary theory can be the exciting arena in which we examine, debate, and specify the cultural and social implications of advances in the natural and social sciences. Textual interpretation, in turn, can reveal the various kinds of social construction of texts and ideologies, and analyze the differences that different forms (and degrees) of construction make. For such analyses to be successful, we need richly detailed accounts of the social bases of error and mystification and of the ways to overcome them. It will be difficult to develop these explanatory accounts if, railing against an outmoded conception of science and scientific method, we adopt an extreme constructivist or skeptical position and assume that objective knowledge is in principle impossible. The positivist ideal of a knowledge based on pure disinterested observation, shorn of all theoretical or subjective bias, was profoundly flawed, but even the deepest critique of positivism does not justify the adoption of an unqualified skepticism toward all knowledge. Such a critique should lead, as I have shown, to an understanding of how a theory-mediated objectivity is possible and how our strongest conception of objective knowledge is informed by the various forms—and contexts—of human inquiry.

"History," as we have seen in various ways in the preceding chapters, poses urgent questions about novelty, difference, and alterity. However, there is no convincing reason to believe that alterity is so absolute, the radically new future so different, that we can make no sense of it at all. At the very least, I want to reiterate one recurring theme of this book— that such unyielding skepticism might ironically be based on a form of dogmatism which denies the social organization of human inquiry and formulates its political views a little too hastily. That intransigence does not make postmodernist skepticism politically conservative, but it does severely restrict the scope of its politics. We need to reexamine our epistemological assumptions and biases if we are to expand the range of our politics and deepen our understanding of its implications.

INDEX

Cézanne, Paul, 191
Cherniak, Christopher, 141–42
Chomsky, Noam, 241n
Cixous, Hélène, 119n
Clifford, James, 30n, 123n
Cohen, G. A., 76n
Collini, Stefan, 4n
Condorcet, Marie Jean Antoine, 77, 122, 245
Connell, R. W., 136n
Conrad, Joseph, 102
constructivism, xi, 10–18, 29–32, 66–72, 90, 98, 171, 194, 251–52
Courtivron, Isabelle de, 119n
Coward, Rosalind, 51n
criticism, 1–9, 117–21, 251–53
Culler, Jonathan, 13n, 14n, 32n, 108n, 144, 145n, 203–4
cultural diversity. See multiculturalism
cultural identity. See identity
culture, 135–42; defined as a field of moral inquiry, 240–51
Cutler, Robert M., 241n

Dante, 46
Davidson, Donald, 138, 151, 191
deconstruction, 28n, 47, 176–84. See also Derrida, Jacques
Deleuze, Gilles, 48n, 104
de Man, Paul, 19, 26–46, 47, 71, 179, 222n; Allegories of Reading, 35–41, 44–46; Blindness and Insight, 3n, 35–37; "The Resistance to Theory," 32–35; "The Rhetoric of Blindness," 36–37; The Rhetoric of Romanticism, 36; "Rhetoric of Tropes (Nietzsche)," 39–41
Derrida, Jacques, 12, 19, 27, 34–35, 44n, 75–76, 83, 100, 174, 176–84; Margins of Philosophy, 178n; Of Grammatology, 34n, 44n; Positions, 180n, 181; "The Principle of Reason," 180n; Writing and Difference, 176n, 182n
Descartes, René, 153
determination, social, 34–35, 48–58. See also causality
Devitt, Michael, 67n, 151n, 164n
Dickens, Charles, 99
Diderot, Denis, 1
Dilthey, Wilhelm, 118, 192
diversity, cultural, xii, 17, 198, 202, 240–51. See also multiculturalism; pluralism
Dostoevsky, Fyodor, 57–58

Dreyfus, Hubert L., 61n
Dupré, Louis, 75n
Durkheim, Emile, 172

Eagleton, Terry, 5
Eco, Umberto, 43–46, 60n, 66–67
Edgley, Roy, 92n
Eliot, T. S., 4
Ellis, John, 51n
Elster, Jon, 50n, 76n
Emerson, Caryl, 52n
emotions, naturalist-realist account of, 206–11, 216–29, 236–39
Engels, Frederick, 49–50, 75
Enlightenment, the, xi–xii, 1–3, 8–11, 242, 245–51
epistemic privilege: and experience, 206–16; and feminist standpoint theory, 212–13, 215; of the oppressed, 232–34; of the proletariat, 80; and the realist theory of identity, 234–40
epistemological privilege. See epistemic privilege
epistemology. See error; knowledge; objectivity
error, 15, 20, 39–42, 65, 70–72, 79–85, 106–15, 145–48, 215–16. See also objectivity
essentialism: about language (de Man), 38; poststructuralist critique of, 84–85, 97, 183; and reference (Kripke), 69–70. See also experience
evaluation. See value
Evans-Pritchard, E. E., 132
experience: and epistemic privilege, 215; essentialist (or idealized) conception of, 202–3, 216, 234; naturalist-realist account of, 205–12, 216, 222–34; postmodernist critique of, 202–5, 216, 234
explanation, 14n, 47, 65, 144–45, 184, 235, 252; and confirmation, 170–75; of error, 146–47; postpositivist realist account of, 184–97; theory of identity as, 202–40. See also causality; objectivity

fact, 18, 45, 62, 98, 251. See also object, the (Peircean); objectivity; value
fallibilism, 23, 172. See also error; objectivity
fallibility. See error
Farr, James, 50n
Felman, Shoshana, 11–13, 27, 31, 108n
Fernbach, David, 78n
Feuerbach, Ludwig, 214
Feyerabend, Paul, 97

interpretation, 4–9, 58, 61; horizon of, 7; textual, 102–5, 252. *See also* hermeneutics; meaning

Jameson, Fredric, 9, 20–21, 28n, 53–54, 79n, 93–115; "The Cultural Logic of Late Capitalism," 108n, 112; *Fables of Aggression*, 102, 105, 113; *Late Marxism*, 111n; *Marxism and Form*, 9n, 28n, 79n, 93n, 94–96, 113; *The Political Unconscious*, 94–106, 113; *Postmodernism, or the Logic of Late Capitalism*, 108n; *The Prison-House of Language*, 94n, 97; "Third World Literature in the Era of Multinational Capitalism," 113n
Jardine, Alice A., 204n
Jay, Martin, 79n
Johnson, Barbara, 27, 29–30
Jordanova, Ludmilla, 2n
Joyce, James, 78

Kant, Immanuel, 1–3, 44, 111, 199, 200n, 248–50; "An Answer to the Question: 'What Is Enlightenment?' " 2n; *Critique of Pure Reason*, 2–3; *Grounding for the Metaphysics of Morals*, 199n
Kaufmann, Walter, 31n, 143n, 204n
Kitcher, Philip, 114n, 147n, 193
Kleist, Heinrich von, 36
knowledge, xi–xiii, 10–24, 30–32, 35–42, 65–66, 91–92, 106–15, 144–97, 204–53. *See also* error; objectivity
Kranz, Michael, 118n
Kripke, Saul, 19, 67, 69–70
Kuhn, Thomas, 10, 22, 157, 166–73, 192, 210; *The Structure of Scientific Revolutions*, 167–70

Lacan, Jacques, 87, 104, 108; *Ecrits: A Selection*, 87
LaCapra, Dominick, 221n, 227, 233–34
Laclau, Ernesto, 120n, 212n
language: Bakhtin's view of, 52–58; de Man's view of, 19, 27–29, 32–46; social basis of, 47–72; and translation, 123–28, 137–38
Leavis, F. R., 5, 9
Leibniz, Gottfried Wilhelm, 179–80
Lemaire, Anika, 87–88
Lentricchia, Frank, 32n
Levins, Richard, 56n, 57n, 249n
Lewis, Philip, 28n, 120n

Lewis, Wyndham, 102, 105
Lewontin, Richard, 56n, 57n, 249n
liberalism, 17–18. *See also* pluralism; relativism
Lichtheim, George, 77n
Livingston, Paisley, 163n
Lloyd, Genevieve, 14n
Locke, John, 153–54
Lorde, Audre, 210n
Lukács, Georg, 35, 76–81, 101, 103, 114n; *History and Class Consciousness*, 76–81
Lukes, Steven, 118n
Lyotard, Jean-François, 12, 27, 104, 108n, 131n, 143–47; *The Postmodern Condition*, 143

MacIntyre, Alasdair, 132
Mandel, Ernst, 110
Manuel, Frank E., 246n
Marcus, George E., 123n
Marks, Elaine, 119n
Marshall, Donald, 7n
Marx, Karl, 8, 48–50, 75–80, 91, 172–73, 196, 214, 232; *Capital*, 79–80; *The Communist Manifesto*, 77; *A Contribution to the Critique of Political Economy*, 48; *The Eighteenth Brumaire of Louis Bonaparte*, 77; *The German Ideology*, 75
Marxism, 56, 75, 90, 94–115. *See also* Althusser, Louis; Bakhtin, Mikhail; Jameson, Fredric; Lukács, Georg; Marx, Karl; naturalism; objectivity
Matthiessen, F. O., 8
McConnell-Ginet, Sally, 206n
McKenna, Andrew, 27
meaning, 29–32, 69–71. *See also* interpretation; Putnam, Hilary; Quine, W. V. O.; reference
Medvedev, Pavel, 52n
Meiland, Jack, 118n
Mepham, John, 75n
Miller, Eugene F., 241n
Miller, Fred D., Jr., 146n
Miller, Richard, 14n, 50n, 92n, 190
Milton, John, 46
Mohanty, Chandra Talpade, 231n
Molière, *L'Ecole des Femmes*, 29
Molina y Vedia, Caroline, 40n
Morrison, Toni, 23, 112n, 203; *Beloved*, 23, 112n, 203, 216–40
Morson, Gary Saul, 53
Mouffe, Chantal, 120n, 199n, 212n

multiculturalism: strong, realist version of, xii–xiii, 21, 24, 198–202, 240–51; weak, relativist definition of, 16–18,144–45, 198. *See also* diversity, cultural; pluralism; relativism

Murdoch, Iris, 244n

narrative, 12, 14n, 102–5. *See also* explanation; objectivity; totality

naturalism, 22–24, 92, 114n, 234–53; Nietzschean view of, 41, 208n; Quinean view of, 162–66, 204n. *See also* realism; Nietzsche, Friedrich; Quine, W. V. O.

needs, human, 90, 93, 208n, 236. *See also* philosophical anthropology

Newton, John, 246

Nicholson, Linda, 14–16, 144

Nietzsche, Friedrich, 31n, 39–44, 64–65, 71, 143, 196, 204n, 208; *On the Genealogy of Morals*, 31n, 40–41, 204n; "On Truth and Falsity in Their Extramoral Sense," 40n; *The Will to Power*, 31n, 143n

Nisbet, Robert, 186n

Noble, James, 50n

normative, the. *See* value

Nussbaum, Martha, 211n

object, the (Peircean), 43–45, 59–64. *See also* fact; reference

objectivity: positivist definition of, 18, 165–66; postpositivist understanding of, 147, 152–53, 162–66, 189–93, 201, 209–16, 242, 247, 251–53. *See also* error

Omi, Michael, 18

O'Neill, Onora, 2n, 200n

Ortony, Andrew, 230n

other, the, 119–121, 161, 182, 191; cultural, 120, 198; otherness, 140–41, 145. *See also* incommensurability

Outhwaite, William, 49n

overdetermination, 34, 64, 83–85

Paul, Ellen Frankel, 146n

Paul, Jeffrey, 146n

pedagogy, 26–32

Peirce, Charles Sanders, 34, 42–46, 58–67, 70, 172

personhood, 139, 197–99, 226

philosophical anthropology, 89, 138, 199–200. *See also* human nature; needs, human

Plato, 29

pluralism, 17–18, 120, 129–31, 197, 246–47. *See also* diversity, cultural; multiculturalism

Popper, Karl, 186, 187n

positivism. *See* knowledge; objectivity

postmodernism, xi–xiii, 10–16, 18–24, 31, 108n, 129–31, 142–48, 202–9, 212n, 234, 251–53. *See also* constructivism; relativism; universalism

poststructuralism. *See* postmodernism; skepticism, epistemological

Poulet, Georges, 35

presuppositions, 22, 41. *See also* objectivity

Proust, Marcel, 46

psychoanalysis, 11, 27, 31–32; Lacanian, 11, 13, 31. *See also* Althusser, Louis; Freud, Sigmund; Lacan, Jacques

Putnam, Hilary, 19, 34, 48, 67–70, 140n, 163n

Quine, W. V. O., 22, 61n, 151–52, 155–73, 185–87, 194, 204n; "Epistemology Naturalized," 162n; *Ontological Relativity and Other Essays*, 160n, 204n; "Speaking of Objects," 159–60; "Two Dogmas of Empiricism," 155n, 158, 160; *Word and Object*, 160

Railton, Peter, 213n, 214n

Rajchman, John, 171n

rationality, xi–xii, 1–3, 9–10, 14n, 116–18, 248–51; instrumental conception of, 248–49; practical, 111, 117, 133–42, 198–201

realism, xii–xiii, 67–72, 92, 114–15, 147–48, 184–97, 198–253. *See also* knowledge; naturalism; objectivity

reason. *See* rationality

reference, 19–20, 40–46, 47–51, 98–100, 107, 146–47, 229–30; causal theory of, 66–72; de Man's conception of, 33–38; epistemic content of, 43–46; as epistemological notion, 70–72; of evaluative terms, 244–45; indeterminacy of, 70–71, 244–45; Peirce's conception of, 58–66. *See also* causality; realism

Reiss, Hans, 2n

relativism: cultural, 21, 116–28, 144, 174; epistemological, 21,142–48; extreme or radical, 117, 129–31, 146, 148; sophisticated, 117, 132–42. *See also* constructivism; multiculturalism; postmodernism; skepticism, epistemological

Rembrandt, 191

Ricardo, David, 50

Richards, I. A., 7

Rocker, Rudolf, 241n

Roemer, John, 76n

Rorty, Amélie Oksenberg, 210n

Rorty, Richard, 22, 25, 117n, 149–61, 163n, 166, 170–75, 194; *Philosophy and the Mirror of Nature*, 149–55, 160; "Solidarity or Objectivity?" 171n

Ross, Andrew, 16n, 199n

Rousseau, Jean-Jacques, 37, 38n

Ruben, D. H., 75n

Russo, Ann, 231n

Ryan, Michael, 27, 30

Sade, Marquis de, 30

Said, Edward, 26, 33

Sartre, Jean-Paul, 78, 79n, 94

Saussure, Ferdinand de, 46, 52

Savan, David, 45n, 59n

Sayre-McCord, Geoffrey, 148n, 197n, 213n

Scarpetta, Guy, 181

Scheman, Naomi, 206–11, 218

Scott, Joan Wallach, 30n, 205n

Seidman, Steven, 30n

Selby-Bigge, L. A., 249n

self-determination, 90–92. *See also* agency, human; freedom

Sellars, Wilfrid, 151, 155

Shaw, William H., 50n

Shelley, Percy Bysshe, 36

sign, the (Peircean), 43–45, 59–66

signification: 60–67; cognitive and epistemic aspects of, 61n; materialist account of, 67. *See also* meaning

Sivanandan, A., 17, 231n

skepticism, epistemological, 14–16, 42n, 142–45, 153–55, 163–64, 184, 215. *See also* foundationalism, epistemological; knowledge; objectivity; relativism

Smith, Adam, 50

Smith, Barbara Herrnstein, 147n, 196n

social location, 148, 202, 206–16, 234. *See also* epistemic privilege; identity

Sontag, Susan, 79

Sousa, Ronald de, 210

Spillers, Hortense, 221n, 226

Spivak, Gayatri Chakravorty, 12–13, 18n, 144, 232n

Sprinker, Michael, 39n

Sterelny, Kim, 67n

Sturgeon, Nicholas L., 146–47, 172n, 197n

subject, the: Althusserian conception of, 81–83, 85–92; as epistemic agent (idealist), 11–12, 106–15; as epistemic agent (naturalist), 114–15, 193; of European humanism, 136–38; Lukácsian conception of, 79–81. *See also* agency, human; human nature

Taylor, Charles, 139n, 140, 145, 191, 237n, 241n, 242–43, 245n

Terdiman, Richard, 27

Torres, Lourdes, 231n

totality, 9, 79–80, 83–85. *See also* explanation; objectivity

Tracy, Destutt de, 77

Trilling, Lionel, 8–9

Trout, J. D., 213n

universalism, 11, 16n, 129, 199–200; moral, xii–xiii, 24, 234–51

value, xi–xiii, 6–9, 18, 20, 23–24, 29–30, 196–97; Althusser's poststructuralist conception of, 91–92; realist conception of, 201–2, 214, 242–52

Van Parijs, Philippe, 50n

Vlastos, Gregory, 200n, 243n

Volosinov, V. N., 52n; *Marxism and the Philosophy of Language*, 52n, 53–55

Voltaire, 1

Waters, Lindsay, 39n

Weber, Max, 172

Weinsheimer, Joel, 7n

West, Cornel, 171n

White, Hayden, 97, 98n

Whiting, Jennifer, 244n

Williams, Raymond, 50–51, 100

Wilson, Bryan R., 123n, 132n

Wilson, Edmund, 8–9

Winant, Howard, 18

Winch, Peter, 132–40

Witt, Charlotte, 166n

Wittgenstein, Ludwig, 127

Wood, Allen, 2n, 76n

Woolf, Virginia, 78

Wordsworth, William, 36

Zinsser, William, 229n